MICROWAVE
COOKING

MICROWAVE COOKING
CECILIA NORMAN

GALLERY BOOKS
An Imprint of W. H. Smith Publishers Inc.
112 Madison Avenue
New York City 10016

NOTES

Standard spoon measurements are used in all recipes.
1 tablespoon = one 15ml spoon
1 teaspoon = one 5ml spoon
All spoon measures are level.

Fresh herbs are used unless otherwise stated. If unobtainable substitute a bouquet garni of the equivalent dried herbs, or use dried herbs instead but halve the quantities stated.

Plain flour should be used unless otherwise stated.

Only one column of measures should be followed; metric and imperial columns are not interchangeable.

First published 1979 by
Octopus Books Limited
59 Grosvenor Street
London W1

This edition published in 1985 by Gallery Books
An imprint of W.H. Smith Publishers Inc.
112 Madison Avenue, New York, N.Y. 10016

ISBN 0 8317 5956 9

Produced by Mandarin Publishers Limited
22a Westlands Road,
Quarry Bay, Hong Kong

Printed in Hong Kong

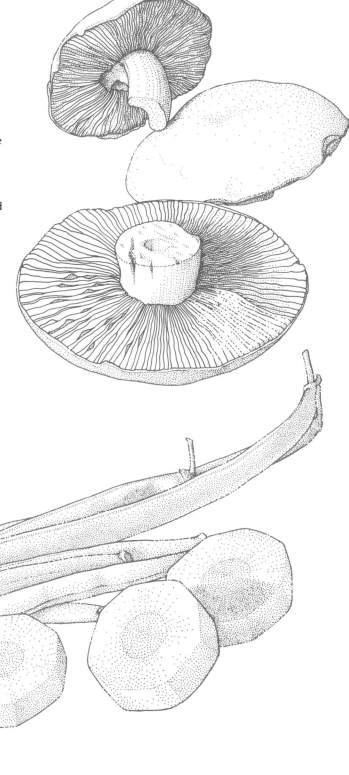

CONTENTS

INTRODUCTION

The Microwave Oven

The microwave oven is one of the most useful and versatile kitchen appliances on the market today. It is portable so it can be used anywhere in the house; it can even be taken on self-catering holidays to ensure you really don't spend much time in the kitchen. It is quick, easy and economical, because it saves on fuel. It also dispenses with the need to use saucepans and many other kitchen items – reducing washing-up. Most foods can be microwaved on the serving dish and, because there is no direct heat involved, food does not become burnt on – so dishes are easy to clean.

A microwave oven enables you to cook soups and casseroles, steam puddings, bake cakes and cook vegetables in a fraction of the time it takes using a conventional cooker. With the aid of a microwave browning skillet, meat can be browned and sealed effectively; some ovens are also fitted with a special browning element.

The microwave oven is an excellent quick defroster – it can thaw a medium-sized chicken in 15 to 20 minutes – and is also ideal for reheating prepared dishes.

How the Microwave Oven Works

When the oven is switched on, the magnetron – the 'heart of the oven' – converts the electrical energy into microwave energy and produces invisible waves. These pass down a channel into the oven and are distributed through the oven by a stirrer. The waves reflect off the sides, top and bottom of the oven, and pass through the container and food.

Microwaves tend to cook in a circle, so that the food around the outside edge cooks more quickly than that in the centre. Foods which cannot be stirred should be arranged so that the thinner parts are nearer the centre.

Each make of oven is, of course, different: they may cook at slightly different speeds, while each will have its own hot and cold spots. To ensure that every part of the dish receives sufficient microwaves, stir or turn the food during cooking.

Microwave ovens which have three or four power levels are usually operated by a pulsator that switches on and off at pre-set intervals of so many seconds. In this way, foods are given short bursts of microwave energy with rests in between, enabling the heat to be distributed evenly through the food.

More sophisticated ovens are also fitted with a probe which is inserted into the centre of the food. This detects when a certain temperature is reached, and ensures that the oven will retain that temperature throughout cooking.

When buying a microwave oven, the choice will ultimately, of course, depend on what you can afford, as well as just what you expect the oven to do. If, for example, you don't mind setting the oven manually with a timer and turning the dishes yourself, you can buy one at quite a reasonable price. These modest types usually have two settings, HIGH and DEFROST.

If you want the oven to have a greater range of power levels and do everything automatically for you – including turning the dishes on a turntable – it will of course cost more. The most expensive ovens are a combination of microwave and conventional which may be used simultaneously or separately.

Safety, Care and Maintenance

All ovens should conform to standard safety regulations, and there should be a label attached to the oven guaranteeing this. As a general safety guide, follow these basic rules.

1. Never switch on an empty microwave oven; if there's no food to absorb the waves, they bounce back to the magnetron and can shorten its life.
2. Don't operate the oven by opening and closing the door as this could result in harmful exposure to microwave energy; always use the controls.
3. Never tamper with the safety locks.
4. Do not place objects between the oven front face and the door.
5. Do not let spilled food accumulate round the door, as this will prevent a tight seal forming when the door is closed.
6. Do not use the oven if it becomes damaged, and *never* try to repair it yourself; always call in a qualified engineer.
7. Never use an abrasive cleaner on the inside of the oven as it can scratch the metallic walls. Avoid aerosol spray cleaners too, as these may penetrate the internal surface. Simply wipe the oven over with a cloth wrung out in soapy water and rinse with a clean cloth. Any persistant smells can be dispelled by heating a cup of lemon juice and water in the oven.

The oven door is fitted with a special seal to ensure minimum microwave leakage. Every oven has at least one cut-out device enclosed in the door so that the energy is automatically switched off when the door is opened and cooking *cannot* take place with your hand in the oven.

What will the Microwave Oven Cook?

The microwave oven is not intended to replace the conventional cooker. It is essentially an additional appliance, particularly useful when quick meals are needed, or when a large variety of food is required at one time. You will soon appreciate which foods are best cooked by microwave and can select the appliance you use according to the dishes you are preparing. Use your conventional cooker for boiling eggs, casseroles, large turkeys, batch cooking, deep-fried foods, foods which require a crisp outside and soft inside – like Yorkshire pudding, pavlovas and éclairs.

Use your microwave oven for vegetables, cakes (when only one or two are required), sauces, syrups, chicken, stewed fruits, fish and meat.

The microwave oven is also invaluable for cutting corners in conventional cooking; it is ideal for blanching vegetables, softening butter, melting chocolate, dissolving gelatine, heating milk and peeling chestnuts.

When cooking entire meals by microwave, pre-cook as much as possible, then reheat in the following order: soup, any joint or composite meat or poultry dish, fish dishes, then vegetables. Those items which take longest to cook retain the heat longest; those which cook quickly cool quickest. Most desserts can be cooked in advance. Desserts to be served hot can either be cooked quickly by microwave or reheated during the main course.

Defrosting and Reheating Food by Microwave

Defrosting by microwave is quick and efficient. Use the HIGH setting for thawing cooked foods and frozen blocks of food. As soon as the block is sufficiently soft, break it up with a fork, moving the frozen parts towards the outside of the dish. Continue to microwave on HIGH, stirring at frequent intervals, until evenly thawed. If the food has been frozen in a polythene (plastic) bag, half-turn it into a dish and leave the bag on the food during defrosting until the block is sufficiently thawed for the bag to be removed without tearing.

When thawing frozen fruit on HIGH, open the bag and place it on the oven shelf; remember to remove any metal tags, which must *never* be left in the oven during cooking. Microwave on HIGH for a few minutes until the surface feels warm, then shake the bag gently to redistribute the fruit before continuing to thaw. Alternatively, turn the fruit into a dish and thaw uncovered, stirring frequently.

To defrost large cuts of frozen meat on HIGH, place in a dish and give 1 minute of microwave energy followed by a 10-minute rest period. Turn the joint over and turn the dish, then repeat until the meat is pliable and a small amount of moisture collects in the dish. To defrost meat and poultry using the DEFROST setting, see chart on page 152.

Oven-ready frozen chickens may be thawed in the bag, provided the metal tag is cut away. Open the bag at the top and defrost in the same way as for meat. When the chicken is thawed, remove the giblets (which may still be frozen) and rinse the cavity well with cold water.

Finished dishes which have been specially arranged in a serving dish before freezing should be given short bursts of microwave energy, then left for a few minutes for the heat to spread through, thus avoiding stirring and spoiling the appearance of the dish. Turn the dish every minute and do not give prolonged microwaving on HIGH until the food is completely thawed. This type of dish should be covered during defrosting.

Food which has been thawed on HIGH should always be allowed a standing time of a few minutes before serving. No rest period is necessary if the LOW or DEFROST setting has been used. However the food should be broken up with a fork and stirred, and the dish should be turned during defrosting.

Food reheated by microwave tastes as though it has been freshly cooked. When reheating a dish like a casserole or stew, cover the container to prevent the food drying out. To check whether the food is hot, feel the underneath of the dish, which will be warmed by the food. Be careful when removing plastic cling film, as the steam trapped inside could cause a nasty scald; snip the plastic film with scissors before removing to allow some steam to escape.

Delicate foods, such as egg custards and cheese dishes, should be reheated on LOW, or given short intermittent bursts of microwave energy on MEDIUM or HIGH, followed by a short rest.

When reheating a plate meal for a latecomer, try to have all the items at the same temperature, cover the plate and microwave on a fairly high setting, turning occasionally. As many as three or four plates may be reheated together by microwave, with the aid of plastic stacking rings. Stack the plates in such a way that similar food items are not arranged above one another, otherwise the food will not reheat evenly. Cover the top plate only and turn the plates occasionally during reheating.

Cooking Utensils

A wide range of cooking utensils and serving dishes can be used in a microwave oven; the only prerequisite is that the material they are made of allows microwaves to be transmitted through to the food.

Metal acts as a barrier to microwaves, so food in metal dishes will not cook. Metal dishes, metallic-glazed dishes and dishes with metallic trims should not be used in a microwave oven. Metal objects can cause 'arcing' which will damage the magnetron; so if by accident you have placed metal in the oven and you see – or hear – sparking, switch off immediately.

In addition to non-metal ovenproof dishes that you would normally use in a conventional oven, you can also use paper, most plastics, straw and wooden items. Wood and straw should only be used for short-term cooking and check before using to make sure there are no metal staples. Similarly, before using cups, jugs or coffee pots, make sure the handles are not secured by metal screws.

Most china and ceramics are suitable; you only need to carry out a quick test once to be sure. Put a half-filled glass of water in the dish. Microwave for 1 minute. The water should be much hotter than the edge of the dish. If the dish is hotter than the water, it will not be microwave proof for any length of time.

A number of manufacturers now produce ranges of special microware, including trays, cake dishes and bun pans. A microwave browning skillet is a very useful accessory, as it seals, sears and browns meat. For details of cookware suitable for use in your microwave oven, refer to the chart on page 156.

Oven Settings and Cooking Times

Microwave cooking times cannot be stated absolutely precisely, since they are affected by a number of factors. Most important is the starting temperature of the food. Obviously the colder the food is before microwaving, the longer it will take to cook. The size and shape of the container can also influence cooking time. As far as possible use straight-sided regular-shaped containers. If you increase the quantities of a recipe, or microwave two dishes simultaneously, the cooking time must be increased accordingly.

Different microwave oven models have different power ratings and this influences cooking times. The recipes in this book have been tested using standard microwave ovens with an output of 600–700 watts. If the wattage of your oven is less, the longest time stated in each recipe will provide the most appropriate guide.

Instructions are given for HIGH, MEDIUM and LOW settings for all recipes; the chart on page 151 will enable you to identify the symbols used to denote settings on your particular oven with these.

As a general guide, HIGH is most suitable for fish, vegetables, sauces and liquids. MEDIUM is best for reheating cooked dishes and roasting poultry and meat. The LOW setting should preferably be used for egg dishes, milk puddings and casseroles.

However, most foods will cook and reheat successfully on HIGH. So, when time is at a premium use this setting, but remember to turn and stir often.

All food continues to cook to a certain degree after it is removed from the oven, and this is taken into account in the recipes. It is sometimes necessary, or advantageous, to have a resting time during cooking, to allow the heat to penetrate through the food. This particularly applies to dishes that cannot be stirred, for example, cheesecakes.

Take care to avoid overcooking food in your microwave oven – timing is crucial. Always check after the minimum time stipulated in each recipe, then microwave for longer if necessary.

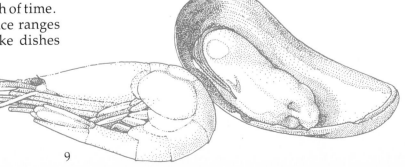

BREAKFASTS

In virtually every household, there is minimum time to prepare breakfast and this is when the microwave oven really becomes invaluable. Sausages, bacon and egg can be cooked in the time it would normally take to toast a slice of bread! Furthermore it can cope with as many as four different breakfast choices, without the need to use every pan in the cupboard.

To save the morning rush breakfasts can be prepared ahead. Bacon, sausages, omelettes, scrambled eggs and porridge, for example, can all be cooked in advance. Leave them covered in a cool place, then reheat for 30 seconds to 1 minute on HIGH. Foods to be reheated should be slightly undercooked. Tomatoes will not reheat successfully but as these cook quickly, they can be arranged on the plate with the other partly cooked items.

If one plate is being reheated, cover it tightly with plastic cling film. Up to four plates can be reheated together with the aid of plastic stacking rings, in which case only the top plate needs to be covered. An extra 30 seconds cooking time must be allowed for each plate. When reheating several composite breakfasts make sure that you do not, for example, have the scrambled egg on one plate directly above the scrambled egg on the plate below, otherwise the food will not be reheated evenly.

To reheat porridge, add 1 or 2 extra tablespoonfuls of water, stir well and MICROWAVE ON HIGH, stirring occasionally, until thoroughly hot. Slightly stale bread or rolls can be refreshed by microwave: wrap in kitchen paper towels and MICROWAVE ON HIGH for 10 to 15 seconds. Large quantities of hard butter can be softened by microwaving on LOW; for smaller quantities, e.g. 1 tablespoon, use the HIGH setting.

Coffee or strained tea can also be reheated if preparation time is at a minimum; 1 cup of tea or coffee will take 1½ to 2 minutes on HIGH and reheating a pot will take up to 5 minutes on HIGH.

PORRIDGE

Porridge oats should be cooked in water or in a mixture of milk and water in the microwave oven. They should never be cooked simply in milk, because the mixture will inevitably boil over. For 'quick' porridge oats reduce the specified microwave cooking time by half.

To cook 1 or 2 portions: Use the quantities of porridge oats and liquid recommended on the packet. Place in a deep bowl and three-quarters cover with plastic cling film. MICROWAVE ON LOW FOR 10 MINUTES.

Alternatively, MICROWAVE ON HIGH FOR 5 TO 6 MINUTES, stirring frequently during cooking.

To cook 4 to 6 portions: Increase the quantities accordingly and MICROWAVE ON LOW FOR AT LEAST 12 MINUTES or MICROWAVE ON HIGH FOR 8 TO 10 MINUTES, stirring frequently.

OATMEAL

METRIC/IMPERIAL	AMERICAN
100 g/4 oz oatmeal	*⅔ cup oatmeal*
½ teaspoon salt	*½ teaspoon salt*
300 ml/½ pint water	*1¼ cups water*
To serve:	**To serve:**
creamy milk	*creamy milk*
sugar to taste	*sugar to taste*

Combine all the ingredients in a large bowl, stir well, then cover the dish with a sheet of greaseproof (waxed) paper. MICROWAVE ON HIGH FOR 3 TO 3½ MINUTES until the mixture boils, stirring 2 or 3 times during cooking. Cover with plastic cling film and leave to stand for 5 minutes. Serve with milk and sugar to taste.

SERVES 4

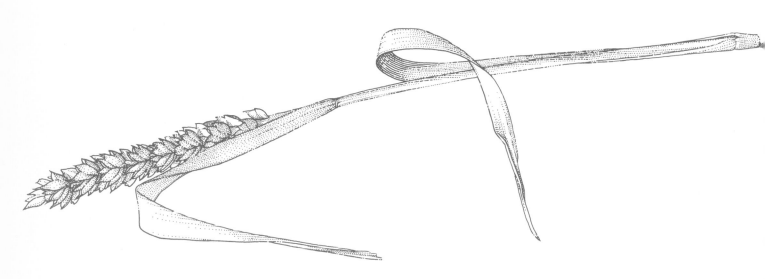

GRANOLA

METRIC/IMPERIAL	AMERICAN
2 tablespoons clear honey	*2 tablespoons clear honey*
1 tablespoon vegetable oil	*1 tablespoon vegetable oil*
100 g/4 oz rolled oats	*1 cup rolled oats*
2 tablespoons wheatgerm	*2 tablespoons wheatgerm*
25 g/1 oz hazelnuts, chopped	*3 tablespoons chopped hazelnuts or filberts*
2 tablespoons desiccated coconut	*2 tablespoons shredded coconut*
25 g/1 oz stoned dates, chopped	*¼ cup chopped dates*
25 g/1 oz raisins	*3 tablespoons raisins*
To serve:	**To serve:**
2–3 bananas, apples or oranges, peeled and chopped	*2–3 bananas, apples or oranges, peeled and chopped*
150 ml/¼ pint natural yogurt, single or soured cream, or milk	*⅔ cup unflavored yogurt, light or sour cream, or milk*

Put the honey and oil in a large bowl and MICROWAVE ON HIGH FOR 30 SECONDS. Gently mix in the oats, wheatgerm, hazelnuts and coconut. Turn onto a sheet of non-stick parchment and carefully lift onto the oven shelf.

MICROWAVE ON HIGH FOR 3 TO 3½ MINUTES until lightly browned; stir frequently during cooking to prevent the centre of the mixture from burning. Granola continues to brown after the oven is switched off, so do not overcook.

Add the dates and raisins, stir well, then leave to stand, covered, for 1 minute. Divide the granola between cereal bowls allowing 1 to 2 tablespoons per person. Serve sprinkled over chopped banana, apple or orange. Top each portion with a little yogurt, cream or milk.

SERVES 6 TO 8

Note: If your oven is fitted with a turntable make sure that the non-stick parchment does not overlap the shelf.

HOT SOUTHERN MUESLI

METRIC/IMPERIAL	AMERICAN
50 g/2 oz porridge oats	½ cup rolled oats
25 g/1 oz brown sugar	3 tablespoons brown sugar
25 g/1 oz flaked peanuts or almonds, toasted	¼ cup flaked peanuts or almonds, toasted
¼ teaspoon grated nutmeg	¼ teaspoon grated nutmeg
1 orange	1 orange
25 g/1 oz sultanas	3 tablespoons golden raisins
½ sharp dessert apple, cored and cut into chunks	½ sharp dessert apple, cored and cut into chunks
150 ml/¼ pint natural yogurt	⅔ cup unflavored yogurt

Combine the oats, sugar, peanuts or almonds, and nutmeg in a dish. MICROWAVE ON HIGH FOR 2 MINUTES, stirring occasionally. Peel the orange, then carefully cut out the segments, with a sharp knife, removing all pith. Chop the flesh roughly.

Add the chopped orange to the oats, and squeeze the juice from the pithy membrane into the bowl. Add the sultanas (golden raisins) and the apple chunks. MICROWAVE ON HIGH FOR 1½ TO 2 MINUTES, stirring occasionally, until the fruit is hot but not soft.

Stir in the yogurt, cover and leave to stand for 1 minute, then spoon into cereal bowls and serve at once.

SERVES 4

Note: For a refreshing summer breakfast, top cereals with sliced peaches, strawberries, raspberries or other seasonal fruits of choice.

FRESH APPLE AND ORANGE COMPOTE

METRIC/IMPERIAL	AMERICAN
2 dessert apples	2 dessert apples
1 tablespoon lemon juice	1 tablespoon lemon juice
2 oranges	2 oranges
4 tablespoons thick honey	4 tablespoons thick honey
2 tablespoons wheatgerm	2 tablespoons wheatgerm

Peel and core the apples and cut into rings. Arrange in a large shallow dish and sprinkle with lemon juice. Grate the orange rind over the apples. Peel the oranges, removing all pith, and slice the flesh, removing the pips. Place the oranges on top of the apples and add the honey and wheatgerm.

Cover with plastic cling film and MICROWAVE ON HIGH FOR 2 MINUTES, until the honey has melted, giving the dish a half-turn after 1 minute. Serve hot or chilled.

SERVES 4

Illustrated on pages 10–11: Fresh apple and orange compote; Granola; Southern meusli; Compote of mixed dried fruit; Breakfast omelettes

COMPOTE OF MIXED DRIED FRUIT

METRIC/IMPERIAL	AMERICAN
100 g/4 oz dried apricots	*½ cup dried apricots*
100 g/4 oz prunes	*¾ cup prunes*
100 g/4 oz dried figs	*½ cup dried figs*
450 ml/¾ pint cold water (approximately)	*2 cups cold water (approximately)*
1 tablespoon lemon juice	*1 tablespoon lemon juice*
4 tablespoons orange juice	*4 tablespoons orange juice*
100 g/4 oz dried apple rings	*¾ cup dried apple rings*
75–100 g/3–4 oz brown sugar	*½–¾ cup brown sugar*
To serve:	**To serve:**
plain yogurt or soured cream (optional)	*unflavored yogurt or sour cream (optional)*

Combined the apricots, prunes and figs in a large deep dish. Add sufficient water to cover, then stir in the lemon and orange juice. Cover with a lid and leave to stand for 2 hours.

Mix in the apple rings and brown sugar. Cover loosely with plastic cling film. MICROWAVE ON HIGH FOR 12 TO 15 MINUTES until the figs are tender, giving the dish a shake occasionally during cooking.

Serve either hot or chilled, topped with a spoonful of yogurt, or soured cream if preferred.

SERVES 6

BACON

Avoid salty bacon rashers (slices) as these are inclined to become brittle.

To cook up to 4 bacon slices: Place between folded sheets of absorbent kitchen paper. To reduce shrinkage, press down well before microwaving. MICROWAVE ON HIGH, allowing approximately 1 MINUTE for each bacon slice. Remove the bacon slices from the paper the moment they are cooked.

To cook up to 500 g/1 lb bacon slices: Arrange the bacon slices either on a bacon rack or in a large shallow dish overlapping, so the fat parts lay over the lean. Cover with a piece of absorbent kitchen paper to prevent splattering. MICROWAVE ON HIGH allowing approximately 12 TO 14 MINUTES for 500 g/1 lb bacon, turning the slices over half-way through cooking and removing each one as soon as it is cooked. The use of a bacon rack will enable excess fat to drain away, avoiding the need to drain the bacon on absorbent kitchen paper again, before serving.

Note: Bacon may also be cooked in a preheated browning skillet without using additional fat.

MUSHROOMS

Mushrooms cook very quickly in the microwave oven. A little butter should be added before cooking them, covered with a lid or plastic cling film. Sprinkle the mushrooms with salt and pepper just before serving.

To cook 3 or 4 small mushrooms: Arrange on a plate, dot with a little butter, cover and MICROWAVE ON HIGH FOR 30 SECONDS.

To cook 100 g/4 oz/1 cup mushrooms: Place in a dish which will catch the juices. Add 15 g/½ oz/1 tablespoon butter and MICROWAVE ON HIGH FOR 2 TO 2½ MINUTES, stirring once during cooking.

Preparing breakfast by microwave, with reusable plastic microware: Bacon; Mushrooms; Baked eggs (see Bacon, Egg and Tomato, page 19); Compote of mixed dried fruit

TOMATOES

Tomatoes must either be pricked thoroughly or halved before microwaving. Arrange in a circle, cut sides up in a shallow dish. Dot with butter, season with salt and pepper and, without covering, MICROWAVE ON HIGH. Microwave timings vary, depending upon the size and ripeness of the tomatoes. One small ripe tomato will be softened in 20 seconds; 4 large under-ripe tomatoes will take 3 to 4 minutes to cook. Each tomato should be removed from the oven as soon as it is cooked.

SAUSAGES

Choose fat pork or beef (link) sausages. Prick them thoroughly and arrange in a circle on a plate. Cover with a piece of absorbent kitchen paper.

To cook 2 sausages: MICROWAVE ON HIGH FOR 1½ TO 2 MINUTES.

To cook 4 sausages: MICROWAVE ON HIGH FOR 3 TO 3½ MINUTES.
Give the plate a half-turn halfway through cooking and leave to stand for 1 minute before serving.

Sausages should not be overcooked in the microwave oven, because cooking continues after the oven is switched off. Pork sausages must be cooked until they are no longer pink inside.

Note: A browner appearance can be achieved by dipping the sausages into gravy browning, dissolved in a little water, before cooking.

CRISPY SAUSAGES

Prick fat pork or beef (link) sausages all over. PREHEAT A LARGE BROWNING SKILLET FOR 5 MINUTES (or according to the manufacturer's instructions). Quickly add a knob (1 teaspoon) of butter, then immediately put in the sausages, turning them over at once to brown both sides.

To cook 2 crispy sausages: MICROWAVE ON HIGH FOR 2½ MINUTES.

To cook 4 crispy sausages: MICROWAVE ON HIGH FOR 4 MINUTES.

Move the sausages to the sides of the dish and turn them over halfway through cooking. Remove and drain on absorbent kitchen paper. Leave to stand for 3 minutes before serving.

EGGS

Beaten egg mixtures are best cooked in the microwave oven on HIGH, but with the exception of fried eggs which are to be cooked in the browning skillet, whole shelled eggs are better cooked in the oven on MEDIUM. This setting permits the yolks and whites to set at the same time.

When eggs are cooked together with other ingredients, the microwave settings are less critical. Although a variation of speeds is recommended, eggs may be microwaved on HIGH with perfectly satisfactory results, provided care is taken.

Eggs should not be cooked or reheated in their shells, as these will burst and cover the oven with tiny pieces of solid egg, which are difficult to clean off.

BREAKFAST OMELETTE

METRIC/IMPERIAL	AMERICAN
15 g/½ oz butter	1 tablespoon butter
2 eggs	2 eggs
3 tablespoons milk	3 tablespoons milk
salt	salt
freshly ground black pepper	freshly ground black pepper

Put the butter in a shallow dish or curved-edge plate. MICROWAVE ON HIGH FOR 45 SECONDS, then swirl the melted butter to completely coat the dish.

Beat the eggs and milk together with salt and pepper to taste, until thoroughly blended. Pour into the prepared dish. MICROWAVE ON MEDIUM FOR 2½ TO 3 MINUTES until almost set, drawing the cooked edges towards the middle 3 times during cooking.

Serve the omelette in the dish, or fold in half and transfer to a heated plate. Place under a preheated hot grill (broiler) for a few seconds to brown the top.

SERVES 1

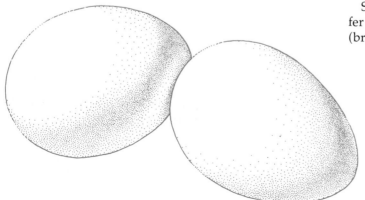

CODDLED EGG

METRIC/IMPERIAL	AMERICAN
150 ml/¼ pint water	⅔ cup water
1 egg (at room temperature)	1 egg (at room temperature)

Pour the water into a glass or jug, whisk with a fork, then MICROWAVE ON HIGH FOR 1¾ TO 2 MINUTES until the water is boiling. Carefully lower the egg into the water and cover the container with a saucer or piece of plastic cling film.

Leave to stand for 5 minutes, then lift out the egg and serve immediately.

SERVES 1

Note: If the eggs have been stored in the refrigerator, place them, one at a time, on the oven shelf and MICROWAVE ON HIGH FOR 5 SECONDS before cooking as above.

To cook 2 coddled eggs: Pour 150 ml/¼ pint/⅔ cup water into each of two glasses, place both in the oven and MICROWAVE ON HIGH FOR 3 MINUTES. As soon as the water boils, carefully lower an egg into each glass, cover as above and leave to stand for 5 minutes before serving.

CRUNCHY EGG FRIES

METRIC/IMPERIAL	AMERICAN
2 slices of bread	2 slices of bread
40 g/1½ oz butter (at room temperature)	3 tablespoons butter (at room temperature)
¼ teaspoon salt	¼ teaspoon salt
2 eggs	2 eggs

Remove the crusts and cut the bread into small cubes. PREHEAT A LARGE BROWNING SKILLET FOR 5 MINUTES (or according to the manufacturer's instructions), adding the butter after 4 minutes. Immediately toss in the bread, turning over quickly with a wooden spoon.

MICROWAVE ON HIGH FOR 30 SECONDS, sprinkle with the salt, stir and MICROWAVE ON HIGH FOR 30 SECONDS. Divide the croûtons in half and move to opposite corners of the skillet. Break an egg over each pile of croûtons. MICROWAVE ON HIGH FOR 30 SECONDS.

Partially cover with a lid and leave to stand for 30 seconds before serving.

SERVES 2

To cook 4 portions: Double the ingredients and increase the microwave cooking times to 45 seconds at each stage. Cook each egg on one quarter of the croûtons at each corner of the skillet.

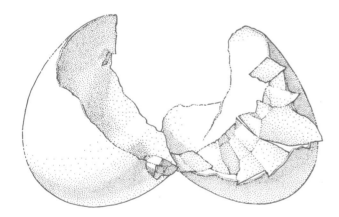

CRISP-FRIED EGGS

METRIC/IMPERIAL	AMERICAN
15 g/½ oz butter	1 tablespoon butter
2 eggs	2 eggs

PREHEAT A LARGE BROWNING SKILLET FOR 3 MINUTES. Add the butter and break the eggs into opposite corners. Puncture the egg yolk, cover and MICROWAVE ON HIGH FOR 1½ TO 2 MINUTES until cooked to taste. Remove with a slotted spoon and transfer to a serving plate.

SERVES 1 OR 2

For each additional crisp-fried egg: Allow an extra 7 g/¼ oz/ 1 teaspoon butter and increase the cooking times by 35 to 45 seconds.

POACHED EGG

METRIC/IMPERIAL
5 tablespoons hot water
¼ teaspoon white vinegar
1 egg
pinch of salt

AMERICAN
⅓ cup hot water
¼ teaspoon white vinegar
1 egg
pinch of salt

Pour the water and vinegar into a ceramic cereal bowl or a 10 cm/4 in custard cup. MICROWAVE ON HIGH FOR 30 SEC-ONDS or until boiling. Carefully break the egg into the water. Add salt and cover loosely with plastic cling film.

MICROWAVE ON MEDIUM FOR 1 MINUTE or MICROWAVE ON HIGH FOR 30 SECONDS until the yolk just starts to change colour. Leave to stand, covered, for 1 minute, then MIC-ROWAVE FOR 15 TO 30 SECONDS according to taste. Remove the egg with a slotted spoon, allowing the water to drain off, then transfer to a serving plate.

SERVES 1

To cook 2 poached eggs: Combine 450 ml/¾ pint/2 cups boiling water, ½ teaspoon white vinegar and ½ teaspoon salt in a large deep dish and MICROWAVE ON HIGH FOR 1 TO 1½ MINUTES until fast boiling. Break the eggs into the water, one at a time. Cover and MICROWAVE ON HIGH FOR 1 TO 1½ MINUTES or MICROWAVE ON HIGH FOR 45 SECONDS TO 1 MINUTE. Allow 2 minutes standing time.

To cook 4 poached eggs: Combine 600 ml/1 pint/2½ cups boiling water, 1 tablespoon white vinegar and 1 teaspoon salt in a large deep dish. MICROWAVE ON HIGH FOR 3 TO 4 MINUTES until fast boiling. Break the eggs into the water, one at a time. Cover and MICROWAVE ON MEDIUM FOR 2½ TO 3 MINUTES or MICROWAVE ON HIGH FOR 1¾ TO 2 MINUTES.

Preparing scrambled eggs and baked eggs (see Bacon, Egg, and Tomato)

Bacon, egg and tomato; Toast (page 21)

SCRAMBLED EGGS

METRIC/IMPERIAL	AMERICAN
2 eggs	2 eggs
2 tablespoons milk	2 tablespoons milk
pinch of salt	pinch of salt
freshly ground black pepper	freshly ground black pepper
2 teaspoons butter	2 teaspoons butter

Lightly beat the eggs, milk, salt, and pepper to taste, together in a small bowl. Add the butter and MICROWAVE ON HIGH FOR 1½ TO 2 MINUTES until almost set, stirring with a fork once or twice during cooking. Leave to stand for 1 minute before serving.

SERVES 1

To cook 4, 6 or 8 scrambled eggs: Increase the quantities accordingly and MICROWAVE ON HIGH, allowing an additional 30 seconds for each extra egg.

BACON, EGG AND TOMATO

METRIC/IMPERIAL	AMERICAN
2 rashers bacon	2 bacon slices
1 medium firm tomato, halved	1 medium firm tomato, halved
1 egg	1 egg

Snip the bacon rind with kitchen scissors in two or three places or trim away. Put the bacon on a plate and MICROWAVE ON HIGH FOR 30 SECONDS. Place the tomato halves on the plate, cut side up.

Break the egg into a greased cup, puncture the yolk with the tip of a sharp knife, cover loosely with plastic cling film and put on the plate with the bacon and tomato. MICROWAVE ON HIGH FOR 1½ MINUTES, giving the plate a quarter-turn every 15 seconds.

Leave to stand for 30 seconds, then carefully remove the plastic cling film and slide the egg on to the plate.

SERVES 1

To cook 4 portions: PREHEAT A LARGE BROWNING SKILLET FOR 3 MINUTES. Arrange the bacon slices, side by side on the skillet and MICROWAVE ON HIGH FOR 3 MINUTES. Remove the bacon and keep warm. REHEAT THE BROWNING SKILLET FOR 2 MINUTES, then break an egg into each corner. Puncture the yolk, cover and MICROWAVE ON HIGH FOR 1½ TO 2 MINUTES, giving the dish a half-turn once during cooking. Leave to stand while cooking the tomatoes; arrange on a plate, cover and MICROWAVE ON HIGH FOR 2½ TO 3 MINUTES, giving the dish a quarter-turn every 30 seconds.

EGG IN THE MIDDLE

METRIC/IMPERIAL	AMERICAN
2 thin slices of bread or toast	2 thin slices of bread or toast
7 g/¼ oz butter	¼ oz butter
7 g/¼ oz anchovy paste	¼ oz anchovy spread
1 egg	1 egg

Using an upturned cup, cut a large circle of bread from the centre of one slice. Spread the whole slice of bread with butter and anchovy paste and place the cut-out slice on top. Spread with the remaining butter and anchovy paste.

Put the sandwich on a plate and break an egg into the hole. Pierce the yolk gently with the tip of a sharp knife. Cover with the circle of bread and MICROWAVE ON HIGH FOR 1 TO 1½ MINUTES. Leave to stand for 1 minute and remove the circle of bread before serving.

SERVES 1

To cook 2 or 4 eggs: Increase the quantities accordingly. Two eggs will take 2 to 2½ minutes to cook. Four eggs will take 3½ to 4 minutes to cook.

QUICK STUFFED TOMATOES WITH BACON

METRIC/IMPERIAL	AMERICAN
2 large tomatoes	2 large tomatoes
2 eggs	2 eggs
2 lean rashers bacon, derinded	2 lean bacon slices, derinded

Cut a slice from the top of each tomato and set aside. Scoop out half the pulp. Arange the tomato shells side by side on a serving plate and carefully break an egg into each one.

Wrap a slice of bacon around each tomato to form a collar, about 1 cm/½ inch taller than the tomato. Spoon the remaining tomato pulp over the egg and top with the tomato lid.

Cover with a piece of absorbent kitchen paper and MICROWAVE ON MEDIUM FOR 4½ TO 5 MINUTES or MICROWAVE ON HIGH FOR 2½ TO 3½ MINUTES, until the egg white just begins to thicken.

Leave to stand for 1 minute before removing the paper and serving.

SERVES 1 TO 2

To cook 4 stuffed tomatoes: Double the quantities. MICROWAVE ON MEDIUM FOR 7½ TO 9 MINUTES or MICROWAVE ON HIGH FOR 4 TO 6 MINUTES, giving the dish a half-turn once during cooking.

SAUSAGES AND BAKED BEANS

METRIC/IMPERIAL	AMERICAN
2 × 50 g/2 oz pork or beef sausages, well-pricked	¼ lb link sausages, well-pricked
4–5 tablespoons baked beans	4–5 tablespoons baked beans

Cook the sausages in the microwave oven (see page 15). Cover and leave to stand while cooking the beans.

Pile the baked beans onto a suitable warmed serving plate. Cover loosely with plastic cling film and MICROWAVE ON HIGH FOR 1 MINUTES. Carefully remove the cling film and place the sausages next to the beans. Serve immediately.

SERVES 1

To cook 2 or 3 portions: Use a 225 g/½ lb can baked beans and divide between the serving plates. Stack the plates so that the piles of beans are staggered, cover the top plate only and MICROWAVE ON HIGH FOR 2½ TO 3 MINUTES. Serve with sausages as above.

KIPPERS

METRIC/IMPERIAL	AMERICAN
2 kippers	2 kippers
cayenne pepper	cayenne pepper

Remove the heads and tails from the kippers, using kitchen scissors. Place the kippers, skin side down, on a plate. Cover loosely with plastic cling film. MICROWAVE ON HIGH FOR 3 TO 4 MINUTES, giving the dish a half-turn once during cooking. Carefully remove the plastic cling film and sprinkle the kippers with cayenne pepper, before serving.

SERVES 1 OR 2

Note: Boil-in-the-bag kipper fillets will take less time to cook. Place the kippers in their bags on a plate. Puncture the top of the bag and cook for half the time specified on the packet.

To cook 4 or 8 kippers: Arrange the kippers, either individually or in pairs, on individual serving plates. Using stacking rings, place these one above the other. Cover the top plate only with plastic cling film. MICROWAVE ON HIGH FOR 6 TO 10 MINUTES, depending on the thickness and the number of kippers being cooked. There is no need to turn the kippers during cooking.

SAUSAGE, BACON AND EGG

METRIC/IMPERIAL	AMERICAN
7 g/¼ oz butter	1 teaspoon butter
2 × 50 g/2 oz sausages, well-pricked	¼ lb link sausages, well-pricked
1 bacon rasher	1 bacon slice
1 egg	1 egg

PREHEAT A LARGE BROWNING SKILLET FOR 5 MINUTES (or according to the manufacturer's instructions). Quickly add the butter and sausages, turning the sausages over once to brown both sides. MICROWAVE ON HIGH FOR 2 MINUTES, then add the bacon and MICROWAVE ON HIGH FOR 1 MINUTE.

Finally, break in the egg and MICROWAVE ON HIGH FOR 1 MINUTE. Cover and leave to stand for 2 minutes. Using a slotted spoon, transfer to a heated plate and serve immediately.

SERVES 1

To cook 2 portions: Double the quantities. Follow the above method, but add the butter to the browning skillet after just 4 minutes. To cook the sausages, MICROWAVE ON HIGH FOR 3½ MINUTES, then add the bacon and MICROWAVE ON HIGH FOR 1½ MINUTES. Add the eggs and MICROWAVE ON HIGH FOR 1½ MINUTES. Leave to stand, as above, before serving.

SMOKED HADDOCK

METRIC/IMPERIAL
500 g/1 lb smoked haddock
  fillet
15 g/½ oz butter
cayenne pepper

AMERICAN
1 lb smoked haddock fillet
1 tablespoon butter
cayenne pepper

Place the smoked haddock, skin side down, in a large shallow dish. Cover loosely with plastic cling film and MICROWAVE ON HIGH FOR 4 TO 4½ MINUTES, giving the dish a half-turn once during cooking. Leave to stand for 2 minutes.

Carefully remove the plastic cling film and test with a fork; the flesh should be creamy white and flake easily. Dot with butter and sprinkle with cayenne pepper before serving.

SERVES 2

TOAST

METRIC/IMPERIAL
25 g/1 oz butter
2 slices bread, crusts
  removed

AMERICAN
2 tablespoons butter
2 slices bread, crusts
  removed

Butter the bread generously on both sides. PREHEAT A LARGE BROWNING SKILLET FOR 5 MINUTES (or according to the manufacturer's instructions). Quickly place the bread in the skillet and MICROWAVE ON HIGH FOR 30 SECONDS. Immediately turn the bread over and MICROWAVE ON HIGH FOR 30 TO 45 SECONDS until lightly browned.

SERVES 1 OR 2

Note: If triangles of toast are required, cut the buttered bread before microwaving. Move the triangles in the centre to the outside edges of the skillet before the second cooking period.

LUNCHES & SNACKS

In this chapter, the emphasis is on quickly assembled one-course meals. Perhaps the most exciting advantage the microwave oven offers is that it permits so many items to be reheated without spoiling. Thus time can be saved by preparing and par-cooking components of a dish in advance.

Where a recipe calls for a sauce, such as Chicken à la King, prepare it ahead and store in the refrigerator until required. Pasta can be reheated successfully provided a spoonful of oil is added to the cooking water and the pasta is well-drained before storing. Pasta can also be frozen, although it takes almost as long to thaw and reheat as it does to cook afresh. Microwave-cooked rice is perfect, whether reheated from cold or frozen.

Stuffed baked potatoes can be cooked and later reheated on HIGH FOR 1½ TO 2 MINUTES. If you intend to serve stuffed peppers, prepare the filling in advance and soften the peppers by microwaving on HIGH FOR 2 TO 3 MINUTES. The dish can later be assembled and cooked quickly.

There are of course other ways to save time by preparing ahead. Grated cheese can be stored in a plastic container in a cool place, or frozen. Bread-crumbs can similarly be kept handy for instant use.

Burgers can be pre-shaped and simply popped into the microwave oven when required.

Most of the recipes give quantities for two persons; should you wish to cook for only one, halve the quantities and cut the cooking time by approximately one-third. So, if the cooking time is 6 minutes, a half-quantity will be cooked in 4 minutes. Similarly, unless otherwise stated, there is no reason why recipes cannot be doubled to serve four. In this case the cooking time should be increased by two-thirds, so a recipe taking 6 minutes to cook will, when doubled, require 10 minutes.

If you wish to serve a vegetable with your lunch, follow the instructions given in the charts on pages 148–9. All that is required in most cases is the addition of a few tablespoons of salted water. Fresh vegetables are extremely successful cooked by microwave. Because cooking periods are short and minimal liquid is used, they retain flavour, colour and nutritive value. Frozen vegetables can also be cooked very quickly in the microwave oven.

In all probability you will round off your lunch with fresh fruit or perhaps cheese, but if you have a little extra time to prepare a dessert turn to the desserts in the Family Meals chapter.

BEETROOT AND CELERY SOUP

METRIC/IMPERIAL	AMERICAN
1 small onion, finely chopped	1 small onion, finely chopped
½ stick celery, finely chopped	½ celery stalk, finely chopped
knob of butter	1 teaspoon butter
1 teaspoon flour	1 teaspoon flour
150 ml/¼ pint water	⅔ cup water
2 tablespoons red wine	2 tablespoons red wine
1 chicken stock cube, crumbled	1 chicken bouillon cube, crumbled
pinch of mustard powder	pinch of mustard powder
pinch of powdered bay leaves	pinch of powdered bay leaves
100 g/4 oz cooked beetroot, finely chopped	¼ lb cooked beet, finely chopped
salt	salt
freshly ground black pepper	freshly ground black pepper
4 tablespoons top of the milk	¼ cup half and half
1 tablespoon chopped chives	1 tablespoon chopped chives

Combine the onion, celery and butter in a bowl and MICROWAVE ON HIGH FOR 3 MINUTES, stirring once during cooking. Mix in the flour, then gradually stir in the water and wine. Add the stock (bouillon) cube, mustard, bay leaves, beetroot, salt and pepper to taste. MICROWAVE ON HIGH FOR 10 MINUTES.

Purée the soup in an electric blender or press through a sieve (strainer). Return to the bowl, add the milk and MICROWAVE ON HIGH FOR 1 TO ¼ MINUTES until hot.

Sprinkle with chopped chives to garnish and serve with crusty bread.

SERVES 2

CONVENIENT CARROT SOUP

METRIC/IMPERIAL	AMERICAN
1 onion	1 onion
1 × 275 g/10 oz can carrots	1 × 10 oz can carrots
1 chicken stock cube	1 chicken bouillon cube
1 teaspoon tomato ketchup	1 teaspoon tomato ketchup
¼ teaspoon salt	¼ teaspoon salt
freshly ground black pepper	freshly ground black pepper
1 tablespoon instant mashed potato powder	1 tablespoon instant mashed potato powder
150 ml/¼ pint cold water	⅔ cup cold water

Place the onion in a bowl, cover and MICROWAVE ON HIGH FOR 2 MINUTES until soft. Shred, using a knife and fork. Add the carrots, together with the liquid from the can; the stock (bouillon) cube, tomato ketchup, salt and pepper to taste.

Cover and MICROWAVE ON HIGH FOR 5 MINUTES, then mash with a fork or potato masher. Blend the potato powder with the water and stir into the soup. MICROWAVE ON HIGH FOR 3 MINUTES, stirring occasionally.

Serve hot, with crusty bread or rolls.

SERVES 2

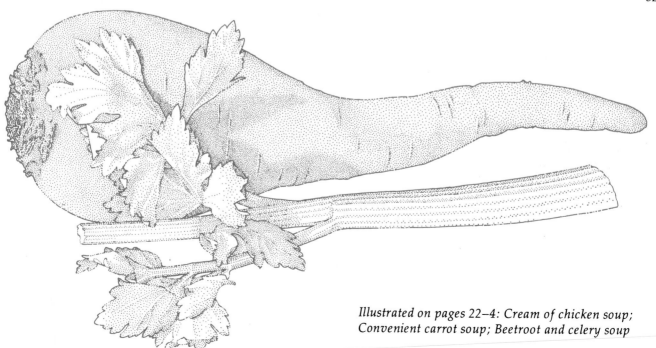

Illustrated on pages 22–4: Cream of chicken soup; Convenient carrot soup; Beetroot and celery soup

CREAM OF CHICKEN SOUP

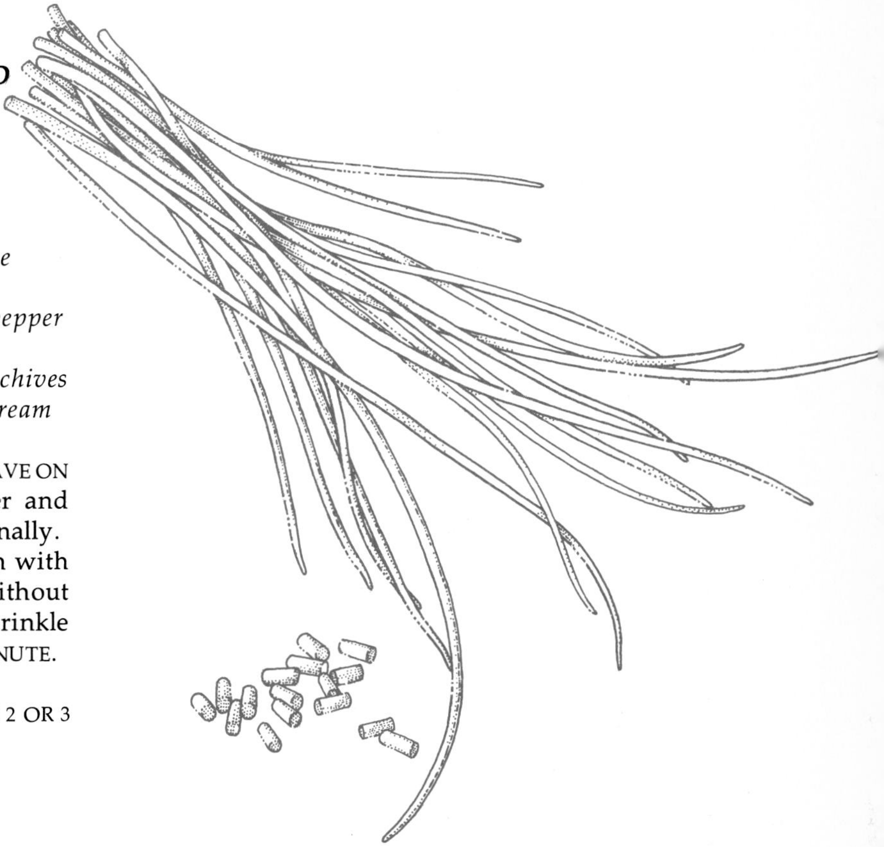

METRIC/IMPERIAL	AMERICAN
25 g/1 oz butter	2 tablespoons butter
25 g/1 oz flour	½ cup flour
450 ml/¾ pint water	2 cups water
1 chicken stock cube	1 chicken bouillon cube
salt	salt
freshly ground black pepper	freshly ground black pepper
100 g/4 oz cooked chicken	¼ lb cooked chicken
1 tablespoon chopped chives	1 tablespoon chopped chives
2 tablespoons double cream	2 tablespoons heavy cream

Put the butter and flour in a large bowl and MICROWAVE ON HIGH FOR 1½ MINUTES. Gradually stir in the water and MICROWAVE ON HIGH FOR 4 MINUTES, stirring occasionally.

Crumble in the stock (bouillon) cube and season with salt and pepper to taste, then add the chicken. Without covering, MICROWAVE ON HIGH FOR 10 MINUTES. Sprinkle with the chives and MICROWAVE ON HIGH FOR 1 MINUTE.

Stir in the cream just before serving.

SERVES 2 OR 3

POTATO SOUP

METRIC/IMPERIAL	AMERICAN
100 g/4 oz peeled potato	¼ lb peeled potato
1 small onion	1 small onion
2 tablespoons frozen peas	2 tablespoons frozen peas
¼ teaspoon powdered bay leaves	¼ teaspoon powdered bay leaves
½ chicken stock cube, crumbled	½ chicken bouillon cube, crumbled
300 ml/½ pint water	1¼ cups water
4 tablespoons milk	¼ cup milk
¼ teaspoon salt	¼ teaspoon salt
freshly ground black pepper	freshly ground black pepper

Cut the potato and onion into thin slices and place in a large bowl. Add the remaining ingredients and stir well. Cover the bowl loosely with plastic cling film and MICROWAVE ON HIGH FOR 10 MINUTES. Purée the soup in an electric blender or press through a sieve. Adjust the seasoning and serve hot.

SERVES 2

For 4 or more servings: Increase the ingredients accordingly and combine all ingredients in the bowl except the milk; stir well. MICROWAVE ON HIGH FOR 15 MINUTES then purée as above. Add the milk to the purée, then MICROWAVE ON HIGH FOR 3 TO 4 MINUTES to reheat, before serving.

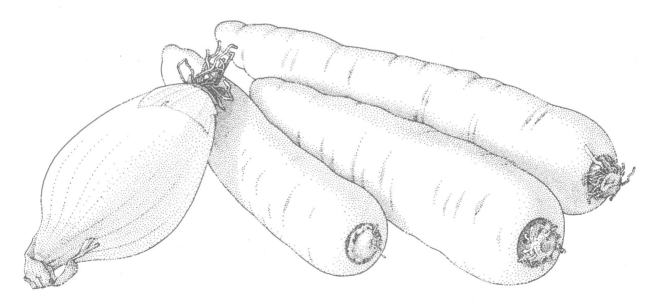

CONSOMMÉ WITH TAGLIATELLE

METRIC/IMPERIAL	AMERICAN
1 × 275 g/10 oz can condensed beef consommé	1 × 10 oz can condensed beef consommé
water to mix	water to mix
1 teaspoon tomato ketchup	1 teaspoon tomato ketchup
25 g/1 oz tagliatelle	1 oz tagliatelle
25 g/1 oz Edam cheese, finely diced	1 oz Edam cheese, finely diced
freshly ground black pepper	freshly ground black pepper

Pour the consommé into a large bowl. Add the required quantity of water, stir well. MICROWAVE ON HIGH FOR 5 TO 5½ MINUTES until boiling.

Add the pasta, then cover and MICROWAVE ON HIGH FOR 5 MINUTES, stirring once during cooking. Add the cheese and sprinkle liberally with black pepper.

Leave to stand for 1 minute to allow the cheese to soften. Serve hot with crusty bread.

SERVES 2 OR 3

Note: If only 1 portion of soup is required, just add cheese and pepper to this serving. The rest of the consommé may be reheated later; add cheese and pepper before serving.

LENTIL SOUP

METRIC/IMPERIAL	AMERICAN
25 g/1 oz dried lentils	2–3 tablespoons dried lentils
½ onion, thinly sliced	½ onion, thinly sliced
450 ml/¾ pint water	2 cups water
¼ teaspoon salt	¼ teaspoon salt
¼ teaspoon black pepper	¼ teaspoon black pepper
½ beef stock cube, crumbled	½ beef bouillon cube, crumbled
1 teaspoon tomato ketchup	1 teaspoon tomato ketchup

Wash the lentils under cold running water, then drain and place in a large bowl. Add all the remaining ingredients, cover loosely with plastic cling film and MICROWAVE ON HIGH FOR 15 MINUTES.

Carefully remove the plastic cling film and stir thoroughly. Without covering, MICROWAVE ON HIGH FOR 5 TO 10 MINUTES until the lentils are soft.

If a smooth soup is preferred, purée in an electric blender. Alternatively, serve directly from the bowl.

SERVES 2

For 4 servings: Double the above quantities. Prepare as above, but add the extra boiling water after MICROWAVING ON HIGH FOR 35 TO 40 MINUTES. Serve immediately.

TOMATO SOUP

METRIC/IMPERIAL	AMERICAN
15 g/½ oz butter	1 tablespoon butter
2 tablespoons flour	2 tablespoons flour
1 × 400 g/14 oz can tomatoes	1 × 14 oz can tomatoes
250 ml/8 fl oz boiling water	1 cup boiling water
1 beef stock cube	1 beef bouillon cube
½ teaspoon dried basil	½ teaspoon dried basil
salt	salt
freshly ground black pepper	freshly ground black pepper

Put the butter and flour in a large bowl and MICROWAVE ON HIGH FOR 1 MINUTE. Stir well until thoroughly blended. Add the tomatoes, together with their juice, and mash well, using a potato masher.

Stir in the water, then crumble in the stock (bouillon) cube. Sprinkle in the basil and salt and pepper to taste. Without covering, MICROWAVE ON HIGH FOR 10 MINUTES, stirring occasionally. Serve immediately, or purée in an electric blender before serving, if a smooth soup is preferred.

SERVES 2 OR 3

TUNA-STUFFED GREEN PEPPERS

METRIC/IMPERIAL	AMERICAN
2 large green peppers	2 large green peppers
1 × 200 g/7 oz can tuna	1 × 7 oz can tuna
1 tablespoon lemon juice	1 tablespoon lemon juice
75 g/3 oz boiled rice	½ cup boiled rice
salt	salt
freshly ground black pepper	freshly ground black pepper
1 egg, beaten	1 egg, beaten
150 ml/¼ pint water	⅔ cup water

Cut a slice from the top of each pepper and set aside, then scoop out the core and seeds. Flake the tuna and mix with the lemon juice, rice and salt and pepper to taste. Bind the stuffing with the beaten egg.

Pile the stuffing into the peppers, replace the lids and put in a shallow dish into which they fit snugly. Pour the water into the dish, cover loosely with plastic cling film and MICROWAVE ON HIGH FOR 10 TO 12 MINUTES until the pepper feels tender when lightly pressed. There is no need to remove the cling film when testing. Leave to stand for 2 minutes then drain off the water. Serve hot.

SERVES 2

Stuffing variations:
The tuna may be replaced with either of the following:—
1. 100 g/¼ lb smoked cod, flaked with 2 chopped hard-boiled (hard-cooked) eggs
2. 100 g/¼ lb minced (ground) cooked beef, with 3 table-spoons tomato purée (paste) and ½ teaspoon onion salt

Left: Consommé with tagliatelle; tomato soup; lentil soup

Below: Tuna-stuffed green peppers

SOFT FISH ROES ON TOAST

METRIC/IMPERIAL	AMERICAN
15 g/½ oz butter	*1 tablespoon butter*
100 g/4 oz soft herring roes	*¼ lb soft herring roes*
lemon juice	*lemon juice*
salt	*salt*
freshly ground black pepper	*freshly ground black pepper*
1–2 slices of bread	*1–2 slices of bread*
cayenne pepper	*cayenne pepper*

Put the butter in a small shallow dish and MICROWAVE ON HIGH FOR 30 SECONDS, until melted. Wash the herring roes and drain thoroughly. Sprinkle with lemon juice and season with salt and pepper to taste.

Add the herring roes to the butter, turning them until thoroughly coated. Arrange in a single layer, cover the dish loosely with plastic cling film and MICROWAVE ON LOW FOR 4 TO 4½ MINUTES.

Leave to stand, covered, while toasting the bread. Pile the herring roes onto the unbuttered toast and sprinkle with cayenne pepper before serving.

SERVES 1 OR 2

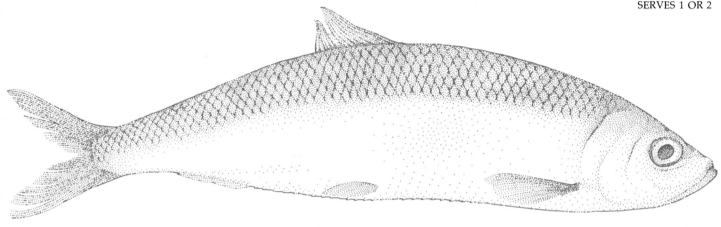

FISH IN CHEESE SAUCE

AMERICAN	METRIC/IMPERIAL
½ lb frozen fish steaks	*225 g/8 oz frozen fish steaks*
1 egg	*1 egg*
1¼ cups milk	*300 ml/½ pint milk*
¼ cup grated Cheddar cheese	*25 g/1 oz Cheddar cheese, grated*
salt	*salt*
freshly ground black pepper	*freshly ground black pepper*

Arrange the fish steaks in a large shallow dish and MICROWAVE ON HIGH FOR 2 MINUTES. Beat the egg, milk, cheese, salt and pepper together. Pour this sauce over the fish. MICROWAVE ON HIGH FOR 6 TO 8 MINUTES or until the custard is just set, stirring occassionally during cooking and breaking the fish into pieces as it becomes tender.

Serve the fish with baked tomatoes, peas or other vegetables of choice.

SERVES 2

QUICK-COOK PLAICE (FLOUNDER) FILLETS

METRIC/IMPERIAL	AMERICAN
2–3 plaice fillets	*2–3 flounder fillets*
15–25 g/½–1 oz butter	*1–2 tablespoons butter*
squeeze of lemon juice	*squeeze of lemon juice*
salt	*salt*
freshly ground black pepper	*freshly ground black pepper*

Arrange the fish fillets, skin side down and with the thinner parts towards the middle, in a single layer on a plate or serving dish. Spread the butter around the outside edges of the fillets. Sprinkle with lemon juice, salt and pepper to taste.

Cover the dish loosely with plastic cling film. MICROWAVE ON HIGH FOR 3½ TO 6 MINUTES, depending on the number and size of the fillets, until the flesh is opaque and flakes when tested with a fork. Carefully remove the plastic cling film and serve immediately.

SERVES 2 OR 3

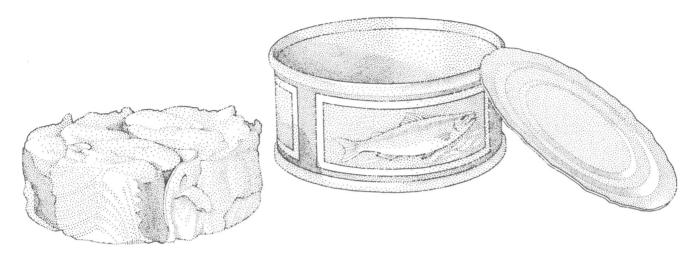

SALMON FISH CAKES

METRIC/IMPERIAL
1 × 100 g/4 oz can pink
   salmon
100 g/4 oz mashed potato
knob of softened butter
1 teaspoon lemon juice
1 tablespoon chopped
   parsley
salt
freshly ground black pepper
1 small egg, beaten
4–5 tablespoons golden
   crumbs
3 tablespoons vegetable oil

AMERICAN
1 × ¼ lb can pink salmon
¼ lb mashed potato
1 teaspoon softened butter
1 teaspoon lemon juice
1 tablespoon chopped
   parsley
salt
freshly ground black pepper
1 small egg, beaten
4–5 tablespoons golden
   crumbs
3 tablespoons vegetable oil

Drain and flake the salmon. Mix thoroughly with the potato, butter, lemon juice and parsley. Add salt and pepper to taste. Bind the mixture with the beaten egg.

Divide the mixture into 4 equal portions and shape each one into a round cake, about 1 cm/½ inch thick. Coat with the crumbs, pressing them on firmly with a palette knife.

Put the oil in a round dish and MICROWAVE ON HIGH FOR 1 MINUTE. Arrange the fish cakes in the dish and MICROWAVE ON HIGH FOR 3 TO 4 MINUTES until thoroughly hot, turning the fish cakes over once during cooking. Drain on absorbent kitchen paper.

Serve the salmon fish cakes, either hot or cold with a mixed salad.

SERVES 2

Note: Either mashed boiled potatoes or reconstituted instant dried potato may be used for these fish cakes.

MUSTARD HERRINGS

METRIC/IMPERIAL
15 g/½ oz butter
1 tablespoon lemon juice
½ teaspoon salt
3 teaspoons whole grain, or
   Dijon mustard
2 herrings, gutted and
   cleaned
1 tablespoon flour

AMERICAN
1 tablespoon butter
1 tablespoon lemon juice
½ teaspoon salt
3 teaspoons whole grain, or
   Dijon mustard
2 herrings, gutted and
   cleaned
1 tablespoon flour

Put the butter into a dish in which the herrings will fit snugly. MICROWAVE ON HIGH FOR 30 SECONDS until melted. Stir in the lemon juice, salt and mustard.

Coat the herrings with the flour, then place in the dish and turn over so that they are completely coated with butter. Arrange them head to tail.

Cover with a piece of greaseproof (waxed) paper and MICROWAVE ON HIGH FOR 3 TO 4 MINUTES until the fish is tender; turn the herrings over once during cooking. Serve hot.

SERVES 1 OR 2

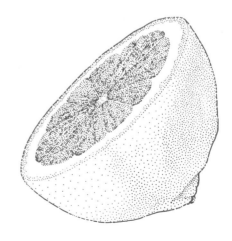

KEDGEREE

METRIC/IMPERIAL	AMERICAN
175 g/6 oz smoked haddock	*6 oz smoked haddock*
20 g/¾ oz butter	*1½ tablespoons butter*
1 hard-boiled egg, chopped	*1 hard-cooked egg, chopped*
225 g/8 oz cooked long-grain rice	*1⅓ cups cooked long-grain rice*
2 tablespoons single cream	*2 tablespoons light cream*
1 tablespoon chopped parsley	*1 tablespoon chopped parsley*
pinch of cayenne pepper	*pinch of cayenne pepper*
¼ teaspoon paprika	*¼ teaspoon paprika*

Place the smoked haddock in a deep pie dish. Cover the dish loosely with plastic cling film and MICROWAVE ON HIGH FOR 2½ TO 3½ MINUTES until the flesh is tender. Remove any skin and flake the fish. Drain the residual juices from the dish.

Put the butter into the hot dish and swirl round until melted. Stir in the flaked fish, chopped egg and rice. MICROWAVE ON HIGH FOR 3 TO 3½ MINUTES until the rice is hot.

Stir in the cream and sprinkle the kedgeree with the parsley, cayenne and paprika before serving.

SERVES 2

CHICKEN PACKETS

METRIC/IMPERIAL	AMERICAN
225 g/8 oz frozen puff pastry	1/2 lb frozen puff pastry
2 thin slices cooked ham	2 thin slices cooked ham
225 g/8 oz boned, cooked chicken, skinned	1/2 lb boneless, cooked chicken, skinned
salt	salt
freshly ground black pepper	freshly ground black pepper
1 egg, beaten	1 egg, beaten

To thaw the pastry, MICROWAVE ON LOW FOR 1 MINUTE, then leave for 5 minutes until it is just pliable. Cut in half and roll each piece to an oblong, approximately 13 × 18 cm/ 5 × 7 inches.

Place a slice of ham on each piece of pastry, leaving a 2½ cm/1 inch border. Dice the chicken and place on top of the ham. Season lightly with salt and pepper. Brush the edges of the pastry with beaten egg. Fold in half to form packets, enclosing the filling. Press the edges together to seal, trimming them if necessary.

Arrange the packets on a piece of greaseproof (waxed) paper, pressing the sealed edges underneath. Cut 2 or 3 slits in the top of the packets, with a sharp knife. Brush with beaten egg. MICROWAVE ON HIGH FOR 5½ MINUTES, then turn over and MICROWAVE ON HIGH FOR 2 MINUTES.

Immediately place under a preheated hot grill (broiler) to brown. Serve hot with parsley sauce if liked, or cold with salad.

SERVES 2

PARSLEY SAUCE

METRIC/IMPERIAL	AMERICAN
15 g/½ oz butter	1 tablespoon butter
2 tablespoons flour	2 tablespoons all-purpose flour
150 ml/¼ pint milk	⅔ cup milk
salt	salt
freshly ground black pepper	freshly ground black pepper
2 tablespoons chopped parsley	2 tablespoons chopped parsley

Put the butter in a large jug and MICROWAVE ON HIGH FOR 30 SECONDS until melted. Mix in the flour, then gradually stir in the milk. MICROWAVE ON HIGH FOR 2 MINUTES.

Add salt and pepper to taste and whisk thoroughly. Stir in the parsley. MICROWAVE ON HIGH FOR 1 TO 1½ MINUTES until the sauce thickens. Whisk thoroughly. Serve with fish or chicken dishes.

SERVES 2

Note: This sauce can be prepared in advance and then reheated in the microwave oven just before serving.

Left: Kedgeree

Below: Preparing Chicken packets

CHICKEN À LA KING

METRIC/IMPERIAL	AMERICAN
40 g/1½ oz butter	*3 tablespoons butter*
25 g/1 oz flour	*¼ cup flour*
150 ml/¼ pint water	*⅔ cup water*
150 ml/¼ pint milk	*⅔ cup milk*
½ chicken stock cube	*½ chicken bouillon cube*
½ teaspoon celery salt	*½ teaspoon celery salt*
freshly ground black pepper	*freshly ground black pepper*
225 g/8 oz cooked chicken, diced	*1 cup diced cooked chicken*
1 thin slice ham, diced	*1 thin slice cooked ham, diced*
100 g/4 oz frozen peas	*¾ cup frozen peas*
175–225 g/6–8 oz boiled long-grain rice	*1–1⅓ cups boiled long-grain rice*

Put the butter in a large shallow dish and MICROWAVE ON HIGH FOR 30 TO 45 SECONDS until melted. Stir in the flour. Add the water, milk, stock (bouillon) cube, celery salt and pepper to taste. MICROWAVE ON HIGH FOR 2 MINUTES, stirring, thoroughly from the sides to the centre of the dish after 1 minute.

Add the chicken, ham and peas to the sauce. Partially cover and MICROWAVE ON HIGH FOR 7 TO 10 MINUTES, stirring occasionally, until the peas are cooked and the chicken is hot.

Remove the cover and arrange the rice in a border around the edges of the dish. MICROWAVE ON HIGH FOR 2 MINUTES or until the rice is hot, giving the dish a half-turn after 1 minute. Serve immediately.

SERVES 2

GRIDDLED LAMB CHOPS

METRIC/IMPERIAL	
2 lamb chops	*2 lamb chops*
15–25 g/½–1 oz butter	*1–2 tablespoons butter*
salt	*salt*
freshly ground black pepper	*freshly ground black pepper*

PREHEAT A LARGE BROWNING SKILLET FOR 5 MINUTES (or according to the manufacturer's instructions). Meanwhile trim the chops and spread both sides with butter. As soon as the oven switches off, place the chops in the skillet with the bones towards the centre.

Cooking time will depend upon the size of the chops; MICROWAVE ON HIGH FOR 1½ TO 2 MINUTES, then turn the chops over and MICROWAVE ON MEDIUM FOR 2½ TO 3½ MINUTES, until just cooked. Remove from the skillet and drain off the fat. Transfer to warm plates and sprinkle with salt and pepper to taste.

SERVES 2

Note: For the second cooking period the chops may be MICROWAVED ON HIGH and the cooking time reduced by about 1 minute, but the chops will not be quite as tender.

To cook 1 chop: Prepare as above, but increase the time for each cooking period by about 1 minute.

To cook 4 chops: Prepare as above, but double the time for each cooking period.

GRIDDLED PORK CHOPS

METRIC/IMPERIAL	AMERICAN
2 × 100 g/4 oz pork chops	*2 × ¼ lb pork chops*
salt	*salt*
freshly ground black pepper	*freshly ground black pepper*
15 g/½ oz butter	*1 tablespoon butter*

Season the chops with salt and pepper to taste. PREHEAT A LARGE BROWNING SKILLET FOR 5 MINUTES (or according to the manufacturer's instructions). Toss in the butter, then quickly add the chops, moving them round quickly so they brown evenly. MICROWAVE ON HIGH FOR 2½ MINUTES.

Turn the chops over, pointing the thin end towards the centre of the dish and MICROWAVE ON HIGH FOR 2½ TO 3 MINUTES until the flesh is no longer pink inside. Leave to stand for 3 minutes before serving, accompanied by vegetables of choice.

SERVES 2

To cook 1 pork chop: MICROWAVE ON HIGH FOR 3½ MINUTES, turning halfway through cooking.

To cook 4 chops: Arrange with the thinnest part of each chop towards the centre of the dish. MICROWAVE ON HIGH FOR 7 TO 8 MINUTES, turning halfway through cooking. Although 4 chops may be cooked simultaneously, they will not brown successfully and should ideally be cooked in 2 batches. To reheat the first batch, MICROWAVE ON HIGH FOR 1 MINUTE.

GRIDDLED STEAKS

METRIC/IMPERIAL	AMERICAN
2 × 175 g/6 oz fillet or rump steaks	*2 × 6 oz fillet or sirloin steaks*
ground steak spice (optional)	*ground steak spice (optional)*
15 g/½ oz butter	*1 tablespoon butter*
salt	*salt*
freshly ground black pepper	*freshly ground black pepper*

PREHEAT A SMALL BROWNING SKILLET FOR 4 MINUTES (or according to the manufacturer's instructions). Sprinkle the steaks with steak spice, if preferred.

Toss in the butter, then quickly add the steaks, turning them over immediately. MICROWAVE ON HIGH, turning the steaks over half-way through cooking. Rare steaks will take approximately 3½ minutes; well done steaks will take about 7 minutes.

Transfer to warm serving plates and sprinkle with salt and pepper to taste.

SERVES 2

To cook 1 steak: Proceed as above. A rare steak will take 2 minutes to cook; a well-done steak will take 4 minutes.

Note: It is not advisable to griddle more than 2 steaks at one time, because they will not brown adequately.

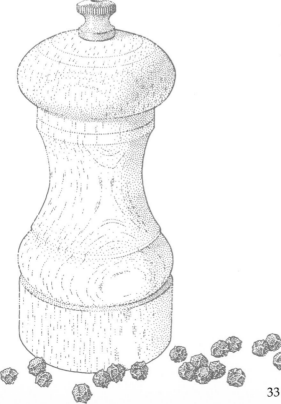

QUICK BEEF SAVOURY

METRIC/IMPERIAL	AMERICAN
225 g/8 oz lean minced beef	1 cup lean ground minced beef
1 teaspoon salt	1 teaspoon salt
¼ teaspoon black pepper	¼ teaspoon black pepper
2 teaspoons flour	2 teaspoons flour
150 ml/¼ pint canned cream of celery soup	⅔ cup canned cream of celery soup

Spread the beef in a small shallow dish. Sprinkle with the salt, pepper and flour. Using the blade of a knife, chop the mixture until the flour is thoroughly incorporated.

Pour the soup over the meat. Without covering, MICROWAVE ON HIGH FOR 5 MINUTES, giving the dish a half-turn after 2½ minutes.

Serve hot, with crusty French bread, potatoes or boiled rice.

SERVES 2

SPAGHETTI BOLOGNESE

METRIC/IMPERIAL	AMERICAN
175 g/6 oz lean minced beef	6 oz lean ground beef
1 onion, chopped	1 onion, chopped
pinch of garlic powder	pinch of garlic powder
1 × 255 g/8 oz can tomatoes	1 × ½ lb can tomatoes
4 tablespoons tomato purée	4 tablespoons tomato paste
1 beef stock cube, crumbled	1 beef bouillon cube, crumbled
150 ml/¼ pint water	⅔ cup water
salt	salt
freshly ground black pepper	freshly ground black pepper
750–900 ml/1 ¼–1 ½ pints boiling water	3–3 ¾ cups boiling water
1 teaspoon salt	1 teaspoon salt
½ teaspoon vegetable oil	½ teaspoon vegetable oil
175 g/6 oz spaghetti	6 oz spaghetti
To serve:	**To serve:**
grated Parmesan or other cheese	grated Parmesan or other cheese

PREHEAT A BROWNING SKILLET FOR 5 MINUTES (or according to the manufacturer's instructions). Quickly stir in the beef, onion and garlic powder. MICROWAVE ON HIGH FOR 5 MINUTES, breaking up the meat with a fork and stirring occasionally during cooking. Add the tomatoes with their juices, tomato purée (paste) and water; stir well. Crumble in the stock (bouillon) cube and season with salt and pepper to taste. Cover with a lid and MICROWAVE ON HIGH FOR 10 MINUTES, stirring once. Leave to stand while cooking the spaghetti.

Pour the boiling water into a large deep dish, add the salt and oil and gently lower in the spaghetti. Stir once and, without covering, MICROWAVE ON HIGH FOR 6 TO 7 MINUTES until just beginning to soften. Cover tightly and leave to stand for 10 minutes.

Meanwhile to reheat the sauce, without covering, MICROWAVE ON HIGH FOR 4 MINUTES, stirring occasionally. Drain the spaghetti thoroughly. Add to the sauce, toss well and sprinkle with grated cheese, before serving.

SERVES 2 OR 3

Spaghetti Bolognese; Gammon (smoked ham slices) and apple

GAMMON (SMOKED HAM SLICES) AND APPLE

METRIC/IMPERIAL	AMERICAN
2 × 175 g/6 oz gammon steaks	2 × 6 oz smoked ham slices
1 dessert apple	1 dessert apple
¼ teaspoon ground allspice	¼ teaspoon ground allspice
2 tablespoons brown sugar	2 tablespoons brown sugar

Remove the rind from the gammon (smoked ham slices) and cut through the fat at 2.5 cm/1 inch intervals, with kitchen scissors, to prevent the meat curling up during cooking. Peel and core the apple, cut into rings and spread in a large shallow dish. Sprinkle with the allspice.

Arrange the gammon steaks (smoked ham slices) on top of the apples and sprinkle with sugar. Cover the dish loosely with plastic cling film and MICROWAVE ON HIGH FOR 5 MINUTES, giving the dish a half-turn after 2½ minutes. Carefully remove the cling film and test the meat with the tip of a sharp knife. If it is not quite tender, MICROWAVE ON HIGH FOR A FURTHER 2 TO 3 MINUTES.

SERVES 2

CHILLI CON CARNE

METRIC/IMPERIAL	AMERICAN
25 g/1 oz butter	2 tablespoons butter
1 large onion, finely chopped	1 large onion, finely chopped
500 g/1 lb lean minced beef	1 lb lean ground beef
1 × 400 g/14 oz can tomatoes	1 × 14 oz can tomatoes
4 tablespoons tomato purée	4 tablespoons tomato paste
150 ml/¼ pint beer	⅔ cup beer
2 teaspoons chilli powder	2 teaspoons chili powder
few drops of Tabasco	few drops of Tabasco
salt	salt
freshly ground black pepper	freshly ground black pepper
1 × 500 g/1 lb can kidney beans, drained	1 × 1 lb can kidney beans, drained
2 tablespoons chopped parsley	2 tablespoons chopped parsley

Put the butter and onion in a large deep dish and MICROWAVE ON HIGH FOR 3 MINUTES, stirring once during cooking. Add the minced beef and MICROWAVE ON HIGH FOR 5 MINUTES, breaking up the meat with a fork twice during cooking.

Stir in the tomatoes and their liquor, the tomato purée (paste), beer, chilli powder, Tabasco, and salt and pepper to taste. Cover with a lid and MICROWAVE ON HIGH FOR 20 MINUTES, stirring occasionally.

Stir in the kidney beans and, without covering, MICROWAVE ON HIGH FOR 5 MINUTES. Sprinkle with chopped parsley to garnish.

SERVES 4 TO 6

Note: The flavour of this dish improves if it is prepared 24 hours in advance and stored in the refrigerator until required. To reheat, cover and MICROWAVE ON HIGH FOR 5 TO 7 MINUTES, stirring occasionally.

LIVER AND ONION CHARLOTTE

METRIC/IMPERIAL	AMERICAN
175 g/6 oz ox liver, sliced	6 oz ox liver, sliced
salt	salt
freshly ground black pepper	freshly ground black pepper
1 onion, chopped	1 onion, chopped
2 tablespoons vegetable oil	2 tablespoons vegetable oil
2 teaspoons gravy powder	2 teaspoons gravy powder
6 tablespoons water	6 tablespoons water
2 tablespoons shredded suet	2 tablespoons shredded suet
8 tablespoons soft fresh breadcrumbs	8 tablespoons soft fresh breadcrumbs
1 small beetroot, thinly sliced (optional)	1 small beet, thinly sliced (optional)

Rinse and dry the liver slices and sprinkle both sides with salt and pepper. Combine the onion and oil in a pie dish and MICROWAVE ON HIGH FOR 3 MINUTES. Stir in the gravy powder and water and MICROWAVE ON HIGH FOR 2 MINUTES, stirring once during cooking.

Add the liver and baste thoroughly with the sauce. Mix the suet and breadcrumbs together, spread evenly over the liver and MICROWAVE ON HIGH FOR 3 MINUTES. Give the dish a half-turn, lightly press the crumbs into the sauce and MICROWAVE ON HIGH FOR 2½ TO 3 MINUTES until the liver is tender.

Serve immediately or, if preferred, cover the top with overlapping beetroot slices and MICROWAVE ON HIGH FOR 1 MINUTE before serving.

SERVES 2

FRIED LIVER AND BACON

METRIC/IMPERIAL
1 small knob of butter
2 rashers bacon, derinded
175 g/6 oz lamb's liver,
    sliced

AMERICAN
1 teaspoon butter
2 bacon slices, derinded
6 oz lamb liver, sliced

PREHEAT A LARGE BROWNING SKILLET FOR 5 MINUTES (or according to the manufacturer's instructions). Add the butter and bacon. Turn the bacon over immediately and move the slices towards opposite sides of the skillet. Arrange the liver in the centre.

MICROWAVE ON HIGH FOR 2½ TO 3 MINUTES until the liver is still just pink inside; turn the liver slices over half-way through cooking. Do not overcook otherwise the liver will toughen.

Serve immediately with mushrooms and baked tomatoes or other vegetables of choice.

SERVES 2

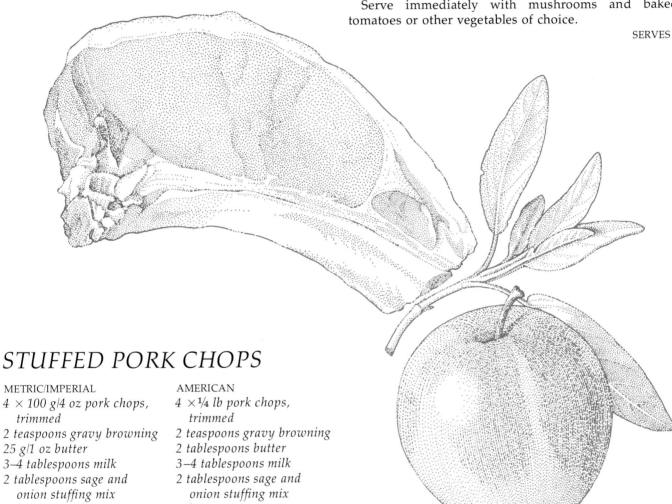

STUFFED PORK CHOPS

METRIC/IMPERIAL
4 × 100 g/4 oz pork chops,
    trimmed
2 teaspoons gravy browning
25 g/1 oz butter
3–4 tablespoons milk
2 tablespoons sage and
    onion stuffing mix
salt
freshly ground black pepper
1 small dessert apple,
    peeled, cored and thinly
    sliced

AMERICAN
4 × ¼ lb pork chops,
    trimmed
2 teaspoons gravy browning
2 tablespoons butter
3–4 tablespoons milk
2 tablespoons sage and
    onion stuffing mix
salt
freshly ground black pepper
1 small dessert apple,
    peeled, cored and thinly
    sliced

Sprinkle one side of each chop with gravy powder. Place the chops, coated side down, in a large shallow dish.

Put the butter in a bowl and MICROWAVE ON HIGH FOR 1 MINUTE. Stir in the dry stuffing mix and sufficient milk to form a soft mixture. Season with salt and pepper to taste.

Spread the stuffing over the chops. Cover the dish loosely with plastic cling film and MICROWAVE ON HIGH FOR 5 TO 6 MINUTES until the chops are no longer pink inside, giving the dish a half-turn once during cooking.

Arrange the apple slices on top of the pork chops and baste with the meat juices. Cover the dish loosely with plastic cling film and MICROWAVE ON HIGH FOR 2 MINUTES.

Serve hot with peas, carrots or other vegetables of your choice.

SERVES 2

Left: Puffy omelette

Right: Cheesy stuffed baked potatoes (page 40); Scrambled eggs and shrimps (page 40); Macaroni cheese with bacon

MACARONI CHEESE WITH BACON

METRIC/IMPERIAL	AMERICAN
100 g/4 oz macaroni	1 cup elbow macaroni
600 ml/1 pint boiling water	2½ cups boiling water
1 teaspoon salt	1 teaspoon salt
15 g/½ oz butter	1 teaspoon butter
2 rashers bacon, derinded and chopped	2 bacon slices, derinded and chopped
25 g/1 oz flour	¼ cup flour
½ teaspoon mustard powder	½ teaspoon mustard powder
300 ml/½ pint milk	1¼ cups milk
100 g/4 oz Cheddar cheese, grated	1 cup grated Cheddar cheese
freshly ground black pepper	freshly ground black pepper
tomato slices to garnish	tomato slices to garnish

Place the macaroni in a deep dish and stir in the water and salt. MICROWAVE ON HIGH FOR 5 MINUTES, then cover and leave to stand while preparing the sauce.

Combine the butter and bacon in a large bowl and MICROWAVE ON HIGH FOR 1 TO 1½ MINUTES until the bacon is lightly cooked. Add the flour and mustard, then gradually stir in the milk. MICROWAVE ON HIGH FOR 3 TO 4 MINUTES, whisking frequently, until the sauce thickens.

Drain the macaroni and stir into the sauce with the cheese. Add pepper and salt to taste. Garnish with tomato slices.

SERVES 2

PUFFY OMELETTE

METRIC/IMPERIAL	AMERICAN
15 g/½ oz butter	1 tablespoon butter
3 eggs, separated	3 eggs, separated
3 tablespoons milk	3 tablespoons milk
¼ teaspoon salt	¼ teaspoon salt
¼ teaspoon black pepper	¼ teaspoon black pepper

Put the butter in a 23 cm/9 inch round pie dish and MICROWAVE ON HIGH FOR 30 SECONDS until melted. Beat the egg whites until stiff peaks form.

In a separate bowl, whisk the egg yolks, milk, salt and pepper together. Gently fold the whisked egg whites into the egg yolk mixture. Turn into the pie dish and MICROWAVE ON LOW FOR 5 TO 6 MINUTES until the middle of the omelette has just set.

Leave to stand for 15 seconds, then fold in half, using a palette knife and turn out on to a serving dish. If desired, place under a preheated hot grill (broiler) to brown. Serve with baked potatoes and a green salad, if liked.

SERVES 2 TO 3

Note: The omelette can be cooked on HIGH FOR 2 TO 3 MINUTES giving the dish a quarter-turn every 30 seconds.

Variations:
1. Add 1 tablespoon chopped chives or parsley to the egg yolk mixture, before folding in the egg whites.
2. Sprinkle grated cheese, chopped cooked ham, finely chopped green pepper, diced cooked bacon or flaked smoked haddock over the omelette, before folding and browning.

WELSH RAREBIT WITH TOMATO

METRIC/IMPERIAL	AMERICAN
1 tomato, skinned and chopped	1 tomato, skinned and chopped
150 g/5 oz Cheddar cheese, grated	1¼ cups grated Cheddar cheese
¼ teaspoon mustard powder	¼ teaspoon mustard powder
¼ teaspoon black pepper	¼ teaspoon black pepper
1 teaspoon cornflour	1 teaspoon cornstarch
2 tablespoons milk	2 tablespoons milk
2 slices of hot buttered toast	2 slices of hot buttered toast

Put the tomato in a small bowl and MICROWAVE ON HIGH FOR 15 SECONDS. Add two-thirds of the cheese, the mustard, pepper and cornflour (cornstarch) then stir in the milk. MICROWAVE ON LOW FOR 2 MINUTES until the cheese has melted. Stir in the remaining cheese. Pile on top of the toast and brown under a preheated grill (broiler).

SERVES 2

SCRAMBLED EGGS AND SHRIMPS

METRIC/IMPERIAL	AMERICAN
20 g/¾ oz butter	1½ tablespoons butter
4 eggs	4 eggs
4 tablespoons milk	4 tablespoons milk
salt	salt
freshly ground black pepper	freshly ground black pepper
50 g/2 oz cooked shelled shrimps	2 oz cooked shelled shrimps
2 slices hot buttered toast paprika	2 slices hot buttered toast paprika

Put the butter in a round shallow dish and MICROWAVE ON HIGH FOR 20 SECONDS. Swirl round the dish. Break in the eggs, milk, salt and pepper and mix with a fork. Add the shrimps. MICROWAVE ON HIGH FOR 3½ TO 4 MINUTES, stirring frequently, until the eggs are soft and just set.

Pile the scrambled egg and shrimps on top of the toast and sprinkle with paprika before serving.

SERVES 2

CHEESY STUFFED BAKED POTATO

METRIC/IMPERIAL	AMERICAN
1 × 200 g/7 oz potato, unblemished	1 × 7 oz potato, unblemished
knob of butter	1 teaspoon butter
3 tablespoons milk	3 tablespoons milk
2 tablespoons grated Cheddar cheese	2 tablespoons grated Cheddar cheese
salt	salt
freshly ground black pepper	freshly ground black pepper
parsley sprig to garnish	parsley sprig to garnish

Scrub and dry the potato, pierce thoroughly and place on a piece of absorbent kitchen paper. MICROWAVE ON HIGH FOR 4 TO 5 MINUTES until just tender, turning the potato over halfway through cooking.

Leave to stand for 1 minute, then cut in half and scoop out the centre of the potato, leaving the skins intact. Mash the potato with the butter, milk, cheese and salt and pepper to taste. Pile the stuffing into the potato shells.

To reheat, MICROWAVE ON HIGH FOR 1 MINUTE. Garnish with parsley and serve hot.

SERVES 1

To cook 2 potatoes: Double the quantities and proceed as above. Cook for 8 to 10 minutes. Reheat for 1½ minutes.

Stuffing variations:
1. 2 tablespoons soured cream, mixed with 1 tablespoon chopped chives, butter, salt and pepper to taste.
2. 15 g/½ oz cream cheese, mixed with ¼ teaspoon nutmeg, salt and pepper to taste.
3. 1 small chopped onion, mixed with a little butter and MICROWAVED ON HIGH FOR 3 MINUTES, then drained and mixed with ¼ teaspoon curry powder.
4. Chopped cooked ham, mixed with 2 tablespoons milk, butter, salt and pepper to taste.
5. Chopped canned pimiento mixed with 1 tablespoon finely chopped nuts, butter, salt and pepper.
6. Sardines mashed with salt and pepper.

TOASTED CHEESE SANDWICH

METRIC/IMPERIAL	AMERICAN
2 slices processed cheese	2 slices processed cheese
¼ teaspoon English mustard	¼ teaspoon English mustard
2 slices buttered toast	2 slices buttered toast

PREHEAT A SMALL BROWNING SKILLET FOR 4 MINUTES (or according to the manufacturer's instructions). Meanwhile sandwich the cheese slices together with mustard and place between the slices of toast, buttered side out. Put into the hot skillet and MICROWAVE ON HIGH FOR 45 SECONDS, turning the sandwich over after 20 seconds.

SERVES 1

Note: Before making a second sandwich REHEAT THE BROWNING SKILLET FOR 2 MINUTES.

Filling variations:
1. Chopped hard-boiled (hard-cooked) egg, mixed with mayonnaise
2. Chopped ham, cream cheese and pickle
3. Sardine mashed with tomato ketchup
4. Crushed sugared raspberries
5. Mashed banana

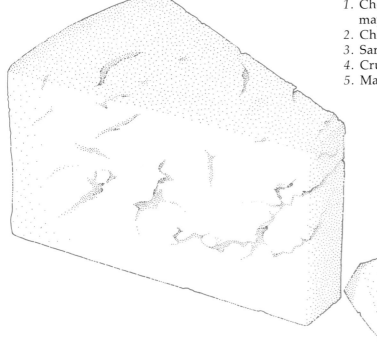

CHEESEBURGERS IN A BUN

METRIC/IMPERIAL	AMERICAN
225 g/8 oz lean minced beef	½ lb lean ground beef
salt	salt
freshly ground black pepper	freshly ground black pepper
2 slices processed cheese	2 slices processed cheese
2 teaspoons tomato ketchup	2 teaspoons tomato ketchup
To serve:	**To serve:**
2 baps, halved and toasted	2 buns, halved and toasted

Divide the meat into 4 equal portions and roll each into a ball then flatten into rounds, about 3 mm/¼ inch thick. Sprinkle liberally with salt and pepper. Sandwich the burgers together in pairs, with a slice of cheese. Press the meat around the edges to seal in the cheese.

Place each cheeseburger on a large plate, lined with absorbent kitchen paper. MICROWAVE ON HIGH FOR 3½ TO 4 MINUTES, giving the plate a half-turn once during cooking. Brush the tops with tomato ketchup, then place in the baps (buns). MICROWAVE ON HIGH FOR 20 SECONDS to reheat before serving.

SERVES 2

BURGERS

METRIC/IMPERIAL
225 g/8 oz lean minced beef
salt
freshly ground black pepper
To serve:
2 baps
few tomato slices

AMERICAN
½ lb lean ground beef
salt
freshly ground black pepper
To serve:
2 buns
few tomato slices

Note: To prepare less crispy burgers, cook on a plate lined with absorbent kitchen paper, giving the plate a half-turn once during cooking. Leave to stand for 2 to 3 minutes until the colour deepens.

Burgers; Nutmeal courgettes; Noodles corvara

PREHEAT A BROWNING SKILLET FOR 5 MINUTES (or according to the manufacturer's instructions). Meanwhile divide the beef into 4 equal portions and roll each into a ball, then flatten to form rounds, about 1 cm/½ inch thick. Sprinkle the burgers liberally with salt and pepper on both sides.

Arrange the burgers on the skillet, cover with a piece of absorbent kitchen paper and MICROWAVE ON HIGH FOR 2½ TO 3 MINUTES, turning the meat over after 1½ minutes.

Split the baps (buns) in half and sandwich together with the burgers and tomato slices. Serve hot with tomato ketchup, brown sauce or mayonnaise.

SERVES 2

NUTMEAL COURGETTES

METRIC/IMPERIAL	AMERICAN
2 large courgettes	2 large zucchini
2 thick slices of bread, crusts removed	2 thick slices of bread, crusts removed
6 tablespoons milk	6 tablespoons milk
15 g/½ oz soft margarine	2 teaspoons soft margarine
4 tablespoons finely chopped nuts	4 tablespoons finely chopped nuts
4 tablespoons grated cheese	4 tablespoons grated cheese
1 egg	1 egg
1 tablespoon chopped parsley	1 tablespoon chopped parsley

Cut the courgettes (zucchini) in half lengthways. Place the bread in a bowl and pour the milk over, then turn the bread over and leave until the milk is absorbed. Mash the bread, then stir in the margarine, nuts, cheese and egg to form a soft stuffing.

Pile the stuffing on top of the courgettes (zucchini). Arrange them, close together, in a dish in which they fit snugly.

MICROWAVE ON HIGH FOR 4 TO 5 MINUTES until the courgettes (zucchini) are just tender. Sprinkle with chopped parsley before serving.

SERVES 2

NOODLES CORVARA

METRIC/IMPERIAL	AMERICAN
100 g/4 oz green noodles	¼ lb green noodles
600 ml/1 pint boiling water	2½ cups boiling water
1 teaspoon salt	1 teaspoon salt
1 teaspoon vegetable oil	1 teaspoon vegetable oil
Sauce:	**Sauce:**
1 small onion, chopped	1 small onion, chopped
2 rashers streaky bacon, derinded and chopped	2 bacon slices, derinded and chopped
1 × 200 g/7 oz can button mushrooms, drained	1 × 7 oz can button mushrooms, drained
2 large tomatoes, quartered	2 large tomatoes, quartered
8 anchovy fillets	8 anchovy fillets
½ teaspoon dried oregano	½ teaspoon dried oregano
¼ teaspoon black pepper	¼ teaspoon black pepper
2 tablespoons water	2 tablespoons water
Garnish:	**Garnish:**
6 stoned black olives	6 pitted ripe olives
1 tablespoon grated Parmesan cheese	1 tablespoon grated Parmesan cheese

Put the noodles in a large deep dish. Pour the water over the noodles and stir in the salt and oil. Without covering, MICROWAVE ON HIGH FOR 5 MINUTES. Cover and leave to stand for 5 minutes, while preparing the sauce.

Combine the onion and bacon in a large deep dish and MICROWAVE ON HIGH FOR 3 MINUTES. Stir in the mushrooms, tomatoes, anchovies, oregano and black pepper. Add the water, then cover and MICROWAVE ON HIGH FOR 4 MINUTES, stirring frequently.

Drain the spaghetti and stir into the sauce. Serve hot, garnished with the olives and sprinkled with cheese.

SERVES 2

CAULIFLOWER BAKE

METRIC/IMPERIAL	AMERICAN
350 g/12 oz frozen cauliflower florets	¾ lb frozen cauliflower florets
Sauce:	**Sauce:**
25 g/1 oz butter	2 tablespoons butter
25 g/1 oz plain flour	¼ cup all-purpose flour
100 g/4 oz curd cheese	½ cup cottage cheese
salt	salt
freshly ground black pepper	freshly ground black pepper
300 ml/½ pint milk	1¼ cups milk
1 egg, beaten	1 egg, beaten
Garnish:	**Garnish:**
25 g/1 oz ham, chopped	2 tablespoons chopped cooked ham
2 slices of toast, cut into triangles	2 slices of toast, cut into triangles

Arrange the frozen cauliflower florets around the edges of a large shallow dish. Cover the dish loosely with plastic cling film and MICROWAVE ON HIGH FOR 5 MINUTES, giving the dish a half-turn after 2 minutes. Leave covered, while preparing the sauce.

Put the butter in a large bowl and MICROWAVE ON HIGH FOR 1 MINUTE. Stir in the flour, then blend in the cheese and add salt and pepper to taste. Add the milk a little at a time, stirring constantly. MICROWAVE ON HIGH FOR 2 MINUTES.

Whisk thoroughly until smooth, then MICROWAVE ON HIGH FOR 1½ MINUTES. Add the egg gradually, stirring continuously, to yield a smooth, glossy sauce. Pour the sauce over the cauliflower and, without covering, MICROWAVE ON HIGH FOR 4 MINUTES, giving the dish a half-turn after 2 minutes.

Sprinkle with the chopped ham to garnish and arrange triangles of toast around the edges of the dish. Serve hot.

SERVES 2

Note: Left-over cooked cauliflower may be used for this dish; it can simply be reheated in the sauce.

FRANKFURTERS, EGG AND BEANS

METRIC/IMPERIAL	AMERICAN
2 frankfurters	2 frankfurters
4 tablespoons baked beans	4 tablespoons baked beans in tomato sauce
1 egg	1 egg

Make 4 or 5 slits along one side of each frankfurter. Bend each one into a curve and arrange on a suitable plate to form a circle. Surround with a border of baked beans and break the egg into the centre of the frankfurter.

Cover the plate loosely with plastic cling film and MICROWAVE ON HIGH FOR 2½ MINUTES, giving a 10 second rest half-way through cooking. Leave to stand, covered, for 1 to 2 minutes until the egg white has set, then serve.

SERVES 2

MONTANA RICE

METRIC/IMPERIAL	AMERICAN
1 small onion, chopped	1 small onion, chopped
2 tablespoons oil	2 tablespoons oil
50 g/2 oz cooked pork, finely chopped	¼ cup finely chopped cooked pork
175 g/6 oz cooked rice	1 cup cooked rice
2 eggs, beaten	2 eggs, beaten
1½ tablespoons soy sauce	1½ tablespoons soy sauce
freshly ground black pepper	freshly ground black pepper

Combine the onion and the oil in a shallow dish and MICROWAVE ON HIGH FOR 2 MINUTES until the onion is soft, stirring once during cooking. Add the pork and rice and mix thoroughly.

Beat the eggs and soy sauce together with a light sprinkling of pepper. Pour evenly over the rice mixture and MICROWAVE ON HIGH FOR 3 TO 4 MINUTES, until the egg has set and the mixture is thoroughly heated. Serve hot, either alone or accompanied by peas, French beans or other vegetable of choice.

SERVES 1 OR 2

Note: The cooking time for the dish will depend on the temperature of the rice. If freshly cooked, still warm rice is used, the dish will, of course, be cooked more quickly than if cold leftover rice is used.

FRANKFURTER RISOTTO

METRIC/IMPERIAL	AMERICAN
100 g/4 oz long-grain rice	⅔ cup long-grain rice
4 tablespoons frozen peas	4 tablespoons frozen peas
1 × 40 g/1½ oz packet instant soup (any variety)	1 × 1½ oz packet instant soup (any variety)
15 g/½ oz butter	1 tablespoon butter
600 ml/1 pint water	2½ cups water
2–3 frankfurters, sliced	2–3 frankfurters, sliced

Combine the rice, peas, soup mix, butter and water in a large bowl and MICROWAVE ON HIGH FOR 12 MINUTES, stirring frequently until most of the liquid is absorbed. Add the frankfurters and MICROWAVE ON HIGH FOR 3 TO 4 MINUTES until the rice is cooked and the frankfurters are hot. Serve immediately.

SERVES 2

SPAGHETTI WITH HAM AND MUSHROOMS

METRIC/IMPERIAL	AMERICAN
15 g/½ oz butter	1 tablespoon butter
50 g/2 oz thinly sliced mushrooms	½ cup thinly sliced mushrooms
2 tomatoes, sliced	2 tomatoes, sliced
175 g/6 oz cooked ham, diced	1 cup diced cooked ham
1 tablespoon sweet pickle (optional)	1 tablespoon sweet pickle (optional)
225 g/8 oz cold cooked spaghetti	2½ cups cold cooked spaghetti
salt	salt
freshly ground black pepper	freshly ground black pepper

Put the butter and mushrooms in a shallow dish and MICROWAVE ON HIGH FOR 2½ MINUTES. Add the tomatoes, turning them over, so they are evenly coated with butter. MICROWAVE ON HIGH FOR 2 MINUTES.

Add the diced ham and sweet pickle and arrange the cold spaghetti on top. Cover the dish loosely with plastic cling film and MICROWAVE ON HIGH FOR 2 TO 3 MINUTES until the spaghetti is hot, giving the dish a half-turn once during cooking. Add salt and pepper to taste and serve immediately accompanied by a crisp green salad, if liked.

SERVES 1 OR 2

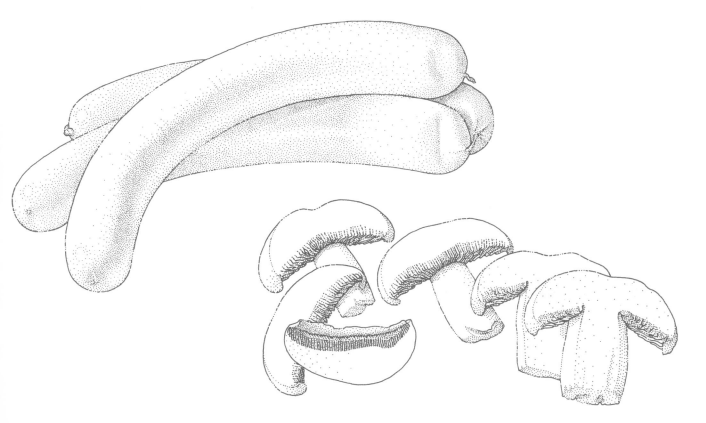

TEA & COFFEE TIME

Delicious tea-time treats can be cooked quickly by microwave and here you will find a wide selection of recipes for breads, cakes, scones, cookies and jams. Don't assume that microwave-baked goods will have a pallid appearance; there are a number of ways to overcome the lack of colour attained in cooking. Browning under the grill (broiler) will improve the appearance without affecting the flavour or texture in any way and is particularly suitable for bread. Cakes containing dark ingredients, such as chocolate, fruit, treacle and brown sugar, will need no further embellishment, but a little food colouring or caramel can always be added to light mixtures before cooking. A little gravy browning or caramel may be used to glaze the top of cakes to enrich the colour. If cakes are to be decorated, the lack of microwave browning is not really relevant. Although plain white bread can be cooked by microwave you may find that better results will be achieved by baking conventionally. However, the microwave oven is ideal for hastening rising.

Cooking containers

Cakes and bread may be cooked in any microwave-suitable container. For even-cooking, round containers not more than 23 cm/9 inches in diameter, are particularly suitable. Square 20 cm/8 inch shapes can also be used, but mixtures may become over-cooked at the corners. To overcome this, check after three-quarters of the minimum cooking time and if necessary, place a small piece of foil over the corners for the remaining cooking time. Soufflé dishes, provided they have no metallic trim, are ideal for cakes. Cardboard boxes are suitable for cakes and cookies; line them loosely with plastic cling film so they can be used again.

Several manufacturers now produce equipment especially for baking in the microwave oven. These include muffin (bun) pans and ring moulds, which are particularly useful as they overcome the problem that microwaves tend to cook mixtures around the edges more quickly than in the middle. If you cannot obtain one of these ring moulds, improvise by standing a jam jar or straight glass in the centre of the dish. To replace a muffin (bun) pan, either cut out even-sized holes around the edges of a circular sheet of corrugated cardboard, or trim paper cups to give shallow containers, about 2.5 cm/1 inch deep. Put paper cases into the holes or cups.

Cakes and cookies

Cakes are cooked when they are just dry on top and should be tested with a skewer. If the cake seems undercooked, leave in the dish for 5 minutes then, if the centre is still soft, cover the edges with a ring of foil and MICROWAVE FOR A FURTHER 1 MINUTE. Cakes should be placed on the wire cooling rack upright.

Cakes cooked by microwave rise more than conventionally baked ones, so cooking containers should not be more than half-filled. Do not be concerned if your cake sinks when the door is opened; it will rise when the oven is switched on again.

Small cakes, shortbread, flapjacks and biscuits cook very rapidly and may burn in the centre if overcooked – so take care! Be sure to mix ingredients thoroughly as lumps of sugar may cause burning.

The most suitable cooking speed is stated for each recipe. Fruit cakes and other rich mixtures are generally cooked more slowly to allow the flavour to develop and ensure even cooking. However all the cakes may be cooked on HIGH if this is the only setting available. Reduce each microwave cooking period by about one-third and allow a few minutes rest, after each quarter of the cooking time.

Preserves

Not only is the microwave method of cooking preserves quick, it dispenses with all those sticky pans and utensils. For microwaving jams and jellies, use the largest heat-resistant bowl which will fit into the microwave oven.

Mixtures must reach a full rolling boil to ensure a good set. If commercial pectin is added to aid setting, be sure to stir it in thoroughly to maintain a good colour. When the boiling mixture is viscose in texture and the bubbles are large, it is time to test for setting. Place a teaspoonful of the jam on a cold saucer, cool, then press gently; if it wrinkles, setting point has been reached. Undercooked jams can always be given extra time. If the jam is overcooked, add 2 to 3 tablespoons water and return to the boil.

If the jam is to be stored for a long period, cover with waxed discs and seal with jam pot covers. Otherwise cover each jar loosely with plastic cling film, replace in the oven and MICROWAVE ON HIGH FOR 1 TO 2 MINUTES until the plastic bubbles up: it will adhere to the surface of the jam as it cools. This method of sealing is only suitable for jams and jellies containing small pieces of fruit.

WHITE BREAD

METRIC/IMPERIAL	AMERICAN
300 ml/½ pint water	1¼ cups water
1 teaspoon sugar	1 teaspoon sugar
1 teaspoon dried yeast	1 teaspoon active dry yeast
500 g/1 lb plain flour	4 cups all-purpose flour
½ teaspoon salt	½ teaspoon salt
2 tablespoons vegetable oil	2 tablespoons vegetable oil
1 tablespoon butter	1 tablespoon butter

Pour the water into a measuring jug and MICROWAVE ON HIGH FOR 15 SECONDS until just hot to the touch. Add the sugar and yeast and mix with a fork until thoroughly blended. Set aside for 10 to 15 minutes until frothy.

Sift the flour and salt together into a mixing bowl and MICROWAVE ON HIGH FOR 30 SECONDS. Make a well in the centre and pour in the yeast liquid and oil. Work the dough mixture with one hand until it leaves the sides of the bowl clean. Turn onto a lightly floured surface and knead for about 5 minutes until smooth.

Shape the dough into a round and replace in the bowl. Cover the bowl with plastic cling film and set aside to rise until doubled in size. To hasten the rising process, MICROWAVE ON HIGH FOR 5 SECONDS occasionally.

Put the butter into a 23 × 10 cm/9 × 4 inch loaf-shaped dish and MICROWAVE ON HIGH FOR 20 SECONDS until melted. Turn the dough onto a lightly floured surface and knead gently for 2 to 3 minutes. Stretch into an oblong the same length as the dish. Ease the bread into the greased dish, then turn over so that the top is also coated with butter.

Leave to stand for 10 minutes. MICROWAVE ON HIGH FOR 1 MINUTE, then give the dish a half-turn. MICROWAVE ON LOW FOR 7 TO 9 MINUTES until the bread is soft but resilient to the touch, giving the dish a quarter-turn occasionally.

Turn out and brown all sides of the loaf under a pre-heated hot grill (broiler) before serving.

MAKES ONE 500 g/1 lb LOAF

SODA BREAD

METRIC/IMPERIAL	AMERICAN
225 g/8 oz plain flour	2 cups all-purpose flour
225 g/8 oz wholemeal flour	2 cups 100% wholewheat flour
2 tablespoons baking powder	2 tablespoons baking powder
1 teaspoon salt	1 teaspoon salt
50 g/2 oz butter	¼ cup butter
300 ml/½ pint milk	1¼ cups milk
1 teaspoon vinegar	1 teaspoon vinegar
2 tablespoons black treacle or molasses	2 tablespoons molasses

Sift the flours, baking powder and salt together into a mixing bowl. Rub in the butter until thoroughly incorporated, then make a well in the centre. Combine the milk, vinegar and treacle or molasses in a jug and MICROWAVE ON HIGH FOR 30 SECONDS. Pour into the flour and work the mixture, using one hand, for 1 to 2 minutes.

Turn onto a lightly floured surface. Knead until smooth, then shape into a 15 cm/6 inch round. Using a floured sharp knife, mark a deep cross on top of the loaf.

Place on a greased plate and MICROWAVE ON HIGH FOR 6 MINUTES, giving the plate a quarter-turn every 1½ minutes. Test by inserting a skewer through the loaf, halfway between the edge and the centre; if it comes out clean the loaf is ready. If necessary, MICROWAVE ON HIGH FOR A FURTHER 1 MINUTE.

Invert the loaf onto a grill (broiler) rack and place under a preheated hot grill (broiler) to brown. Turn the loaf over and brown the top. Serve, cut into wedges.

MAKES ONE LARGE ROUND LOAF

Soda Bread – illustrated on page 46

CORN BREAD

METRIC/IMPERIAL	AMERICAN
100 g/4 oz coarse yellow cornmeal	1 cup coarse yellow cornmeal
100 g/4 oz plain flour	1 cup all-purpose flour
2 tablespoons baking powder	2 tablespoons baking powder
½ teaspoon salt	½ teaspoon salt
1 tablespoon sugar	1 tablespoon sugar
50 g/2 oz soft margarine	¼ cup soft margarine
1 egg, beaten	1 egg, beaten
250 ml/8 fl oz milk	1 cup milk

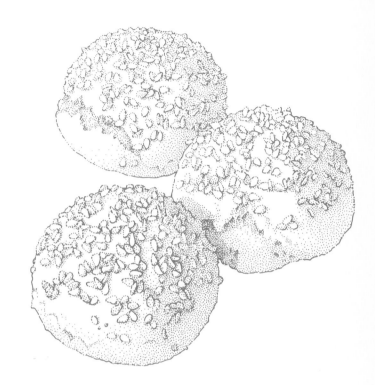

Sift the cornmeal, flour, baking powder and salt together into a mixing bowl. Stir in the sugar, then mix in the margarine with a fork until thoroughly blended. Add the egg and milk and beat to form a smooth dough which has a soft dropping consistency.

Line a 23 × 10 cm/9 × 4 inch loaf-shaped dish with plastic cling film. Spoon the dough into the dish and spread evenly. MICROWAVE ON HIGH FOR 4 MINUTES until just dry on top, giving the dish a quarter-turn every 1 minute. Lift the bread out of the dish with the cling film. Leave to cool a little, then remove the cling film. Brown the bread on all sides under a preheated hot grill (broiler) before serving, if desired.

MAKES 1 MEDIUM LOAF

BROWN ROLLS

METRIC/IMPERIAL	AMERICAN
300 ml/½ pint milk	1¼ cups milk
2 teaspoons dried yeast	2 teaspoons active dry yeast
1 teaspoon sugar	1 teaspoon sugar
350 g/12 oz wholemeal flour	3 cups wholewheat flour
100 g/4 oz plain flour	1 cup all-purpose flour
1 teaspoon salt	1 teaspoon salt
2 teaspoons malt extract	2 teaspoons malt extract
2 tablespoons vegetable oil	2 tablespoons vegetable oil
Topping:	**Topping:**
beaten egg to glaze	beaten egg to glaze
sesame seeds	sesame seeds

Put the milk in a measuring jug and MICROWAVE ON HIGH FOR 30 TO 40 SECONDS until just hot to the touch. Add the yeast and sugar and beat with a fork until thoroughly blended. Set aside for 10 to 15 minutes until frothy.

Sift the flours and salt into a mixing bowl and MICROWAVE ON HIGH FOR 30 SECONDS. Make a well in the centre and pour in the yeast liquid, malt extract and 1 tablespoon oil. Work the dough mixture with one hand until it leaves the sides of the bowl clean.

Turn onto a lightly floured surface and knead until the dough is smooth and no longer sticky. Add a little more liquid if it is too dry. Cover the bowl with plastic cling film and leave until doubled in size. To hasten the rising process, MICROWAVE ON HIGH FOR 5 SECONDS occasionally.

Turn the dough on to a lightly floured surface and knead lightly, then divide into 16 equal-sized pieces. Shape each one into rolls. Brush with the remaining oil and leave to rise for 20 to 30 minutes until the dough springs back when lightly pressed with the fingertip.

Arrange half the rolls, well spaced out, on a greased baking tray or on the oven shelf lined with non-stick parchment. MICROWAVE ON HIGH FOR 3 TO 3½ MINUTES, turning the rolls over once during cooking. MICROWAVE the remaining rolls in the same way.

While the rolls are still hot, brush the tops with beaten egg to glaze and sprinkle with sesame seeds. Brown under a preheated hot grill (broiler) if desired.

MAKES 16 ROLLS

YEAST PANCAKES

METRIC/IMPERIAL	AMERICAN
5 tablespoons milk	1/3 cup milk
1 teaspoon sugar	1 teaspoon sugar
1 teaspoon dried yeast	1 teaspoon active dry yeast
100 g/4 oz plain flour	1 cup all-purpose flour
pinch of salt	pinch of salt
65 g/2 1/2 oz butter, at room temperature	1/4 cup + 1 tablespoon butter, at room temperature
2 eggs, beaten	2 eggs, beaten

Put the milk in a jug and MICROWAVE ON HIGH FOR 10 TO 15 SECONDS until just hot to the touch. Add the sugar and yeast and beat with a fork until thoroughly blended. Set aside for 10 to 15 minutes until frothy.

Sift the flour and salt into a mixing bowl and MIC-ROWAVE ON HIGH FOR 20 SECONDS. Make a well in the centre and pour in the yeast liquid. Flick some of the flour over the top of the liquid. Cover and set aside for 30 minutes until the yeast mixture is spongy.

Cut the butter into small pieces and add to the mixture with the beaten eggs. Beat thoroughly for 5 minutes until the batter is smooth and elastic.

Place spoonfuls of the yeast batter well apart on the oven shelf, lined with non-stick parchment. MICROWAVE ON HIGH, allowing 20 seconds for each pancake. Transfer the pancakes to a wire rack as soon as they are dry on top.

Serve while still warm, spread with butter and jam.

MAKES 16 TO 20 PANCAKES

HONEY BREAD

METRIC/IMPERIAL	AMERICAN
350 g/12 oz plain flour	3 cups all-purpose flour
1 teaspoon bicarbonate of soda	1 teaspoon baking soda
1 teaspoon baking powder	1 teaspoon baking powder
1/4 teaspoon salt	1/4 teaspoon salt
1/2 teaspoon ground ginger	1/2 teaspoon ground ginger
1/2 teaspoon mixed spice	1/2 teaspoon ground mixed spice
6 tablespoons clear honey	6 tablespoons clear honey
175 ml/6 fl oz milk	3/4 cup milk
2 tablespoons vegetable oil	2 tablespoons vegetable oil
1 egg	1 egg

Sift the dry ingredients into a mixing bowl. Combine the honey and milk in a jug and MICROWAVE ON HIGH FOR 30 SECONDS. Beat in the oil and egg. Pour onto the flour mixture and beat vigorously for at least 3 minutes.

Turn the mixture into a greased 18 × 10 cm/7 × 4 inch loaf-shaped dish and MICROWAVE ON HIGH FOR 2 MINUTES. Give the dish a half-turn and MICROWAVE ON LOW FOR 8 TO 10 MINUTES until just dry on top. Remove the loaf from the dish and place under a preheated hot grill (broiler) to brown the top.

Slice and serve warm, generously spread with butter, or leave to cool, then slice and toast.

MAKES ONE 350 g/3/4 lb TEA LOAF

Right: Honey bread; Raisin and walnut loaf

Below: Yeast pancakes

RAISIN AND WALNUT LOAF

METRIC/IMPERIAL
150 ml/¼ pint orange juice
1 teaspoon bicarbonate of
  soda
25 g/1 oz butter
½ teaspoon vanilla essence
75 g/3 oz raisins
75 g/3 oz soft brown sugar
1 large egg, beaten
175 g/6 oz plain flour
1 teaspoon baking powder
¼ teaspoon salt
75 g/3 oz shelled walnuts,
  chopped

AMERICAN
⅔ cup orange juice
1 teaspoon baking soda
2 tablespoons butter
½ teaspoon vanilla extract
½ cup raisins
½ cup soft brown sugar
1 large egg, beaten
1½ cups all-purpose flour
1 teaspoon baking powder
¼ teaspoon salt
¾ cup chopped walnuts

Grease the sides of a 23 × 10 cm/9 × 4 inch loaf dish and
line the base with non-stick parchment. Put the orange
juice in a mixing bowl and MICROWAVE ON HIGH FOR 1 TO
1½ MINUTES until hot.

Stir in the bicarbonate of soda (baking soda) and butter,
then add the vanilla essence (extract), raisins and sugar.
Stir in the beaten egg, a little at a time. Sift the flour,
baking powder and salt together over the top. Fold in the
nuts.

Turn the mixture into the prepared dish and smooth the
top. MICROWAVE ON HIGH FOR 7 TO 8 MINUTES until just dry
on top, giving the dish a quarter-turn every 2 minutes.
Transfer to a wire rack to cool.

Serve, sliced and buttered, preferably soon after cooling.

MAKES ONE 500 g/1 lb TEA LOAF

51

MALT LOAF

METRIC/IMPERIAL	AMERICAN
2 teaspoons dried yeast	2 teaspoons active dry yeast
1 teaspoon sugar	1 teaspoon sugar
120 ml/4 fl oz water, hand hot	½ cup water, hand hot
2 teaspoons black treacle	2 teaspoons molasses
2 tablespoons malt extract	2 tablespoons malt extract
15 g/½ oz butter	1 tablespoon butter
100 g/4 oz wholemeal flour	1 cup wholewheat flour
100 g/4 oz strong plain white flour, sifted	1 cup strong white bread flour, sifted
½ teaspoon salt	½ teaspoon salt
25 g/1 oz sultanas	3 tablespoons golden raisins
1 tablespoon clear honey	1 tablespoon clear honey

Cream the yeast, sugar and water together in a small bowl. Set aside for 10 to 15 minutes until frothy. Put the treacle, malt extract and butter in a small bowl and MICROWAVE ON HIGH FOR 1 MINUTE until melted.

Place the flours and salt in a large mixing bowl and MICROWAVE ON HIGH FOR 30 SECONDS. Stir in the yeast liquid and the syrup mixture, then add the sultanas (golden raisins). Mix to a sticky dough, adding a little more warm water if necessary.

Turn on to a lightly floured surface and knead until smooth. Roll into a ball, replace in the mixing bowl and cover with plastic cling film. Leave in the microwave oven until doubled in bulk; MICROWAVE ON LOW FOR 5 TO 10 SECONDS every 10 minutes to hasten rising.

Grease a 23 × 10 cm/9 × 4 inch loaf-shaped dish or similar-sized box and line the base with non-stick parchment. Press the dough evenly into the dish and cover with plastic cling film. Leave in the microwave oven for 10 minutes, then MICROWAVE ON LOW FOR 5 SECONDS. Leave to rise for a further 10 minutes.

Remove the cover and MICROWAVE ON HIGH FOR 1 MINUTE. Give the dish a half-turn and MICROWAVE ON LOW FOR 4 TO 5 MINUTES until well risen and just dry on top.

Transfer the loaf to a wire cooling rack and brush the top with clear honey to glaze while still hot. Serve, spread with butter.

MAKES ONE 500 g/1 lb MALT LOAF

FRUIT LOAF

METRIC/IMPERIAL	AMERICAN
175 g/6 oz plain flour	1½ cups all-purpose flour
2 teaspoons baking powder	2 teaspoons baking powder
½ teaspoon salt	½ teaspoon salt
25 g/1 oz butter	2 tablespoons butter
2 tablespoons brown sugar	2 tablespoons brown sugar
1 egg, beaten	1 egg, beaten
150 ml/¼ pint natural yogurt	⅔ cup unflavored yogurt
¼ teaspoon bicarbonate of soda	¼ teaspoon baking soda
50 g/2 oz raisins	⅓ cup raisins
25 g/1 oz currants	3 tablespoons currants
caramel colouring (see page 69)	caramel coloring (see page 69)

Sift the flour, baking powder and salt into a mixing bowl. Rub in the butter until the mixture resembles fine breadcrumbs. Add the sugar, egg, yogurt and bicarbonate of soda (baking soda) and mix to form a smooth, soft dough. Mix in the raisins and currants.

Line the base of an 18 × 10 cm/7 × 4 inch loaf-shaped dish with non-stick parchment. Spoon in the mixture and smooth the top with a palette knife. MICROWAVE ON HIGH FOR 4 TO 4½ MINUTES until just dry on top, giving the dish a quarter-turn every 1 minute.

Turn out the loaf. Place, top side down, on a grill (broiler) rack. Brown under a preheated grill (broiler). Turn over and brush the top with caramel before browning. Serve warm or cold, sliced and buttered.

MAKES ONE 350 g/¾ lb FRUIT LOAF

MADEIRA CAKE

METRIC/IMPERIAL	AMERICAN
175 g/6 oz butter	¾ cup butter
50 g/2 oz lard	¼ cup vegetable shortening
225 g/8 oz sugar	1 cup sugar
3 large eggs, beaten	3 large eggs, beaten
175 g/6 oz self-raising flour	1½ cups self-rising flour
50 g/2 oz plain flour	½ cup all-purpose flour
3–4 tablespoons evaporated milk	3–4 tablespoons evaporated milk
Glaze:	**Glaze:**
1 tablespoon evaporated milk	1 tablespoon evaporated milk
1 tablespoon dark brown sugar	1 tablespoon dark brown sugar
½ teaspoon arrowroot	½ teaspoon arrowroot flour

Grease the sides of an 18 cm/7 inch round deep dish and line the base with non-stick parchment. Cream the butter, lard (shortening) and sugar together until light and fluffy. Beat in the egg, a little at a time. Sift the flours together, then fold into the mixture, together with the evaporated milk.

Turn the mixture into the prepared dish and smooth the top with a palette knife. MICROWAVE ON HIGH FOR 5 TO 6 MINUTES until just dry on top, giving the dish a quarter-turn every 1 minute. Leave the cake in the dish for 2 minutes, then turn out and cool on a wire rack.

To make the glaze, blend the evaporated milk, sugar and arrowroot together. Brush over the top of the cake. Place under a preheated moderate grill (broiler) to lightly brown the top.

MAKES ONE 18 cm/7 inch ROUND CAKE

FRUIT CAKE

METRIC/IMPERIAL	AMERICAN
100 g/4 oz butter	½ cup butter
100 g/4 oz soft brown sugar	⅔ cup soft brown sugar
3 eggs, beaten	3 eggs, beaten
175 g/6 oz plain flour	1½ cups all-purpose flour
2½ teaspoons baking powder	2½ teaspoons baking powder
2 teaspoons mixed spice	2 teaspoons ground mixed spice
25 g/1 oz currants	3 tablespoons currants
25 g/1 oz raisins	3 tablespoons raisins
100 g/4 oz sultanas	⅔ cup golden raisins
25 g/1 oz chopped mixed peel	3 tablespoons chopped candied peel
5 glacé cherries, chopped	5 candied cherried, chopped
40 g/1½ oz ground almonds	⅓ cup ground almonds
1 teaspoon caramel colouring (see page 69), or gravy browning	1 teaspoon caramel coloring (see page 69), or gravy browning
3–4 tablespoons milk	3–4 tablespoons milk
2 tablespoons sieved apricot jam, warmed	2 tablespoons sieved apricot preserve, warmed
4 tablespoons toasted flaked almonds	4 tablespoons toasted flaked almonds

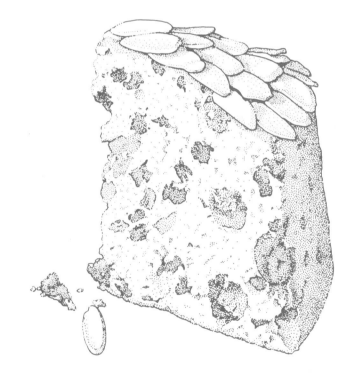

Grease the sides of an 18 cm/7 inch round deep cake dish and line the base with non-stick parchment. Cream the butter and sugar together in a bowl until light and fluffy. Add the beaten eggs, a little at a time, beating thoroughly between each addition.

Sift the flour, baking powder and mixed spice together over the mixture. Add the dried fruit, peel, cherries and ground almonds and lightly fold into the mixture, adding the caramel and sufficient milk to give a firm dropping consistency.

Turn the mixture into the prepared dish and smooth the top with a palette knife. MICROWAVE ON HIGH FOR 6 TO 8 MINUTES until the cake is just dry on top, giving the dish a quarter-turn every 1½ minutes.

Leave to cool in the dish, then turn out and brush the top with warmed apricot jam to glaze. Sprinkle with the almonds.

MAKES ONE 18 cm/7 inch ROUND CAKE

ORANGE STREUSEL CAKE

METRIC/IMPERIAL

Streusel topping:
25 g/1 oz plain flour
1 teaspoon ground cinnamon
2 teaspoons cocoa powder
50 g/2 oz chilled butter
75 g/3 oz brown sugar

Cake base:
50 g/2 oz butter
150 g/5 oz sugar
175 g/6 oz plain flour
2 teaspoons baking powder
pinch of salt
*grated rind and juice of 1
    orange*
*5 tablespoons milk
    (approximately)*
1 egg, beaten

AMERICAN

Streusel topping:
¼ cup all-purpose flour
*1 teaspoon powdered
    cinnamon*
*2 teaspoons unsweetened
    cocoa*
¼ cup chilled butter
½ cup brown sugar

Cake base:
¼ cup butter
⅔ cup sugar
1½ cups all-purpose flour
2 teaspoons baking powder
pinch of salt
*grated rind and juice of 1
    orange*
*5 tablespoons milk
    (approximately)*
1 egg, beaten

To prepare the streusel topping, sift the flour, cinnamon and cocoa into a bowl. Cut the butter into small pieces and lightly rub into the dry ingredients. Stir in the sugar.

To make the cake base, cream the butter and sugar together in a mixing bowl until light and fluffy. Sift the flour with the baking powder and salt over the creamed mixture and add the grated orange rind. Make up the orange juice to ¼ pint/⅔ cup with milk, then add to the mixture, together with the beaten egg. Beat for 2 minutes until smooth.

Turn the mixture into a greased 18 cm/7 inch round deep cake dish. MICROWAVE ON HIGH FOR 3 MINUTES, giving the dish a quarter-turn every 45 seconds. Sprinkle the streusel evenly over the top. MICROWAVE ON HIGH FOR 3 MINUTES, giving the dish a half-turn after 1½ minutes. When a skewer inserted into the centre of the cake comes out clean, the cake is ready. Turn out onto a wire rack to cool.
MAKES ONE 18 cm/7 inch ROUND CAKE

Christmas cake; Orange streusel cake

CHRISTMAS CAKE

METRIC/IMPERIAL
225 g/8 oz butter
175 g/6 oz dark brown sugar
4 eggs, beaten
225 g/8 oz plain flour
pinch of salt
1 teaspoon mixed spice
25 g/1 oz ground almonds
75 g/3 oz mixed shelled
    almonds and walnuts,
    chopped
10 glacé cherries, quartered
50 g/2 oz candied peel, finely
    chopped
225 g/8 oz currants
100 g/4 oz raisins
175 g/6 oz sultanas
50 g/2 oz stoned dates,
    chopped
grated rind and juice of 1
    large orange
1 teaspoon caramel
    colouring (see page 69)
3 tablespoons brandy
To finish:
500 g/1 lb almond paste
575 g/1¼ lb royal icing

AMERICAN
1 cup butter
1 cup dark brown sugar
4 eggs, beaten
2 cups all-purpose flour
pinch of salt
1 teaspoon ground mixed
    spice
¼ cup ground almonds
¼ cup chopped mixed
    almonds and walnuts
10 candied cherries,
    quartered
¾ cup finely chopped
    candied peel
1 cup currants
⅔ cup raisins
1 cup golden raisins
⅓ cup chopped pitted dates
grated rind and juice of 1
    large orange
1 teaspoon caramel coloring
    (see page 69)
3 tablespoons brandy
To finish:
1 lb almond paste
1¼ lb royal icing

Grease the sides of a 20 cm/8 inch round deep dish and line the base with a circle of non-stick parchment.

Cream the butter and sugar together in a large bowl until fluffy. Add the beaten egg, a little at a time, beating well between each addition. Sift the flour, salt and spice into the mixture and stir well. Add the ground almonds, chopped nuts, cherries, peel, dried fruit, orange rind and juice. Fold into the mixture gently. Stir in the caramel and brandy.

MICROWAVE ON LOW FOR 5 MINUTES. Draw the mixture in from the sides to the middle with a fork. MICROWAVE ON LOW FOR 15 MINUTES. Leave to stand for 15 minutes, then MICROWAVE ON LOW FOR 15 TO 20 MINUTES until the cake is just dry on top. If the cake seems to be cooking too fast around the edge, cut out a circular piece of foil, about 2.5 cm/1 inch wide; place over the edge of the cake for the final 5 minutes. This will enable the middle of the cake to 'catch up'.

Slide a knife around the edge of the cake and leave in the dish to cool slightly, before turning out onto a wire rack. When completely cold, wrap in foil, seal tightly and store in a cool place until a few weeks before Christmas. Cover with almond paste, leave to dry for 3 to 4 days, then cover with royal icing.

MAKES ONE 20 cm/8 inch ROUND CAKE

APPLE RING CAKE

METRIC/IMPERIAL	AMERICAN
1 × 300 g/12 oz packet plain cake mix	1 × 12 oz package yellow cake mix
150 g/6 oz cooking apple, peeled, cored and chopped	2½ cups peeled, chopped baking apple
3 heaped tablespoons apricot jam, sieved	6 tablespoons apricot preserve, sieved
2 tablespoons water	2 tablespoons water
1 red-skinned dessert apple, cored and sliced	1 red-skinned dessert apple, cored and sliced

Make up the cake mixture according to the directions on the packet. Add the chopped cooking apple and mix well. Turn into a greased 750 ml/1¼ pints/3 cup ring mould, suitable for use in the microwave oven. MICROWAVE ON HIGH FOR 4 TO 5 MINUTES until the cake is just dry on top and a skewer, inserted into the centre, comes out clean. Turn onto a sheet of non-stick parchment and leave to cool.

Combine the jam and water in a bowl. MICROWAVE FOR 1½ MINUTES until boiling briskly. Spread half the jam over the top and sides of the cake.

Arrange the apple slices, overlapping, on the top of the cake. Coat with the remaining jam. Allow to cool, then transfer the cake to a serving plate.

SERVES 6 TO 8

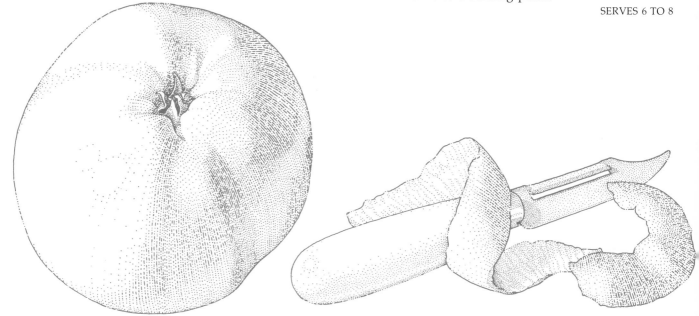

CHOCOLATE AND ORANGE CHEQUERED CAKE

METRIC/IMPERIAL	AMERICAN
1 × 350 g/12 oz packet plain cake mix	1 × 12 oz package plain yellow cake mix
2 teaspoons water	2 teaspoons water
2 tablespoons cocoa powder, sifted	2 tablespoons unsweetened cocoa, sifted
2 teaspoons orange juice	2 teaspoons orange juice
few drops of orange food colouring	few drops of orange food coloring
200 g/7 oz can apricot pie filling	¾ cup canned apricot pie filling
100 g/4 oz plain cooking chocolate	¼ lb semi-sweet cooking chocolate
orange jelly slices to decorate	orange jelly slices to decorate

Grease two 18 cm/7 inch straight-sided round dishes and line the bases with greased greaseproof paper or non-stick parchment. Prepare the cake mix according to the directions on the packet. Divide the mixture in half. Add the water and cocoa to one half, and the orange juice and colouring to the other.

Place alternate spoonfuls of chocolate and orange mixture in each dish and separately MICROWAVE ON HIGH FOR 2 MINUTES, giving the dish a quarter-turn every 15 seconds. Leave for 5 minutes before turning out on to a wire rack to cool. When cold, sandwich the cakes together with the pie filling.

Put the chocolate on a sheet of greaseproof paper and MICROWAVE ON HIGH FOR 1½ TO 2 MINUTES until melted but still holding its shape. Pour over the cake and smooth over the top and sides, with a palette knife. Allow to set, then decorate with orange jelly slices.

MAKES ONE 18 cm/7 inch ROUND CAKE

CAKE MIX SANDWICH CAKE

METRIC/IMPERIAL
1 × 350 g/12 oz packet plain
   cake mix
4 tablespoons jam

AMERICAN
1 × ¾ lb package yellow
   cake mix
4 tablespoons jam

Prepare the cake mix according to the instructions on the packet, adding the required amount of eggs and liquid. Line the bases of two 18 cm/7 inch round shallow dishes with non-stick parchment and grease the sides. Divide the mixture evenly between the dishes.

Cook the cakes separately: MICROWAVE ON LOW FOR 4 MINUTES or MICROWAVE ON HIGH FOR 2 MINUTES, until the top is just dry, giving the dish a quarter-turn every 1 minute. Leave to cool in the dishes for 5 minutes, then run a knife round the edge of each cake and turn out onto a wire rack. When cool carefully remove the parchment.

Place one cake under a preheated grill (broiler) to brown the top. Spread the other cake layer with the jam and place the browned cake layer on top.

MAKES ONE 18 cm/7 inch ROUND CAKE

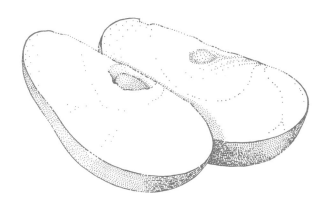

CHOCOLATE CHERRY CAKE

METRIC/IMPERIAL
100 g/4 oz butter
100 g/4 oz sugar
2 eggs, beaten
100 g/4 oz self-raising flour
50 g/2 oz cocoa powder
50 g/2 oz ground almonds
4 tablespoons clear honey
4 tablespoons milk
8 to 10 glacé cherries,
   halved
Icing:
2 tablespoons milk
50 g/2 oz unsalted butter
1 tablespoon cocoa powder
½ teaspoon vanilla essence
200 g/7 oz icing sugar, sifted

AMERICAN
½ cup butter
½ cup sugar
2 eggs, beaten
1 cup self-rising flour
2 tablespoons unsweetened
   cocoa
½ cup ground almonds
4 tablespoons clear honey
4 tablespoons milk
8 to 10 candied cherries,
   halved
Icing:
2 tablespoons milk
¼ cup sweet butter
1 tablespoon unsweetened
   cocoa
½ teaspoon vanilla extract
1 ½ cups confectioners'
   sugar, sifted

Line a 15 cm/6 inch round deep cake dish with plastic cling film. Cream the butter and sugar together in a bowl until light and fluffy. Beat in the eggs, a little at a time. Sift the flour and cocoa onto the mixture. Stir in the ground almonds, honey and sufficient milk to form a consistency which easily shakes from a spoon.

Turn the mixture into the cake dish and smooth the top with a palette knife. MICROWAVE ON HIGH FOR 5 TO 6 MINUTES until just dry on top, giving the dish a quarter-turn every 1½ minutes during cooking. Turn out onto a wire rack set over a tray. Cover the top of the cake with the halved glacé (candied) cherries, then leave to cool.

To make the icing, place the milk, butter, cocoa and vanilla essence (extract) in a bowl and MICROWAVE ON HIGH FOR 1½ MINUTES. Stir in the icing (confectioners') sugar and beat until smooth. Pour the icing over the cake, spreading it over the top and sides. Leave to set before transferring to a serving plate.

MAKES ONE 15 cm/6 inch ROUND CAKE

VIENNESE CHERRY CAKES

METRIC/IMPERIAL	AMERICAN
225 g/8 oz plain flour	2 cups all-purpose flour
3 tablespoons custard powder	3 tablespoons custard powder
65 g/2½ oz sugar	⅓ cup sugar
175 g/6 oz butter	¾ cup butter
To decorate:	**To decorate:**
150 ml/¼ pint double cream, whipped	⅔ cup heavy cream, whipped
12 glacé cherries	12 candied cherries

Sift the flour and custard powder together into a mixing bowl. Add the sugar, then rub in the butter until the mixture clings together. Knead until smooth. Divide the mixture between 12 paper cake cases, pressing the mixture down with the back of a teaspoon.

Place six of the cakes in a bun or muffin dish. MICROWAVE ON HIGH FOR 2 TO 2½ MINUTES giving the dish a half-turn after 1 minute. Test every cake before removing from the oven by inserting a skewer into the centre; if it comes out clean the cake is cooked. Transfer to a wire rack to cool. MICROWAVE the remaining cakes in the same way.

Leave the cakes until cold. Unwrap to show the fluted edges or serve in the paper cases. Before serving, decorate each cake with a piped swirl of whipped cream and top with a glacé (candied) cherry.

MAKES 12

Note: When fresh cherries are in season, use stoned (pitted) ones in place of glacé (candied) cherries.

GENOESE ICED FANCIES

METRIC/IMPERIAL	AMERICAN
4 eggs	4 eggs
100 g/4 oz sugar	½ cup sugar
50 g/2 oz butter	¼ cup butter
100 g/4 oz plain flour	1 cup all-purpose flour
1 teaspoon baking powder	1 teaspoon baking powder
Icing:	**Icing:**
5 tablespoons orange juice	5 tablespoons orange juice
50 g/2 oz butter	¼ cup butter
500 g/1 lb icing sugar, sifted orange and yellow food colouring	1 lb confectioners' sugar, sifted orange and yellow food coloring
To decorate:	**To decorate:**
crystalized orange and lemon slices	candied orange and lemon slices

Line two 20 cm/8 inch square dishes or boxes with plastic cling film. Using an electric beater or rotary whisk, whisk the eggs and sugar together in a large mixing bowl until very thick and creamy. The mixture is beaten sufficiently when a fork drawn through the top leaves a channel.

Put the butter in a jug and MICROWAVE ON HIGH FOR 30 TO 45 SECONDS until just melted. Sift the flour and baking powder together over the creamed mixture and pour the melted butter round the edge of the bowl. Using a metal spoon, gently fold in the flour and butter, using a figure-of-eight movement, until thoroughly incorporated.

Divide the mixture between the lined dishes, tilting them so the batter spreads evenly and reaches the corners. Cook the cakes one at a time: MICROWAVE ON HIGH FOR 3½ TO 4 MINUTES until spongy and just dry on top, giving the dishes a half-turn once during cooking. Leave to stand until cold before turning out and decorating.

To make the icing, put the orange juice and butter in a large bowl and MICROWAVE ON HIGH FOR 1½ MINUTES. Add the icing (confectioners') sugar and beat thoroughly until smooth. Divide the icing in half. Beat the orange colouring into one portion and the yellow colouring into the other.

Spread the orange icing over one cake and the yellow icing over the other cake. Leave until set, then cut the cakes into 5 cm/2 inch squares. Decorate each one with orange and lemon slices.

MAKES 32 SMALL CAKES

Note: These cakes should be stored in an airtight container in a cool place. They may also be frozen successfully.

Left: Preparing Viennese cherry cakes

Right: Gingerbread; Tea scones; Viennese cherry cakes; Cornish wholewheat scones; Genoese iced fancies

TEA SCONES

METRIC/IMPERIAL	AMERICAN
225 g/8 oz plain flour	2 cups all-purpose flour
pinch of salt	pinch of salt
2 teaspoons baking powder	2 teaspoons baking powder
50 g/2 oz butter	¼ cup butter
25 g/1 oz sugar	2 tablespoons sugar
25 g/1 oz currants	3 tablespoons currants
1 egg	1 egg
4–6 tablespoons milk	4–6 tablespoons milk

Sift the flour, salt and baking powder into a mixing bowl and rub in the butter until the mixture resembles bread-crumbs. Add the sugar and currants. Stir in the beaten egg and sufficient milk to form a smooth, soft dough which drops from a spoon.

Shape the dough into a ball, then flatten to form a round, about 1 cm/½ inch thick. Cut into 3 cm/1½ inch rounds. Place on a piece of non-stick parchment in the oven, spacing them well apart.

MICROWAVE ON HIGH FOR 3 TO 3½ MINUTES, moving the scones around from time to time. Insert a skewer into the centre of each scone; if it comes out clean, the scones are cooked. Return any uncooked scones to the oven and MICROWAVE ON HIGH FOR A FURTHER 30 SECONDS or until cooked.

Place the scones upside down on a grill (broiler) rack. Brown under a preheated hot grill (broiler). Turn over and brown the tops. Serve warm, split and buttered.

MAKES 6 TO 8 SCONES

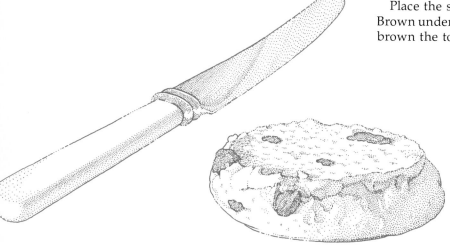

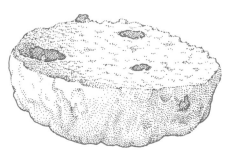

CORNISH WHOLEWHEAT SCONES

METRIC/IMPERIAL	AMERICAN
100 g/4 oz wholemeal flour	1 cup 100% wholewheat flour
100 g/4 oz self-raising flour	1 cup self-rising flour
pinch of salt	pinch of salt
1 teaspoon sugar	1 teaspoon sugar
50 g/2 oz butter	¼ cup butter
½ teaspoon bicarbonate of soda	½ teaspoon baking soda
1 teaspoon cream of tartar	1 teaspoon cream of tartar
2 tablespoons natural yogurt	2 tablespoons unflavoured yogurt
1 egg, beaten	1 egg, beaten
4–6 tablespoons milk	4–6 tablespoons milk
To serve:	**To serve:**
raspberry or strawberry jam	raspberry or strawberry preserve
whipped cream or butter	whipped cream or butter

Place the flours, salt and sugar in a mixing bowl. Rub in the butter until the mixture resembles fine breadcrumbs. Mix the bicarbonate of soda (baking soda) and cream of tartar with the yogurt, then stir into the flour mixture, together with the beaten egg. Add sufficient milk to form a soft dough which easily drops from a spoon.

Grease a 6-holed bun or muffin dish. Two-thirds fill each hollow with scone mixture. MICROWAVE ON HIGH FOR 3 TO 3½ MINUTES until the scones are well-risen, giving the dish a quarter-turn every 45 seconds. Insert a skewer into the centre of each one; if it comes out clean the scones are cooked. Return to the oven for a little longer, if necessary.

Transfer the cooked scones to a grill (broiler) rack, placing them top side down. Place under a preheated hot grill (broiler) until brown. Turn over and brown the tops.

Serve warm with jam and whipped cream, or butter.

MAKES 6 TO 8 SCONES

Note: Refill the bun or muffin dish with any remaining mixture. MICROWAVE ON HIGH, allowing 30 seconds for each scone.

BROWNIES

METRIC/IMPERIAL	AMERICAN
75 g/3 oz plain chocolate, broken	3 squares semi-sweet chocolate, broken
100 g/4 oz butter	½ cup butter
2 eggs	2 eggs
225 g/8 oz sugar	1 cup sugar
1 teaspoon vanilla essence	1 teaspoon vanilla extract
100 g/4 oz plain flour, sifted	1 cup all-purpose flour, sifted
100 g/4 oz mixed nuts, chopped	1 cup chopped mixed nuts

Line a 20 cm/8 inch square box or dish with plastic cling film. Put the chocolate and butter in a bowl and MICROWAVE ON HIGH FOR 1½ TO 2 MINUTES until the chocolate is melted.

In another bowl, beat the eggs, sugar and vanilla essence (extract) together until thick and creamy. Fold in the flour and chocolate mixture in alternate spoonfuls. Fold in the nuts.

Turn the mixture into the lined box and spread smoothly. MICROWAVE ON HIGH FOR 5 TO 6 MINUTES until a skewer inserted into the centre comes out clean; give the dish a quarter-turn every 1 minute during cooking.

Leave in the box or dish until cold, then turn out and cut into squares.

MAKES 16 TO 20 BROWNIES

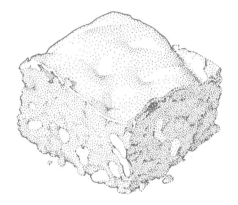

GINGERBREAD

METRIC/IMPERIAL	AMERICAN
1½ teaspoons vinegar	1½ teaspoons vinegar
4 tablespoons milk	4 tablespoons milk
100 g/4 oz plain flour	1 cup all-purpose flour
1 teaspoon baking powder	1 teaspoon baking powder
¼ teaspoon bicarbonate of soda	½ teaspoon baking soda
pinch of salt	pinch of salt
1 teaspoon ground ginger	1 teaspoon ground ginger
½ teaspoon ground cinnamon	½ teaspoon ground cinnamon
¼ teaspoon ground allspice	¼ teaspoon ground allspice
50 g/2 oz butter	¼ cup butter
50 g/2 oz brown sugar	¼ cup brown sugar
1 egg, beaten	1 egg, beaten
175 g/6 oz black treacle	½ cup molasses
whipped cream to decorate (optional)	whipped cream to decorate (optional)

Mix the vinegar and milk together and set aside. Sift together the flour, baking powder, bicarbonate of soda (baking soda), salt, ginger, cinnamon and allspice together.

Cream the butter with the sugar until light and fluffy. Add the beaten egg, a little at a time, beating thoroughly after each addition. Fold the sifted dry ingredients into the mixture, together with the black treacle (molasses), vinegar and milk mixture.

Turn the batter into a greased 20 cm/8 inch square dish or similar-sized box. Cover with a piece of greaseproof (waxed) paper. MICROWAVE ON HIGH FOR 4 TO 5 MINUTES until the colour deepens and the cake is just dry on top; give the dish a quarter-turn every 1½ minutes during cooking.

Leave to stand for 10 minutes before turning out. Cut into squares and serve while still slightly warm, or store uncut in an airtight tin until required. Before serving, top each square with a spoonful of whipped cream, if desired.

MAKES 16 SQUARES

FLAPJACKS

METRIC/IMPERIAL	AMERICAN
75 g/3 oz butter	⅓ cup butter
75 g/3 oz soft brown sugar	½ cup soft brown sugar
100 g/4 oz porridge oats	1¼ cups rolled oats

Put the butter into an 18 cm/7 inch round shallow dish. MICROWAVE ON HIGH FOR 1 TO 1½ MINUTES until melted. Stir in the sugar and oats and mix thoroughly. Press down evenly.

MICROWAVE ON HIGH FOR 4 TO 5 MINUTES until a skewer inserted into the centre comes out clean; give the dish a quarter-turn every 1 minute during cooking. Leave in the dish to cool slightly until firm, then mark into wedges.

Turn out onto a wire rack. Cut into wedges when cold.

MAKES 12 FLAPJACKS

BUTTERSCOTCH SLICES

METRIC/IMPERIAL	AMERICAN
50 g/2 oz butter	¼ cup butter
175 g/6 oz brown sugar	1 cup brown sugar
75 g/3 oz plain flour	¾ cup all-purpose flour
1 teaspoon baking powder	1 teaspoon baking powder
1 egg, beaten	1 egg, beaten
½ teaspoon vanilla essence	½ teaspoon vanilla extract
25 g/1 oz chopped nuts	¼ cup chopped nuts

Put the butter in a large bowl and MICROWAVE ON HIGH FOR 1 MINUTE until melted. Stir in the sugar and MICROWAVE ON HIGH FOR 2 MINUTES. Leave to cool.

Sift the flour and baking powder onto the mixture, then add the egg, vanilla essence (extract) and nuts. Beat until the mixture is smooth.

Grease a 20 cm/8 inch square dish and spread the mixture over the base. MICROWAVE ON HIGH FOR 2½ TO 3½ MINUTES until the cake is just dry on top. Leave to cool, then cut into slices.

MAKES 12 TO 16 SLICES

CHOCOLATE BISCUITS

METRIC/IMPERIAL	AMERICAN
50 g/2 oz wholemeal flour	½ cup wholewheat (100%) flour
50 g/2 oz self-raising flour	½ cup self-rising flour
100 g/4 oz porridge oats	1¼ cups rolled oats
25 g/1 oz dark brown sugar	3 tablespoons dark brown sugar
½ teaspoon salt	½ teaspoon salt
½ teaspoon bicarbonate of soda	½ teaspoon baking soda
100 g/4 oz butter, softened	½ cup butter, softened
4 tablespoons milk	¼ cup milk
350 g/12 oz plain chocolate	¾ lb semi-sweet chocolate

Combine all the ingredients except the chocolate in a large bowl. Mix thoroughly and knead to form a soft dough. Roll out on a floured surface to a thickness of 5 mm/¼ inch and cut out 5 cm/2 inch rounds. Reroll the trimmings and cut out as necessary.

Line a tray or the oven shelf with non-stick parchment or a folded roaster bag. Arrange 9 biscuits in a circle around the edges. MICROWAVE ON HIGH FOR 4 MINUTES, turning the tray occasionally. The biscuits are ready when they can be removed from the tray without easily breaking. Transfer each one to a wire cooling rack as soon as it is cooked. Repeat with the remaining biscuits.

Put the chocolate in a bowl and MICROWAVE ON HIGH FOR 3 TO 3½ MINUTES until just melting. Dip the biscuits into the chocolate one at a time, to coat completely. Lift out with a fork and place on the non-stick parchment.

Chill in the refrigerator until the chocolate has set, then trim the edges to neaten. Store in an airtight container in a cool place until required.

MAKES 18 BISCUITS

Preparing Butterscotch slices, Flapjacks and Chocolate biscuits

JAM TARTS

METRIC/IMPERIAL
175 g/6 oz packet shortcrust
pastry
caramel colouring (see page
69)
6 tablespoons jam

AMERICAN
6 oz package basic pastry
caramel coloring (see page
69)
6 tablespoons jam

Roll out the pastry thinly and cut out six 6 cm/3½ inch circles, using a pastry cutter. Carefully place the pastry circles in a 6-holed bun or muffin dish, suitable for use in the microwave oven. Lightly press the pastry into the base and sides of each mould to form tartlet cases. Prick the base of the pastry tartlets with a fork.

MICROWAVE ON HIGH FOR 4 TO 4½ MINUTES until the pastry is puffed and just firm. Brush each tartlet case with caramel and half-fill with jam. MICROWAVE ON HIGH FOR 30 SECONDS. Allow to cool before serving.

MAKES 6 TARTS

DATE AND RAISIN BARS

METRIC/IMPERIAL
175 g/6 oz self-raising flour
175 g/6 oz ground rice
75 g/3 oz brown sugar
175 g/6 oz butter
100 g/4 oz block stoned dates
100 g/4 oz sultanas
2 tablespoons honey
1 tablespoon lemon juice
2 tablespoons water
¼ teaspoon ground nutmeg
¼ teaspoon ground
cinnamon

AMERICAN
1½ cups self-rising flour
1 cup ground rice
½ cup brown sugar
¾ cup butter
¼ lb block pitted cooking
dates
⅔ cup golden raisins
2 tablespoons honey
1 tablespoon lemon juice
2 tablespoons water
¼ teaspoon ground nutmeg
¼ teaspoon ground
cinnamon

Combine the flour, rice and sugar in a large bowl, then rub in the butter until the mixture forms large crumbs. Put the dates, sultanas (golden raisins), honey, lemon juice and water in a shallow dish and MICROWAVE ON HIGH FOR 1 MINUTE.

Break up the dates and mash lightly with a fork, adding a few drops of water to moisten if necessary. Stir in the nutmeg and cinnamon. Without covering, MICROWAVE ON HIGH FOR 1 TO 1½ MINUTES until the mixture thickens.

Grease a shallow 20 cm/8 inch square dish. Spread half of the crumble mixture evenly over the base. Cover with the date spread, then top with the remaining crumbs. Press the mixture down firmly, then MICROWAVE ON HIGH FOR 5½ TO 6 MINUTES, giving the dish a half-turn after 3 minutes. To test the mixture, insert a skewer into the centre; if it comes out clean, the mixture is cooked.

Allow to cool slightly, then mark into bars. Cool completely before serving.

MAKES 15 BARS

Note: The crumble mixture may seem very soft immediately after removing from the oven, but it becomes firm during cooling.

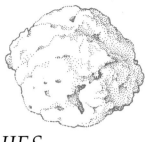

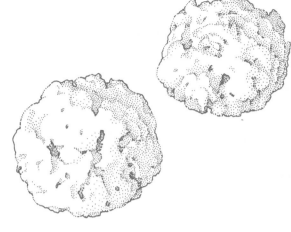

CORNFLAKE CRUNCHIES

METRIC/IMPERIAL	AMERICAN
1 egg white	1 egg white
½ teaspoon vanilla essence	½ teaspoon vanilla extract
65 g/2½ oz sugar	5 tablespoons sugar
40 g/1½ oz ground almonds	⅓ cup ground almonds
25 g/1 oz cornflakes, lightly crushed	1 cup cornflakes, lightly crushed
2–3 sheets rice paper	2–3 sheets rice paper

Whisk the egg white until stiff, then fold in the vanilla essence (extract), sugar, ground almonds and cornflakes. Divide the mixture into 12 pieces, each about the size of a walnut. Roll each piece into a ball.

Line the oven shelf with rice paper and arrange the crunchies on top, spacing them well apart. MICROWAVE ON MEDIUM FOR 5 TO 6 MINUTES, giving the sheets a half-turn after 2½ minutes. To test the crunchies, insert a skewer into the centre of each one; if it comes out clean the crunchie is cooked.

Transfer to a wire rack and allow to cool before serving.

MAKES 12 CRUNCHIES

Note: The crunchies may seem very soft when they are initially removed from the oven, but cooking will continue after they are removed, so take care not to leave in the oven too long. The crunchies will taste best when they are just brown inside.

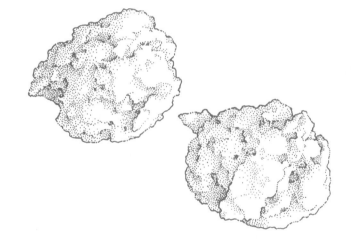

COCONUT COOKIES

METRIC/IMPERIAL	AMERICAN
50 g/2 oz soft margarine	¼ cup soft margarine
65 g/2½ oz sugar	5 tablespoons sugar
1 small egg, beaten	1 small egg, beaten
few drops of vanilla essence	few drops of vanilla extract
75 g/3 oz plain flour	¾ cup all-purpose flour
25 g/1 oz desiccated coconut	⅓ cup shredded coconut
pinch of salt	pinch of salt
1 tablespoon raspberry or strawberry jam	1 tablespoon raspberry or strawberry jam

Beat the margarine and sugar together until light and fluffy. Stir in the egg and vanilla essence (extract), then add the flour, coconut and salt; mix thoroughly. Knead until a smooth, pliable dough is formed.

Divide the dough into 16 pieces. Roll each piece into a ball and press the end of a table knife handle into the centre of each one, to make a hollow. Arrange half of the cookies in a circle on a large plate, lined with plastic cling film. MICROWAVE ON HIGH FOR 3½ TO 4½ MINUTES, giving the plate a quarter-turn every minute, until the cookies are just firm.

Carefully transfer the cookies to a wire cooling rack and spoon a little jam into the centre of each one. Repeat with the remaining cookies. Allow to cool before serving.

MAKES 16 COOKIES

Lemon curd; Orange preserve; Apple jelly; Strawberry preserve

LEMON CURD

METRIC/IMPERIAL	AMERICAN
grated rind and juice of 3 lemons	*grated rind and juice of 3 lemons*
75 g/3 oz unsalted butter	*⅓ cup sweet butter*
225 g/8 oz sugar	*1 cup sugar*
3 large eggs, beaten	*3 large eggs, beaten*

Put the lemon rind, juice and butter in a large bowl and MICROWAVE ON HIGH FOR 3 MINUTES until the butter is melted. Stir in the sugar and MICROWAVE ON HIGH FOR 2 MINUTES. Stir until the sugar is dissolved, then strain in the eggs, stirring constantly.

Without covering, MICROWAVE ON LOW FOR 12 TO 14 MINUTES, stirring occasionally, until the mixture is thick enough to coat the back of a spoon. Spoon into dry jars, cover with plastic cling film and secure. Store in a cool place.

MAKES 750 g/1½ lb LEMON CURD

ORANGE PRESERVE

METRIC/IMPERIAL	AMERICAN
2 large oranges	*2 large oranges*
1 lemon	*1 lemon*
300 ml/½ pint water	*1¼ cups water*
500 g/1 lb sugar	*2 cups sugar*

Cut the oranges and lemon in half; place in a large bowl with the water. Cover loosely with plastic cling film and MICROWAVE ON HIGH FOR 10 MINUTES. Remove the fruit carefully and leave to stand for 5 minutes.

Discard the pips (seeds), shred the oranges finely and squeeze the juice from the lemon. Return to the bowl, stir in the sugar and leave for 10 minutes until completely dissolved. MICROWAVE ON HIGH FOR 20 TO 25 MINUTES, stirring occasionally, until a spoonful of the syrup wrinkles when dropped on to a cold plate.

Pour into hot sterilized jars, leaving a 2.5 cm/1 inch space at the top. Cover loosely with plastic cling film and MICROWAVE ON HIGH FOR 1 MINUTE until the cling film bubbles up. Remove from the oven, using oven gloves. Allow to cool. Store in a cool place.

MAKES 750 g/1½ lb PRESERVE

APPLE JELLY

METRIC/IMPERIAL	AMERICAN
750 ml/1 ¾ pints apple juice	3 cups apple juice
1 kg/2 lb sugar	4 cups sugar
1 teaspoon lemon juice	1 teaspoon lemon juice
150 ml/¼ pint commercial pectin	⅔ cup commercial pectin
few drops of green food colouring	few drops of green food coloring

Combine the apple juice, sugar and lemon juice in a large bowl. Cover the MICROWAVE ON HIGH FOR 10 MINUTES, stirring occasionally. Stir in the pectin. Without covering, MICROWAVE ON HIGH FOR 7 TO 10 MINUTES until a drop of the syrup forms a thread when suspended from a wooden spoon.

Stir in the green colouring and allow to cool slightly. Pour into hot sterilized jars, leaving a 2.5 cm/1 inch space at the top. Cover loosely with plastic cling film, return to the oven and MICROWAVE ON HIGH FOR 30 SECONDS TO 1 MINUTE until the cling film bubbles up. Remove the jars from the oven, using oven gloves.

Allow to cool, then store in a cool place until required.

MAKES 1–1.25 kg/2–2½ lb JELLY

STRAWBERRY PRESERVE

METRIC/IMPERIAL	AMERICAN
1 kg/2 lb large strawberries	2 lb large strawberries
1.5 kg/3 lb sugar	3 lb sugar
3 tablespoons lemon juice	3 tablespoons lemon juice

Hull the strawberries, then rinse and dry thoroughly. Put the strawberries and sugar into a large bowl, toss gently, then cover and leave for 24 hours.

Add the lemon juice and stir thoroughly. Without covering, MICROWAVE ON HIGH FOR 10 TO 15 MINUTES, stirring 2 or 3 times during cooking, until the mixture reaches a full rolling boil. MICROWAVE ON HIGH FOR 5 TO 10 MINUTES, stirring occasionally until the syrup is thick.

Leave to cool slightly, then pour into warm sterilized jars. Seal with jam pot covers or plastic cling film. Allow to cool, then store in a cool place until required.

MAKES ABOUT 1.75 kg/4 lb JAM

Note: This recipe produces a preserve of whole strawberries in a thick syrup, not a thick jam.

BERRY AND APPLE JAM

METRIC/IMPERIAL	AMERICAN
100 g/4 oz blackcurrants or blueberries	1 cup black currants or blueberries
100 g/4 oz redcurrants	1 cup redcurrants
225 g/8 oz red gooseberries	2 cups red gooseberries
225 g/8 oz cooking apples	½ lb tart baking apples
150 ml/¼ pint water	⅔ cup water
1 kg/2 lb sugar	2 lb sugar

Wash, top and tail the soft fruit. Peel, core and slice the apples. Combine all the fruit in a large bowl and stir in the water. Cover loosely with plastic cling film and MICROWAVE ON HIGH FOR 7 TO 8 MINUTES. Leave to stand for 30 minutes.

Add the sugar to the fruit and stir until dissolved. Cover with a piece of greaseproof (waxed) paper and MICROWAVE ON HIGH FOR 15 TO 20 MINUTES, stirring occasionally, until a spoonful of the syrup wrinkles when placed on a cold plate.

Leave to cool for a few minutes, then pour into hot sterilized jars, leaving 2.5 cm/1 inch space at the top. Cover loosely with plastic cling film and MICROWAVE ON HIGH FOR 30 SECONDS TO 1 MINUTE until the cling film bubbles up. Remove the jars from the oven, using oven gloves. Allow to cool, then store in a cool place until required.

MAKES 1.25 kg/2½ lb JAM

PLUM JAM

METRIC/IMPERIAL	AMERICAN
1 kg/2 lb juicy plums	2 lb juicy plums
150 ml/¼ pint water	⅔ cup water
¼ teaspoon almond essence	¼ teaspoon almond extract
1 kg/2 lb sugar	2 lb sugar

Put the plums in a large bowl with the water and almond essence (extract). Cover with greaseproof (waxed) paper and MICROWAVE ON HIGH FOR 15 MINUTES, stirring occasionally. Remove as many of the stones (pits) as possible, with a slotted spoon.

Stir in the sugar and leave to stand for 30 minutes, stirring occasionally until dissolved. MICROWAVE ON HIGH FOR 30 TO 40 MINUTES, stirring occasionally, until a spoonful of the syrup wrinkles when placed on a cold plate. Remove any remaining stones (pits).

Leave to cool slightly, then pour into hot sterilized jars. Seal with jam pot covers or cover loosely with plastic cling film, return to the oven and MICROWAVE ON HIGH FOR 1 TO 1½ MINUTES until the cling film bubbles up. Remove from the oven, using oven gloves. Allow to cool, then store in a cool place until required.

MAKES 1.5 kg/ 3 lb JAM

DAMSON PRESERVE

METRIC/IMPERIAL	AMERICAN
2.25 kg/5 lb damsons	5 lb damsons
150 ml/¼ pint + 2 tablespoons water	¾ cup water
1 kg/2 lb sugar	2 lb sugar

Wash the fruit, dry thoroughly and place in a large bowl. Add the water. Cover loosely with plastic cling film and MICROWAVE ON HIGH FOR 15 MINUTES. Press through a sieve (strainer) to remove the stones (pits). Stir in the sugar.

Partially cover with plastic cling film. MICROWAVE ON HIGH FOR 20 TO 25 MINUTES, stirring occasionally, until the preserve is thick enough to leave a channel when stirred with a wooden spoon.

Leave to cool slightly, then pour into hot sterilized jars. Seal with jam pot covers, or cover loosely with plastic cling film. Return to the oven and MICROWAVE ON HIGH FOR 1 TO 1½ MINUTES until the cling film bubbles up. Remove from the oven with oven gloves. Allow to cool, then store in a cool place until required.

MAKES 1.75 kg/4 lb PRESERVE

TANGY CHOCOLATE SPREAD

METRIC/IMPERIAL	AMERICAN
50 g/2 oz butter	*¼ cup butter*
225 g/8 oz sugar	*1 cup sugar*
juice of 1 lemon	*juice of 1 lemon*
1 oz cocoa powder	*¼ cup unsweetened cocoa*
1 tablespoon evaporated milk	*1 tablespoon evaporated milk*
1 large egg, beaten	*1 large egg, beaten*

Put the butter and sugar in a large jug and MICROWAVE ON HIGH FOR 2 MINUTES. Beat thoroughly then stir in the lemon juice, cocoa powder and evaporated milk. Beat thoroughly, strain in the beaten egg and beat again.

MICROWAVE ON LOW FOR 4 MINUTES, stirring once during cooking, then MICROWAVE ON HIGH FOR 2 MINUTES until the mixture boils. Leave to cool, then pour into small pots, cover and leave until cold. Store in the refrigerator until required.

Serve as a spread for bread or scones, or use as a cake filling.

MAKES 225 g/½ lb CHOCOLATE SPREAD

CARAMEL COLOURING

METRIC/IMPERIAL	AMERICAN
100 g/4 oz sugar	*½ cup sugar*
4 tablespoons water	*4 tablespoons water*
1 teaspoon vegetable oil	*1 teaspoon vegetable oil*

Combine the sugar and 4 tablespoons/¼ cup cold water in a 600 ml/1 pint/2½ cup heat-resistant jug. MICROWAVE ON HIGH FOR 6 MINUTES, without stirring.

Pour 3 tablespoons of water into a glass or cup and put in the microwave oven beside the syrup. MICROWAVE ON HIGH FOR 1½ TO 2 MINUTES until the water is boiling and the syrup is a very dark brown colour.

Protecting the hands with oven gloves, gradually add the boiling water to the syrup, then stir in the oil. Leave to cool, then pour into a screw-top bottle. Use as required.

MAKES 100 g/¼ lb CARAMEL COLOURING

Note: Caramel colouring keeps indefinitely and may be added in small quantities to fruit cakes, sauces, stews or other dishes which require more depth of colour.

FAMILY MEALS

The aim of this chapter is to provide inexpensive meals that are neither time-consuming nor difficult to prepare. Most dishes are cooked on HIGH, so meals can be ready relatively quickly. You will find a wide selection of soups and starters, main courses, vegetables and desserts.

Meat, and in particular beef, must either be of top quality or tenderized in one of several ways if it is to be microwaved in one piece using the HIGH setting. Cuts of meat generally sold for frying or grilling (broiling) can be used in casseroles to be cooked on HIGH without further treatment. Economical cuts should first be beaten with a mallet or rolling pin to tenderize, then marinated or sprinkled with meat tenderizer. Tougher cuts may be casseroled on LOW; this takes about half the conventional casseroling time and is a suitable method for cooking large quantities.

Suitable cuts of meat can be roasted easily and quickly. If you enjoy cold roast meat, buy a slightly larger joint, remembering that any left-over meat can always be minced (ground) for use in other dishes. For best results from microwave roasting, choose evenly-shaped pieces of meat. Boned and rolled roasts are evenly shaped and therefore ideal. When microwaving a leg of lamb cover the pointed end with a small piece of foil half-way through cooking to prevent burning.

Minced (ground) meat cooks successfully on HIGH, but remember the cheapest is not always the most economical to buy because it usually has a high fat content. In microwave cookery, fat tends to be less well absorbed, so it is better to choose lean minced (ground) meat. You may also prefer to drain off excess fat after the initial cooking.

Whole chicken, duck or turkey all cook well on HIGH but require less turning during cooking if a MEDIUM setting is used for part of the time. Tips of wings and legs should be covered with small twists of foil as soon as these bony parts are cooked. Do,

however, make sure the foil does not touch the oven walls. Whole birds should ideally be cooked in roaster bags with the addition of a little stock or water which will render the meat more tender. Roaster bags may either be sealed with a plastic clip or the open ends can be tucked underneath; metal closures must never be used, as they are made from a type of metal which sparks easily in the microwave oven.

Meat and poultry dishes are easily and safely reheated in the microwave oven. Fish, too, can be reheated, but this is generally unnecessary as it can be cooked so quickly from raw. Sauces to enhance the flavour of your main course dish can be prepared quickly by microwave, and, because no direct heat is involved, there is no risk of a lumpy sauce!

With the exception of tiny French beans, all vegetables can be cooked from fresh or frozen, or reheated in the microwave oven. Apart from spinach, onions and baked potatoes, which require no additional moisture, a few tablespoonfuls of water should be added to vegetables before microwaving. Because cooking liquid and time are both minimal, microwaved vegetables retain more colour, flavour and vitamins than those cooked conventionally. Delicious roast potatoes can be prepared in less than half the normal time: place peeled, quartered potatoes in a roaster bag and soften in the microwave before roasting in a conventional oven. Quantities up to 500 g/1 lb can alternatively be finished off in the microwave oven by browning, with 2 tablespoons of butter added, in a preheated browning skillet.

To complete your family meal, you will find a variety of desserts to choose from. Fruit dishes can, of course, be varied according to taste and the season. For example pears or apricots may be used instead of pineapple in Pineapple Upside Down Pudding *(see page 101)*. All fresh and frozen fruits can be stewed in the same way as plums *(see page 109)*, although a few tablespoonfuls of water should be added to firm fruits and the quantity of sugar will need adjusting according to the sweetness of the chosen fruit.

FRENCH ONION SOUP GRATINÉE

METRIC/IMPERIAL
500 g/1 lb large Spanish
   onions, thinly sliced
1 clove garlic, crushed
½ teaspoon sugar
40 g/1 ½ oz butter
2 tablespoons flour
pinch of powdered mustard
1 beef stock cube
600 ml/1 pint boiling water
300 ml/½ pint canned beef
   consommé
½ teaspoon Worcestershire
   sauce
salt
freshly ground black pepper
6 thick slices of French
   bread, toasted
50 g/2 oz Cheddar cheese,
   grated

AMERICAN
1 lb large Spanish onions,
   thinly sliced
1 clove garlic, minced
½ teaspoon sugar
3 tablespoons butter
2 tablespoons all-purpose
   flour
pinch of powdered mustard
1 beef bouillon cube
2 ½ cups boiling water
1 ¼ cups canned condensed
   beef consommé
½ teaspoon Worcestershire
   sauce
salt
freshly ground black pepper
6 thick slices of French
   bread, toasted
½ cup Cheddar cheese,
   grated

Combine the onions, garlic, sugar and butter in a large bowl and MICROWAVE ON HIGH FOR 6 TO 8 MINUTES until the onions are golden; stir occasionally during cooking.

Stir in the flour, mustard, stock (bouillon) cube, water, consommé and Worcestershire sauce. Partially cover with plastic cling film and MICROWAVE ON HIGH FOR 20 MINUTES, stirring occasionally. Leave to stand for 5 minutes, then add salt and pepper to taste.

Sprinkle the toast with cheese and brown under the grill. Pour the soup into individual bowls, add a slice of toast to each one and serve immediately.

SERVES 6

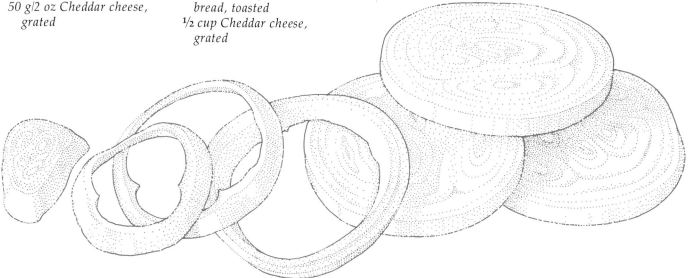

SKIERS SOUP

METRIC/IMPERIAL
225 g/8 oz minced beef
1 large onion, finely
   chopped
1 small green pepper, cored,
   seeded and chopped
1 large potato, peeled and
   diced
1 × 500 g/1 lb can tomatoes
4 tablespoons tomato purée
750 ml/1 ¼ pints hot beef
   stock
1 tablespoon paprika
½ teaspoon black pepper
salt

AMERICAN
1 cup ground beef
1 large onion, finely
   chopped
1 small green pepper, cored,
   seeded and chopped
1 large potato, peeled and
   diced
1 × 1 lb can tomatoes
¼ cup tomato paste
3 cups hot beef stock
1 tablespoon paprika
½ teaspoon black pepper
salt

PREHEAT A LARGE BROWNING SKILLET FOR 5 MINUTES (or according to the manufacturer's instructions). Add the meat, stir briskly and MICROWAVE ON HIGH FOR 3 MINUTES. Add the onion and green pepper and MICROWAVE ON HIGH FOR 4 MINUTES.

Cover and leave to stand for 5 minutes, then, using a slotted spoon, transfer the mixture to a large bowl. Add the potato, tomatoes with their juice, tomato purée (paste), stock, paprika and pepper. Partially cover with plastic cling film and MICROWAVE ON HIGH FOR 25 MINUTES, stirring occasionally.

Add salt to taste and crush the soup with a potato masher to break up the tomatoes. Serve hot.

SERVES 4 TO 6

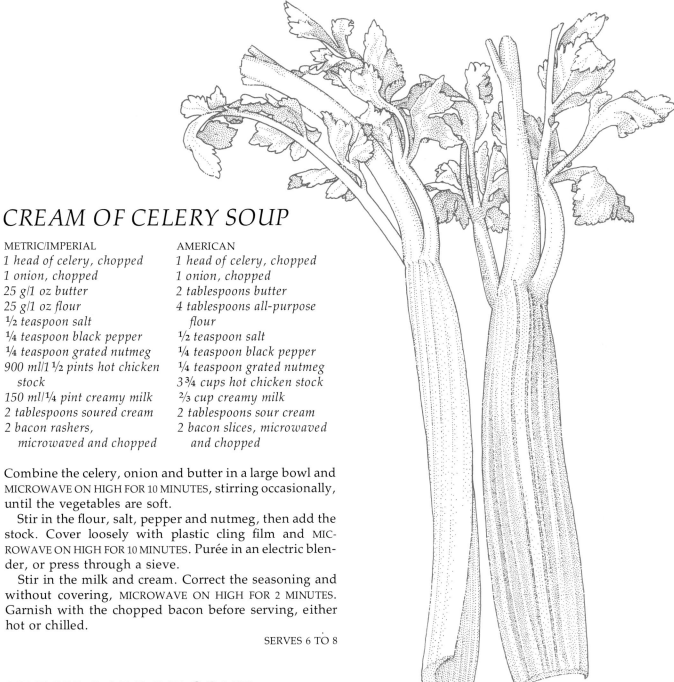

CREAM OF CELERY SOUP

METRIC/IMPERIAL	AMERICAN
1 head of celery, chopped	1 head of celery, chopped
1 onion, chopped	1 onion, chopped
25 g/1 oz butter	2 tablespoons butter
25 g/1 oz flour	4 tablespoons all-purpose flour
½ teaspoon salt	½ teaspoon salt
¼ teaspoon black pepper	¼ teaspoon black pepper
¼ teaspoon grated nutmeg	¼ teaspoon grated nutmeg
900 ml/1½ pints hot chicken stock	3¾ cups hot chicken stock
150 ml/¼ pint creamy milk	⅔ cup creamy milk
2 tablespoons soured cream	2 tablespoons sour cream
2 bacon rashers, microwaved and chopped	2 bacon slices, microwaved and chopped

Combine the celery, onion and butter in a large bowl and MICROWAVE ON HIGH FOR 10 MINUTES, stirring occasionally, until the vegetables are soft.

Stir in the flour, salt, pepper and nutmeg, then add the stock. Cover loosely with plastic cling film and MICROWAVE ON HIGH FOR 10 MINUTES. Purée in an electric blender, or press through a sieve.

Stir in the milk and cream. Correct the seasoning and without covering, MICROWAVE ON HIGH FOR 2 MINUTES. Garnish with the chopped bacon before serving, either hot or chilled.

SERVES 6 TO 8

FRESH CARROT SOUP

METRIC/IMPERIAL	AMERICAN
500 g/1 lb carrots, thinly sliced	1 lb carrots, thinly sliced
1 onion, chopped	1 onion, chopped
600 ml/1 pint hot chicken stock	2½ cups hot chicken stock
½ teaspoon salt	½ teaspoon salt
¼ teaspoon black pepper	¼ teaspoon black pepper
¼ teaspoon sugar	¼ teaspoon sugar
2 bay leaves	2 bay leaves
1 tablespoon cornflour	1 tablespoon cornstarch
3 tablespoons cold water	3 tablespoons cold water

Combine the carrots, onion and stock in a large bowl and add the salt, pepper, sugar and bay leaves. Cover loosely with plastic cling film and MICROWAVE ON HIGH FOR 15 MINUTES until the carrots are soft.

Remove the bay leaves and purée the soup in an electric blender, or press through a sieve. Blend the cornflour (cornstarch) with the water and stir into the soup.

Without covering, MICROWAVE ON HIGH FOR 3 TO 5 MINUTES, stirring occasionally until the soup boils. If the soup is too thick, add more water and bring back to the boil. Adjust the seasoning before serving, either hot or chilled.

SERVES 6 TO 8

ORANGE TOMATO SOUP

METRIC/IMPERIAL	AMERICAN
2 large onions, chopped	2 large onions, chopped
15 g/½ oz butter	1 tablespoon butter
1 orange	1 orange
½ small red pepper, cored, seeded and chopped	½ small red pepper, cored, seeded and chopped
3 mint sprigs	3 mint sprigs
600 ml/1 pint water	2½ cups water
1 chicken stock cube	1 chicken bouillon cube
1 × 500 g/1 lb can tomatoes	1 × 1 lb can tomatoes
salt	salt
freshly ground black pepper	freshly ground black pepper
2 teaspoons cornflour	2 teaspoons cornstarch
1 tablespoon lemon juice	1 tablespoon lemon juice
1 teaspoon Worcestershire sauce	1 teaspoon Worcestershire sauce
mint sprigs to garnish	mint sprigs to garnish

Combine the onions and butter in a large bowl. MICROWAVE ON HIGH FOR 5 MINUTES.

Peel the orange, remove pith and pips and chop the flesh. Add to the onions with the chopped pepper, mint, water, stock (bouillon) cube, tomatoes and their liquor, and a light sprinkling of salt and pepper. Partially cover and MICROWAVE ON HIGH FOR 15 MINUTES.

Without removing the mint, purée the soup in an electric blender, or press through a sieve. Blend the cornflour (cornstarch), lemon juice and Worcestershire sauce with 1 tablespoon of cold water. Stir into the soup and MICROWAVE ON HIGH FOR 5 MINUTES, stirring once.

Stir briskly and adjust the seasoning before serving hot, garnished with mint sprigs.

SERVES 4 TO 6

BEEF SHAMI

METRIC/IMPERIAL	AMERICAN
225 g/8 oz lean minced beef	½ lb lean ground beef
1 onion, grated	1 onion, minced
2 teaspoons curry paste	2 teaspoons curry paste
½ teaspoon cumin powder	½ teaspoon cumin powder
½ teaspoon salt	½ teaspoon salt
1 tablespoon flour	1 tablespoon flour
1 tablespoon vegetable oil	1 tablespoon vegetable oil

Combine all the ingredients, except the oil, and mix well. Divide into eight equal-size pieces and, with floured hands, shape into rolls about 1.5 cm/¾ inch thick.

PREHEAT A MEDIUM BROWNING SKILLET FOR 4 MINUTES (or according to the manufacturer's instructions). Immediately add the oil and the beef rolls. MICROWAVE ON HIGH FOR 4 MINUTES, turning the meat over after 2 minutes. Serve hot on a bed of rice.

SERVES 4

Left: Beef shami; Orange tomato soup

Right: Country pâté

COUNTRY PÂTÉ

METRIC/IMPERIAL	AMERICAN
1 onion, chopped	1 onion, chopped
50 g/2 oz butter	¼ cup butter
100 g/4 oz chicken livers, chopped	¼ lb chicken livers, chopped
100 g/4 oz gammon or smoked ham, chopped	¼ lb raw smoked ham, chopped
1 teaspoon chopped sage	1 teaspoon chopped sage
1 tablespoon brandy	1 tablespoon brandy
2 tablespoons double cream	2 tablespoons heavy cream
salt	salt
freshly ground black pepper	freshly ground black pepper
bay leaves to garnish	bay leaves to garnish

Place the onion and half of the butter in a large shallow dish. MICROWAVE ON HIGH FOR 3 MINUTES. Stir in the chicken livers, gammon or ham, and sage. Cover with a piece of greaseproof paper or non-stick parchment and MICROWAVE ON HIGH FOR 5 TO 7 MINUTES, stirring occasionally, until the meat is cooked.

Blend in an electric blender until smooth, or press through a sieve. Stir in the brandy, cream and salt and pepper to taste. Spoon into a serving dish, or divide between 4 ramekin dishes. Top each with a bay leaf.

Put the remaining butter in a bowl and MICROWAVE ON HIGH FOR 30 SECONDS TO 1 MINUTE until melted, then pour over the paté. Chill in the refrigerator until the butter hardens.

SERVES 4

QUICHE LORRAINE

METRIC/IMPERIAL	AMERICAN
Pastry:	**Pastry:**
100 g/4 oz plain flour	*1 cup all-purpose flour*
pinch of salt	*pinch of salt*
25 g/1 oz butter	*2 tablespoons butter*
15 g/½ oz lard	*1 tablespoon shortening*
2½–3 tablespoons cold	*2½–3 tablespoons cold*
water	*water*
Filling:	**Filling:**
6 bacon rashers,	*6 bacon slices, microwaved*
microwaved and crumbled	*and crumbled*
50 g/2 oz Gruyère cheese,	*½ cup grated Gruyère*
grated	*cheese*
3 spring onions, thinly sliced	*3 scallions, thinly sliced*
¼ teaspoon salt	*¼ teaspoon salt*
¼ teaspoon grated nutmeg	*¼ teaspoon grated nutmeg*
pinch of Cayenne pepper	*pinch of Cayenne pepper*
1½ tablespoons flour	*1½ tablespoons all-purpose*
450 ml/¾ pint single cream	*flour*
4 eggs, lightly beaten	*2 cups light cream*
Garnish:	*4 eggs, lightly beaten*
1 tablespoon fried	**Garnish:**
breadcrumbs	*1 tablespoon fried*
1 bacon rasher, microwaved	*breadcrumbs*
and crumbled	*1 bacon slice, microwaved*
1 tablespoon chopped	*and crumbled*
parsley	*1 tablespoon chopped*
	parsley

To make the pastry, sift the flour and salt into a mixing bowl. Rub in the butter and lard (shortening) until the mixture resembles fine breadcrumbs. Mix in sufficient water to form a firm dough. Cover and chill for 30 minutes.

Roll out the pastry thinly and use to line a 23 cm/9 inch round dish. MICROWAVE ON HIGH FOR 4 TO 5½ MINUTES, giving the dish a half-turn once during cooking. Sprinkle the bacon, cheese and onion into the pastry case.

Combine the salt, nutmeg, Cayenne pepper, flour and cream in a large bowl. MICROWAVE ON MEDIUM FOR 7 MINUTES, stirring frequently. Stir into the beaten eggs, then pour into the pastry case. MICROWAVE ON MEDIUM FOR 4 MINUTES.

Sprinkle with the garnish ingredients. Give the dish a half-turn, then MICROWAVE ON MEDIUM FOR 2 MINUTES or until almost set. Leave to stand for 5 minutes before serving hot, or serve cold.

SERVES 4 TO 6

Quiche Lorraine – illustrated on page 70

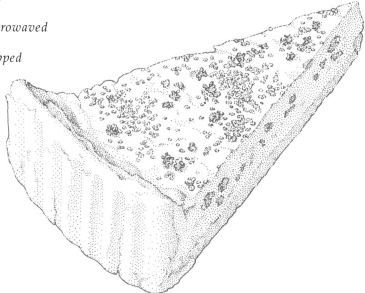

SURPRISE PATTIES

METRIC/IMPERIAL	AMERICAN
100 g/4 oz cold boiled	*¼ lb cold boiled potatoes*
potatoes	*¼ cup all-purpose flour*
25 g/1 oz flour	*1 tablespoon butter, softened*
15 g/½ oz butter, softened	*½ cup grated cheese*
50 g/2 oz cheese, grated	*2 oz cooked chicken, beef,*
50 g/2 oz cooked chicken,	*lamb, ham or fish*
beef, lamb, ham or fish	*salt*
salt	*freshly ground black pepper*
freshly ground black pepper	*beaten egg for binding*
beaten egg for binding	*6–8 tablespoons golden*
6–8 tablespoons golden	*breadcrumbs*
breadcrumbs	*4 tablespoons vegetable oil*
4 tablespoons vegetable oil	

Mash the potatoes and mix with the flour, butter, cheese and meat. Season with salt and pepper to taste. Bind with the egg. Shape into 6 or 8 patties and coat with the breadcrumbs, pressing them on with a palette knife.

Put the oil in a large shallow dish and MICROWAVE ON HIGH FOR 2 MINUTES. Using a palette knife, carefully transfer the patties to the oil and MICROWAVE ON HIGH FOR 2 MINUTES. Turn over and change the position of the patties. MICROWAVE ON HIGH FOR 2 TO 3 MINUTES until thoroughly hot.

Drain on absorbent kitchen paper. Serve hot with bottled fruit sauce.

SERVES 4 TO 6

TUNA SNACKS

METRIC/IMPERIAL	AMERICAN
1 × 200 g/7 oz can tuna fish	1 × 7 oz can tuna fish
1½ teaspoons lemon juice	1½ teaspoons lemon juice
2 tablespoons mayonnaise	2 tablespoons mayonnaise
½ small green pepper, cored, seeded and finely chopped	½ small green pepper, cored, seeded and finely chopped
cayenne pepper	cayenne pepper
butter for spreading	butter for spreading
6 slices wholemeal bread	6 slices wholewheat bread
6 black olives (optional)	6 ripe olives (optional)

Place the fish, lemon juice, mayonnaise, chopped pepper and cayenne pepper in a bowl and mash well.

Butter the bread generously on both sides, remove the crusts and cut each slice in half. Arrange in a circle on a piece of non-stick parchment on the oven shelf. MICROWAVE ON HIGH FOR 5 MINUTES until the bread is crisp, giving the paper a half-turn after 1 minute.

Pile the tuna mixture in a pyramid on each slice; MICROWAVE ON HIGH FOR 1 MINUTE. Garnish with olives, if liked, and serve hot.

SERVES 4 TO 6

MARINATED COD STEAKS

METRIC/IMPERIAL	AMERICAN
25 g/1 oz butter	2 tablespoons butter
4 spring onions, thinly sliced	¼ cup sliced scallions
4 × 100 g/4 oz frozen cod steaks	4 × ¼ lb frozen cod steaks
6 tablespoons white wine	6 tablespoons white wine
1 tablespoon medium sherry	1 tablespoon medium sherry
1 tablespoon brandy	1 tablespoon brandy
½ teaspoon dried mixed herbs	½ teaspoon dried mixed herbs
½–1 teaspoon salt	½–1 teaspoon salt
½ teaspoon black pepper	½ teaspoon black pepper
100 g/4 oz mushrooms, sliced	1 cup sliced mushrooms
2 tablespoons double cream	2 tablespoons heavy cream
parsley sprigs to garnish	parsley sprigs to garnish

Place the butter and spring onions (scallions) in a large shallow dish and MICROWAVE ON HIGH FOR 3 MINUTES. Arrange the fish steaks in the dish, in a single layer. Baste thoroughly.

Mix the wine, sherry, brandy, herbs, salt and pepper together and pour over the fish. Cover and leave in the refrigerator for 24 hours, basting the fish occasionally.

Add the mushrooms to the fish and, without covering, MICROWAVE ON HIGH FOR 8 TO 10 MINUTES, giving the dish a half-turn and basting after 4 minutes.

Transfer the fish to a heated serving dish. Blend the cream into the liquid. Taste and adjust the seasoning, then pour the sauce over the fish. Garnish with parsley before serving.

SERVES 4

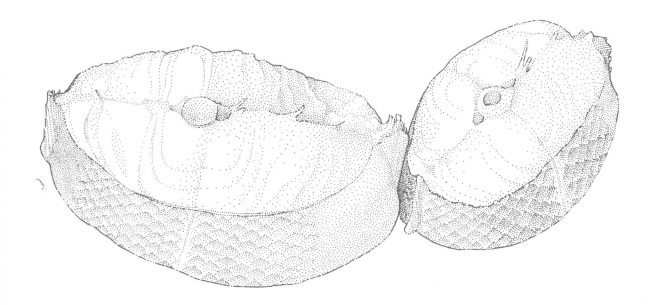

BUTTERED PLAICE (FLOUNDER)

METRIC/IMPERIAL	AMERICAN
1 × 500 g/1 lb plaice	1 × 1 lb flounder
1 teaspoon salt	1 teaspoon salt
½ teaspoon black pepper	½ teaspoon black pepper
2 tablespoons flour	2 tablespoons flour
50 g/2 oz butter	¼ cup butter

Remove the head and skin from the fish. Sprinkle with salt and pepper and coat with the flour. Place the butter in a large shallow dish and MICROWAVE ON HIGH FOR 4 MINUTES.

Put the plaice in the dish and turn to coat with the butter. MICROWAVE ON HIGH FOR 5 MINUTES, turning the fish over and giving the dish a half-turn, half-way through cooking. Test with a skewer, then cover and leave to stand for 3 minutes.

Transfer to a heated serving plate and spoon the butter over the fish, before serving.

SERVES 2

SOLE GRILLÉ

METRIC/IMPERIAL	AMERICAN
4 × 350 g/12 oz fresh or frozen sole, skinned and trimmed	4 × ¾ lb fresh or frozen sole, skinned and trimmed
25 g/1 oz butter, softened	2 tablespoons butter, softened
salt	salt
freshly ground black pepper	freshly ground black pepper

If using frozen fish, thaw before cooking.

Place 2 fish side by side and head to tail in a large shallow dish. Dot with butter and sprinkle with salt and pepper. Cover loosely with plastic cling film and MICROWAVE ON HIGH FOR 6 MINUTES, giving the dish a quarter-turn every 1½ minutes.

Set aside while cooking the remaining sole in the same way. To reheat, MICROWAVE ON HIGH FOR 2 MINUTES. Do not overcook.

SERVES 4

CRISPY CRUMBED HADDOCK

METRIC/IMPERIAL	AMERICAN
1 × 500 g/1 ½ lb piece of filleted haddock	1 × 1 ½ lb piece of filleted haddock
salt	salt
freshly ground black pepper	freshly ground black pepper
1 large egg, beaten	1 large egg, beaten
6–8 tablespoons golden breadcrumbs	½–¾ cup golden breadcrumbs
4 tablespoons vegetable oil	4 tablespoons vegetable oil

Cut the fish into 4 or 6 serving pieces and season with salt and pepper. Dip into the beaten egg and coat with breadcrumbs. Put the oil into a large shallow dish and MICROWAVE ON HIGH FOR 3 MINUTES.

Arrange the fish in the dish in a single layer. Cover with a piece of greaseproof paper or non-stick parchment and MICROWAVE ON HIGH FOR 4 TO 6 MINUTES until the fish is cooked through.

Drain on absorbent kitchen paper. Serve hot or cold.

SERVES 4 TO 6

RUSSIAN FISH BALLS

METRIC/IMPERIAL
1 × 750 g/1 ½ lb piece of
   filleted haddock, skinned
1 large onion
1 large carrot
1 ¼ teaspoons salt
¾ teaspoon black pepper
40 g/1 ½ oz fresh white
   breadcrumbs
40 g/1 ½ oz ground almonds
150 ml/¼ pint milk
150 ml/¼ pint water
2 bay leaves

AMERICAN
1 × 1 ½ lb pieces of filleted
   haddock, skinned
1 large onion
1 large carrot
1 ¼ teaspoons salt
¾ teaspoon black pepper
¾ cup fresh white
   breadcrumbs
⅓ cup ground almonds
⅔ cup milk
⅔ cup water
2 bay leaves

Finely mince (grind) the fish with the onion and the carrot. Stir in the salt, pepper, breadcrumbs and almonds. Divide into even-sized pieces and roll into balls.

Combine the milk, water and bay leaves in a large shallow dish and MICROWAVE ON HIGH FOR 2½ MINUTES until boiling. Arrange the fish balls around the edge of the dish. MICROWAVE ON LOW FOR 12 TO 13 MINUTES, turning the fish balls over halfway through cooking. Discard the bay leaves.

Serve hot or cold, moistened with the cooking liquor if liked.

SERVES 3 TO 4

Note: Russian fish balls can be reheated successfully. Leave the fish balls in the liquid, cover loosely with plastic cling film and MICROWAVE ON HIGH FOR 5 MINUTES, giving the dish a half-turn after 2½ minutes.

Preparing Sole grillé and Russian fish balls

VEAL AND TOMATO CASSEROLE

METRIC/IMPERIAL	AMERICAN
1 kg/2 lb boned shoulder or breast of veal	2 lb boned shoulder or breast of veal
25 g/1 oz flour	¼ cup all-purpose flour
4 tablespoons vegetable oil	¼ cup vegetable oil
2 onions, chopped	2 onions, chopped
1 clove garlic, crushed	1 clove garlic, minced
1 teaspoon salt	1 teaspoon salt
1 teaspoon black pepper	1 teaspoon black pepper
450 ml/¾ pint boiling water	2 cups boiling water
1 chicken stock cube, crumbled	1 chicken bouillon cube, crumbled
1 bouquet garni	1 bouquet garni
1 × 400 g/14 oz can tomatoes	1 × 14 oz can tomatoes

Slice the veal thinly or cut into small cubes. Blend the flour and oil together in a large deep dish and MICROWAVE ON HIGH FOR 5 MINUTES, stirring once during cooking.

Add the veal, salt and pepper. MICROWAVE ON HIGH FOR 5 MINUTES. Add the water, stock (bouillon) cube, bouquet garni, tomatoes and their liquor. Cover and MICROWAVE ON HIGH FOR 20 MINUTES, or MICROWAVE ON MEDIUM FOR 35 MINUTES, stirring occasionally. Remove the bouquet garni.

Leave to stand for 5 minutes before serving.

SERVES 6

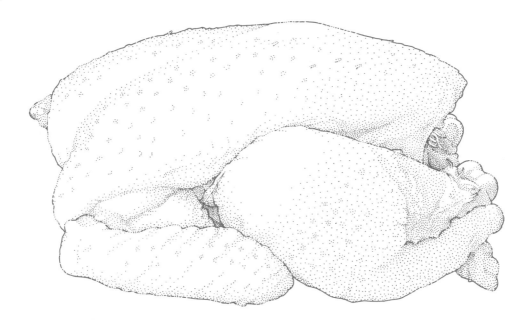

ISADORA'S CHICKEN

METRIC/IMPERIAL	AMERICAN
4 frozen chicken quarters	4 frozen chicken quarters
salt	salt
freshly ground black pepper	freshly ground black pepper
1 × 500 g/1 lb can lentil soup	1 × 1 lb can lentil soup

Arrange the frozen chicken quarters on a double sheet of absorbent kitchen paper and MICROWAVE ON LOW FOR 10 MINUTES until thawed, turning the pieces over after 5 minutes.

Rinse the chicken under cold running water. Drain, then season lightly on both sides with salt and pepper. Place, skin side down, in a large deep casserole. Pour the soup over the chicken, cover with a lid and MICROWAVE ON LOW FOR 30 MINUTES, turning the chicken over and giving the dish a half-turn occasionally.

Leave to stand, covered, for 10 minutes. Test each chicken quarter with the tip of a sharp knife and if the juices do not run clear, MICROWAVE ON HIGH FOR A FURTHER 3 TO 4 MINUTES. The chicken may be served without further standing time.

SERVES 4

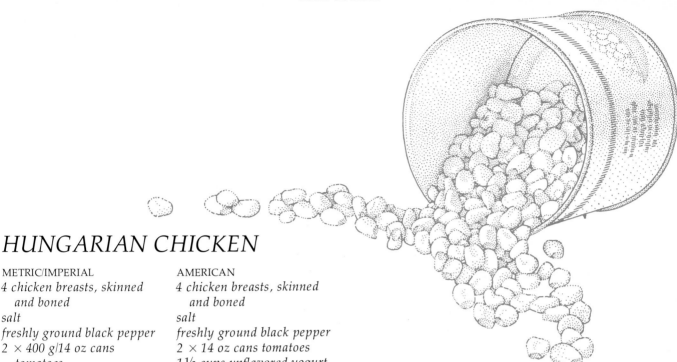

HUNGARIAN CHICKEN

METRIC/IMPERIAL
4 chicken breasts, skinned
    and boned
salt
freshly ground black pepper
2 × 400 g/14 oz cans
    tomatoes
250 ml /1/2 pint natural
    yogurt
3 tablespoons paprika
1 green pepper, cored,
    seeded and thinly sliced
1 red pepper, cored, seeded
    and thinly sliced
1 onion, thinly sliced into
    rings

AMERICAN
4 chicken breasts, skinned
    and boned
salt
freshly ground black pepper
2 × 14 oz cans tomatoes
1 1/3 cups unflavored yogurt
3 tablespoons paprika
1 green pepper, cored,
    seeded and thinly sliced
1 red pepper, cored, seeded
    and thinly sliced
1 onion, thinly sliced into
    rings

Season the chicken breasts with salt and pepper. Drain
the tomatoes and set aside. Blend the tomato liquid with
the yogurt and paprika.

Place the chicken in a large deep dish, cover with
tomatoes, peppers and onion rings and pour the tomato
liquid over the top. Cover and MICROWAVE ON HIGH FOR 30
MINUTES, turning the dish occasionally. Serve hot.

SERVES 4

CHICKEN AND CORN IN
CREAMY SAUCE

METRIC/IMPERIAL
50 g/2 oz butter
1 small onion, chopped
50 g/2 oz flour
600 ml/1 pint hot chicken
    stock
few drops of Tabasco
1/2 teaspoon salt
1/4 teaspoon black pepper
1 × 175 g/6 oz can sweet
    corn, drained
500 g/1 lb cooked chicken,
    diced
2 tablespoons double cream
3 hard-boiled eggs, finely
    chopped
2 teaspoons paprika

AMERICAN
1/4 cup butter
1 small onion, chopped
1/2 cup flour
2 1/2 cups hot chicken stock
few drops of Tabasco
1/2 teaspoon salt
1/4 teaspoon black pepper
1 × 6 oz can kernel corn,
    drained
1 lb cooked chicken, diced
2 tablespoons heavy cream
3 hard-cooked eggs, finely
    chopped
2 teaspoons paprika

FOR 10 TO 12 MINUTES, stirring occasionally. Stir in the
cream and adjust the seasoning.

Combine the chopped egg and paprika, and sprinkle
over the top. MICROWAVE ON LOW FOR 3 MINUTES, giving
the dish a half-turn after 1 1/2 minutes.

Serve immediately, with rice or baked potatoes and
green vegetables of choice.

SERVES 4 TO 6

Combine the butter and onion in a large deep dish and
MICROWAVE ON HIGH FOR 4 MINUTES, stirring occasionally.
Stir in the flour, then gradually mix in the stock, Tabasco,
salt and pepper, corn and chicken. MICROWAVE ON MEDIUM

CHICKEN PIMENTO PIE

METRIC/IMPERIAL
1 × 1.5 kg/3 lb oven-ready
  chicken, cut into 8 pieces
20 g/¾ oz butter
3 tablespoons flour
300 ml/½ pint milk
salt
freshly ground black pepper
1 × 200 g/7 oz can red
  pimentos, drained and
  shredded
1 egg, beaten
225 g/8 oz packet puff
  pastry (see note)

AMERICAN
1 × 3 lb oven-ready chicken,
  cut into 8 pieces
1½ tablespoons butter
3 tablespoons all-purpose
  flour
1¼ cups milk
salt
freshly ground black pepper
1 × 7 oz can red pimentos,
  drained and shredded
1 egg, beaten
½ lb package puff pastry
  (see note)

Put the chicken into a deep pie dish, cover and MIC-ROWAVE ON HIGH FOR 12 TO 15 MINUTES, stirring occasionally. Skin and bone the chicken and replace in the dish.

Put the butter in a large bowl and MICROWAVE ON HIGH FOR 30 SECONDS until melted. Stir in the flour and MICROWAVE ON HIGH FOR 30 SECONDS. Whisk in the milk gradually and MICROWAVE ON HIGH FOR 4 MINUTES, stirring occasionally. Add salt and pepper to taste.

Add the pimentos to the chicken and spoon the sauce over the top. Brush the edges of the pie dish with beaten egg. Roll out the pastry to make a pie lid, 2.5 cm/1 inch larger than the dish. Place over the dish, folding the edges under to form a double thickness. Brush the pastry with the beaten egg. Using a sharp knife, make 3 slits on top of the pie and vertical cuts 1 cm/½ inch apart around the edges. Decorate with the pastry trimmings.

MICROWAVE ON HIGH FOR 6 MINUTES until the pastry is puffed-up and holding its shape. Immediately place under a preheated hot grill (broiler) to brown the top. Serve hot.

SERVES 4

Note: To thaw frozen puff pastry, MICROWAVE ON LOW FOR 1 MINUTE, then leave to stand for 5 minutes.

Chicken pimento pie; Chicken casserole

CHICKEN CASSEROLE

METRIC/IMPERIAL	AMERICAN
1 ×1.5 kg/3½ lb oven-ready chicken, cut into 8 pieces	1 × 3½ lb oven-ready chicken, cut into 8 pieces
25 g/1 oz flour	¼ cup all-purpose flour
6 bacon rashers, derinded and chopped	6 bacon slices, derinded and chopped
2 onions, finely chopped	2 onions, finely chopped
1 × 300 g/11 oz can condensed mushroom soup	1 × 11 oz can condensed mushroom soup
450 ml/¾ pint chicken stock or water	2 cups chicken stock or water
½ teaspoon salt	½ teaspoon salt
¼ teaspoon black pepper	¼ teaspoon black pepper
1 teaspoon paprika	1 teaspoon paprika

Dust the chicken pieces with the flour. Place the bacon in a large deep dish and MICROWAVE ON HIGH FOR 5 MINUTES. Add the onions and MICROWAVE ON HIGH FOR 3 MINUTES until they soften.

Stir in the soup, stock, salt and pepper. And the chicken pieces, arranging them so that the thicker pieces are round the outside. Cover and MICROWAVE ON HIGH FOR 15 TO 18 MINUTES, stirring 2 or 3 times during cooking.

Leave to stand covered for 10 minutes. Test with the tip of a sharp knife and, if the chicken is not quite cooked, MICROWAVE ON HIGH FOR A FURTHER 3 TO 4 MINUTES before serving, sprinkled with paprika.

SERVES 4

QUICK ROAST CHICKEN

METRIC/IMPERIAL	AMERICAN
1 × 1.5 kg/3½ lb oven-ready chicken	1 × 3½ lb oven-ready chicken

Place the chicken, breast-side down, in a large deep dish. Cover with a piece of greaseproof paper or non-stick parchment. MICROWAVE ON HIGH FOR 10 MINUTES. Pour off surplus dripping. Turn the chicken over and cover the legs and wing tips with small pieces of foil, making sure they do not touch the oven walls.

MICROWAVE ON HIGH FOR 11 TO 14 MINUTES until a meat thermometer registers 82°C/180°F, or until the flesh near the bone is opaque. Give the dish a quarter-turn occasionally during cooking.

Transfer the chicken to a heated carving dish and leave to stand for 10 minutes before serving. If a crisp brown skin is preferred, place under a grill (broiler) to brown before serving.

SERVES 6

Note: See chart on page 152 for instructions on defrosting poultry.

SAVOURY ONION STUFFING

METRIC/IMPERIAL	AMERICAN
2 Spanish onions, finely chopped	2 Spanish onions, finely chopped
25 g/1 oz butter	2 tablespoons butter
150 ml/¼ pint chicken stock	⅔ cup chicken stock
50 g/2 oz fresh breadcrumbs	1 cup fresh soft breadcrumbs
2 teaspoons dried sage, thyme or parsley	2 teaspoons dried sage, thyme or parsley
¼ teaspoon salt	¼ teaspoon salt
¼ teaspoon black pepper	¼ teaspoon black pepper

Combine the onions and butter in a bowl and MICROWAVE ON HIGH FOR 3 MINUTES. Add the stock, cover and MICROWAVE ON HIGH FOR 5 MINUTES. Stir in the breadcrumbs, herbs, salt and pepper. MICROWAVE ON HIGH FOR 1 MINUTE.

Use to stuff chicken or any other type of poultry.

MAKES ENOUGH STUFFING FOR A 1.5 KG/ 3½ LB CHICKEN

Quick roast chicken with savoury stuffing; Braised onions (page 96); Glazed carrots (page 97); Steamed Brussel sprouts (page 94); Gravy

FAST COOK ROASTS

METRIC/IMPERIAL	AMERICAN
1 × 1.5 kg/3 lb even-shaped joint of beef, lamb, pork or veal	*1 × 3 lb even-shaped piece of beef, lamb, pork or veal for roasting*

Put the joint, fat side down, in a large deep dish. Cover with a piece of greaseproof paper or non-stick parchment and MICROWAVE ON HIGH FOR 12 MINUTES. Pour off the surplus dripping. Turn the joint over and MICROWAVE ON HIGH FOR 12 TO 15 MINUTES until a meat thermometer, inserted in the centre, registers 70°C/160°F.

To serve rare, transfer to a heated carving dish, cover and stand for 5 minutes. Leave to stand for 20 minutes if a well-cooked joint is preferred.

The joint may be browned during the standing time, under a preheated grill (broiler) or in a hot oven.

SERVES 6

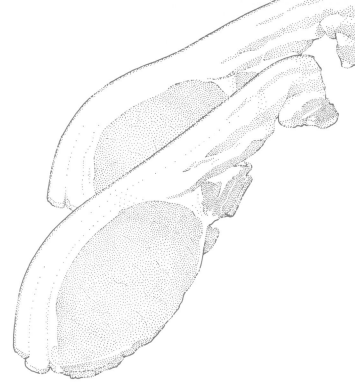

GRAVY

METRIC/IMPERIAL	AMERICAN
juices from the roasting dish	*juices from the roasting dish*
1–2 tablespoons flour	*1–2 tablespoons all-purpose flour*
300 ml/½ pint hot beef stock	*1¼ cups hot beef stock*
1 beef stock cube, crumbled	*1 beef bouillon cube, crumbled*
salt	*salt*
freshly ground black pepper	*freshly ground black pepper*

Pour away the surplus dripping from the roasting dish and stir in enough flour to absorb the remaining fat. MICROWAVE ON HIGH FOR 3 MINUTES, until the flour browns. Gradually stir in the stock and stock (bouillon) cube. MICROWAVE ON HIGH FOR 2 TO 3 MINUTES until the gravy boils. Add salt and pepper to taste.

MAKES 300 ml/½ pint/1¼ cups GRAVY

SWEET AND SOUR PORK

METRIC/IMPERIAL	AMERICAN
1 onion, sliced	*1 onion, sliced*
15 g/½ oz butter	*1 tablespoon butter*
750 g/1½ lb lean boned pork	*1½ lb lean boneless pork*
1 × 225 g/8 oz can pineapple cubes	*1 × 8 oz can pineapple cubes*
2 tablespoons malt vinegar	*2 tablespoons malt vinegar*
4 tablespoons soy sauce	*4 tablespoons soy sauce*
25 g/1 oz cornflour	*¼ cup cornstarch*
1 teaspoon salt	*1 teaspoon salt*
½ teaspoon black pepper	*½ teaspoon black pepper*
½ red pepper, cored, seeded and shredded	*½ red pepper, cored, seeded and shredded*

Place the onion and butter in a large dish and MICROWAVE ON HIGH FOR 3 MINUTES. Cut the pork into 2.5 cm/1 inch cubes and add to the dish, spooning the onion over the meat. MICROWAVE ON HIGH FOR 7 MINUTES.

Drain the liquor from the pineapple into a measuring jug. Add the vinegar and soy sauce, then make up to 600 ml/1 pint/2½ cups with water.

Mix the cornflour (cornstarch) with the salt and pepper, then blend with a little of the pineapple liquid. Stir in the remaining liquid, then pour over the meat and stir well. Cover and MICROWAVE ON HIGH FOR 5 MINUTES or until the sauce boils.

Stir in the pineapple cubes, re-cover and MICROWAVE ON LOW FOR 25 TO 30 MINUTES until the meat is tender, stirring occasionally during cooking.

Garnish with the shredded red pepper and serve with boiled noodles or rice.

SERVES 4 TO 6

Note: To cook this dish more quickly MICROWAVE ON HIGH FOR 15 TO 18 MINUTES after adding the pineapple.

KIDNEY CASSEROLE

METRIC/IMPERIAL	AMERICAN
750 g/1 ½ lb ox kidney	1 ½ lb beef kidney
3 lean rashers bacon, derinded and chopped	3 lean bacon slices, derinded and chopped
1 onion, chopped	1 onion, chopped
20 g/¾ oz butter	1 ½ tablespoons butter
2 tablespoons flour	2 tablespoons flour
150 ml/¼ pint beef stock	⅔ cup beef stock
150 ml/¼ pint red wine	⅔ cup red wine
2 tablespoons tomato purée	·2 tablespoons tomato paste
1 teaspoon salt	1 teaspoon salt
½ teaspoon black pepper	½ teaspoon black pepper
1 × 225 g/8 oz can butter beans, drained	1 × 8 oz can butter beans, drained
Garnish:	**Garnish:**
2 tablespoons chopped parsley	2 tablespoons chopped parsley
triangles of French toast (see page 21)	triangles of French toast (see page 21)

Wash the kidney in cold salted water. Drain well and pat with absorbent kitchen paper. Skin, core and cut the kidney into small pieces.

Combine the bacon, onion and butter in a large deep dish and MICROWAVE ON HIGH FOR 5 MINUTES, stirring occasionally. Stir in the flour, then add the stock, wine, tomato purée (paste), salt and pepper. Cover with a lid and MICROWAVE ON MEDIUM FOR 10 MINUTES, stirring occasionally.

Add the beans, adjust the seasoning, then replace the lid. MICROWAVE ON LOW FOR 15 TO 20 MINUTES until the kidney is tender, stirring occasionally during cooking. Leave to stand for 5 minutes.

Arrange triangles of French toast around the edge of the dish, and sprinkle the casserole with chopped parsley to garnish.

SERVES 4 TO 6

Note: Peas, mushrooms or carrots can be used instead of butter beans if preferred.

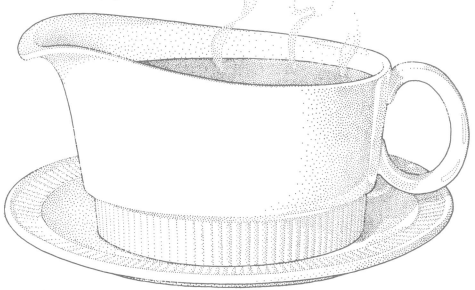

THIRTY FIVE MINUTE IRISH STEW

METRIC/IMPERIAL	AMERICAN
750 g/1 ½ lb stewing lamb	1 ½ lb stewing lamb
2 large onions	2 large onions
2 large potatoes, scrubbed and pricked	2 large potatoes, scrubbed and pricked
300 ml/½ pint hot chicken stock	1 ¼ cups hot chicken stock
½ teaspoon salt	½ teaspoon salt
¼ teaspoon black pepper	¼ teaspoon black pepper
few parsley sprigs	few parsley sprigs

Trim away surplus fat and cut the lamb into cubes. Put the onions into a large deep casserole, cover and MICROWAVE ON HIGH FOR 3 MINUTES. Leave in the dish and separate the onion layers, with a knife and fork. Spread the lamb over the onions. Cover and MICROWAVE ON HIGH FOR 10 MINUTES, stirring occasionally. Set aside while preparing the potatoes.

Put the potatoes on the oven shelf and MICROWAVE ON HIGH FOR 5 MINUTES. Slice and arrange on top of the meat. Season the stock with salt and pepper and pour over the potatoes. Add the parsley. Cover tightly and MICROWAVE ON HIGH FOR 15 MINUTES, giving the dish a half-turn once during cooking. Serve hot.

SERVES 4

BAKED LAMB AND VEGETABLES

METRIC/IMPERIAL	AMERICAN
6–8 lamb chops	6–8 lamb chops
8 small tomatoes, pierced	8 small tomatoes, pierced
1 large potato, peeled and diced	1 large potato, peeled and diced
2 large onions, sliced	2 large onions, sliced
salt	salt
freshly ground black pepper	freshly ground black pepper

Trim away the surplus fat and arrange the chops in a single layer round the edge of a large deep dish. Pile the tomatoes in the centre. Spread the potato and onions over the chops and sprinkle with salt and pepper.

Cover loosely with plastic cling film and MICROWAVE ON LOW FOR 45 MINUTES until the meat is tender, giving the dish a half-turn, half-way through cooking. Serve hot.

SERVES 4 TO 6

Note: For ovens without a fitted low or defrost button, MICROWAVE ON HIGH FOR 10 MINUTES, leave to stand for 5 MINUTES, then MICROWAVE ON HIGH FOR 5 TO 7 MINUTES until the meat and vegetables are cooked.

SUCCULENT LAMB STEW

METRIC/IMPERIAL	AMERICAN
750 g/1 ½ lb stewing lamb	1 ½ lb stewing lamb
1 tablespoon gravy powder	1 tablespoon gravy powder
2 sticks celery, thinly sliced	2 stalks celery, thinly sliced
225 g/8 oz carrots, thinly sliced	½ lb carrots, thinly sliced
2 large onions, thinly sliced	2 large onions, thinly sliced
2 large potatoes, thinly sliced	2 large potatoes, thinly sliced
300 ml/½ pint hot chicken stock	1 ¼ cups hot chicken stock
½ teaspoon salt	½ teaspoon salt
¼ teaspoon black pepper	¼ teaspoon black pepper
1 tablespoon chopped parsley	1 tablespoon chopped parsley
1 teaspoon chopped thyme	1 teaspoon chopped thyme

Trim away the fat and cut the lamb into cubes. Put in a large deep casserole and sprinkle with the gravy powder. Stir and MICROWAVE ON HIGH FOR 5 MINUTES.

Add all the remaining ingredients to the meat, cover with a lid and MICROWAVE ON LOW FOR 50 MINUTES, stirring occasionally, until the meat and vegetables are tender.

SERVES 6

Right: Succulent lamb stew; Baked lamb and vegetables

Below: Casserole of beef in rich brown gravy

CASSEROLE OF BEEF IN RICH BROWN GRAVY

METRIC/IMPERIAL	AMERICAN
500 g /1 lb chuck steak	1 ¼ lb chuck steak
4 tablespoons vegetable oil	4 tablespoons vegetable oil
25 g/1 oz flour	¼ cup all-purpose flour
350 ml/12 fl oz hot beef stock	1 ½ cups hot beef stock
1 × 400 g/14 oz can tomatoes	1 × 14 oz can tomatoes
225 g/8 oz carrots, thinly sliced	½ lb carrots, thinly sliced
225 g/8 oz onions, thinly sliced	½ lb onions, thinly sliced
1 clove garlic, crushed	1 clove garlic, minced
1 bay leaf	1 bay leaf
1 teaspoon salt	1 teaspoon salt
½ teaspoon black pepper	½ teaspoon black pepper

Trim the beef and cut into 2 cm/¾ inch cubes. Blend the oil and flour in a large deep dish and MICROWAVE ON HIGH FOR 5 MINUTES until beige in colour. Add the meat all at once, stir and MICROWAVE ON HIGH FOR 5 MINUTES, stirring after 2 minutes.

Add all the remaining ingredients. Cover and MICROWAVE ON HIGH FOR 35 MINUTES, stirring occasionally during cooking, to scrape away any gravy sticking to the sides of the dish.

Leave to stand covered for 15 minutes before serving.

SERVES 4

STUFFED BEEF ROLL

METRIC/IMPERIAL	AMERICAN
500 g/1 lb lean minced beef	1 lb lean ground beef
2 teaspoons Worcestershire sauce	2 teaspoons Worcestershire sauce
1 teaspoon salt	1 teaspoon salt
½ teaspoon black pepper	½ teaspoon black pepper
1 egg, beaten	1 egg, beaten
1–2 tablespoons flour	1–2 tablespoons all-purpose flour
4 tablespoons sage and onion stuffing mix	4 tablespoons sage and onion stuffing mix
8 tablespoons water (approximately)	⅓ cup water (approximately)
1 teaspoon gravy powder	1 teaspoon gravy powder

Mix the beef, Worcestershire sauce, salt, pepper and egg together. Roll out on a floured working surface to a rectangle about 15 × 20 cm/6 × 8 inches.

Make up the stuffing according to the directions on the packet, and bind the mixture with the water. Form into a sausage shape, the same width as the meat, and place along one edge. Roll up, enclosing the stuffing, and press the edges of the meat together to seal.

Transfer the meat roll to a shallow dish into which it fits snugly. Sprinkle with the gravy powder and MICROWAVE ON HIGH FOR 10 MINUTES, turning the meat over half-way though cooking.

SERVES 3 TO 4

STEAK AND KIDNEY PUDDING

METRIC/IMPERIAL	AMERICAN
Filling:	**Filling:**
225 g/8 oz ox kidney	½ lb beef kidney
500 g/1 lb chuck steak	1 lb chuck steak
25 g/1 oz butter	2 tablespoons butter
25 g/1 oz flour	¼ cup all-purpose flour
200 ml/⅓ pint hot water	1 cup hot water
2 onions, grated	2 onions, grated
1 beef stock cube, crumbled	1 beef bouillon cube, crumbled
1 teaspoon salt	1 teaspoon salt
¼ teaspoon black pepper	¼ teaspoon black pepper
Pastry:	**Pastry:**
225 g/8 oz plain flour	2 cups all-purpose flour
2 teaspoons baking powder	2 teaspoons baking powder
1 teaspoon salt	1 teaspoon salt
100 g/4 oz shredded suet	¾ cup shredded suet
8–10 tablespoons cold water	8–10 tablespoons cold water

Rinse the kidney under cold running water, remove the core and chop the kidney finely. Cut the meat into small even-sized cubes. Place the butter in a large deep dish and MICROWAVE ON HIGH FOR 30 SECONDS. Blend in the flour and MICROWAVE ON HIGH FOR 1 MINUTE.

Stir in the water, then add the remaining filling ingredients, cover and MICROWAVE ON HIGH FOR 20 MINUTES, stirring occasionally during cooking. MICROWAVE ON LOW FOR 15 MINUTES, stirring occasionally.

Meanwhile prepare the pastry. Sift the flour, baking powder and salt into a mixing bowl, then stir in the suet. Mix to a soft dough with the water. Roll out three-quarters of the pastry and use to line a 1 litre/1¾ pint/2 quart pudding basin. Fill with the steak and kidney mixture.

Roll out the remaining pastry to form a lid. Dampen the rim of the pie and place the pastry lid over the top, pressing the pastry edges together to seal. Make 2 or 3 slits in the pastry with a sharp knife. Cover very loosely with plastic cling film and MICROWAVE ON LOW FOR 15 MINUTES, giving the basin a half-turn 3 or 4 times during cooking. Leave to stand for 10 minutes before serving.

SERVES 4 TO 6

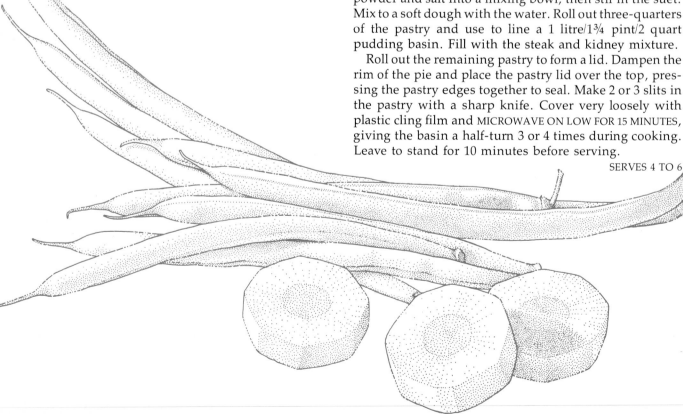

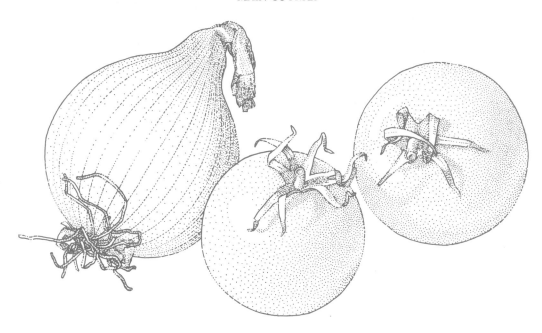

SHEPHERDS' PIE

METRIC/IMPERIAL	AMERICAN
1 large onion, finely chopped	1 large onion, finely chopped
1 tablespoon tomato purée	1 tablespoon tomato paste
1 beef stock cube, crumbled	1 beef bouillon cube, crumbled
300 ml/½ pint beef stock	1¼ cups beef stock
350 g/12 oz cooked minced beef	1½ cups cooked ground beef
1 tablespoon flour	1 tablespoon all-purpose flour
salt	salt
freshly ground black pepper	freshly ground black pepper
500 g/1 lb potatoes, peeled and cubed	1 lb potatoes, peeled and cubed
4 tablespoons water	¼ cup water
15 g/½ oz butter	1 tablespoon butter
6 tomatoes, pricked	6 tomatoes, pricked

Place the onion, tomato purée (paste), stock (bouillon) cube and stock in a large shallow dish. Cover and MICROWAVE ON HIGH FOR 10 MINUTES, stirring occasionally. Toss the meat in the flour, then stir into the onion mixture. Cover and MICROWAVE ON HIGH FOR 10 MINUTES, stirring occasionally. Add salt and pepper to taste. Leave to stand while cooking the potatoes.

Put the potatoes in a large shallow dish, add the water and cover loosely with plastic cling film. MICROWAVE ON HIGH FOR 10 TO 12 MINUTES until soft, shaking the dish vigorously 2 or 3 times during cooking. Drain and mash the potatoes with the butter, adding salt and pepper to taste.

Arrange the tomatoes on top of the meat mixture. Cover with the mashed potato. MICROWAVE ON HIGH FOR 5 MINUTES, giving the dish a quarter-turn every minute. Place under a preheated grill (broiler) to brown, before serving.

SERVES 4 TO 6

BURGER AND DRY VEGETABLE CURRY

METRIC/IMPERIAL	AMERICAN
4 × 50 g/2 oz frozen beefburgers	4 × 2 oz frozen beef patties
225 g/8 oz carrots, thinly sliced	¾ cup thinly sliced carrots
100 g/4 oz French beans, trimmed	¼ lb green beans, trimmed
2 onions, thinly sliced	2 onions, thinly sliced
6–8 cauliflower florets	6–8 cauliflower florets
1 teaspoon salt	1 teaspoon salt
3 tablespoons tomato purée	3 tablespoons tomato paste
2 tablespoons curry paste	2 tablespoons curry paste

Arrange the frozen beefburgers on a folded sheet of absorbent kitchen paper and MICROWAVE ON HIGH FOR 4 MINUTES. Cut into cubes and combine with all the remaining ingredients in a large deep dish.

Cover tightly and MICROWAVE ON HIGH FOR 10 TO 12 MINUTES, stirring occasionally, adding a little water during cooking if the curry seems too dry. Serve hot.

SERVES 4

Note: Fresh or frozen vegetables are equally suitable for this dish.

BEEF À LA MEXICAINE

METRIC/IMPERIAL	AMERICAN
2 tablespoons vegetable oil	2 tablespoons vegetable oil
1 onion, chopped	1 onion, chopped
1 teaspoon chilli powder	1 teaspoon chili powder
1 teaspoon salt	1 teaspoon salt
350 g/12 oz lean minced beef	¾ lb lean ground beef
1 × 225 g/8 oz can tomatoes	1 × ½ lb can tomatoes
1 × 65 g/2½ oz can tomato purée	¼ cup tomato paste
1 tablespoon lemon juice	1 tablespoon lemon juice
6–8 taco shells	6–8 taco shells
50 g/2 oz Cheddar cheese, grated	½ cup grated Cheddar cheese
1 red pepper, cored, seeded and sliced into rings	1 red pepper, cored, seeded and sliced into rings

PREHEAT A LARGE BROWNING SKILLET FOR 5 MINUTES (or according to the manufacturer's instructions). Mix the oil and onion together in a small basin then quickly stir into the skillet. MICROWAVE ON HIGH FOR 2 MINUTES.

Mix in the chilli powder and salt and MICROWAVE ON HIGH FOR 2 MINUTES. Stir in the meat, breaking it up with a fork. MICROWAVE ON HIGH FOR 5 MINUTES, stirring once during cooking. Drain off any surplus fat.

Add the tomatoes, tomato purée (paste) and lemon juice to the meat. Cover with the lid and MICROWAVE ON HIGH FOR 5 MINUTES. Leave to stand for 5 minutes.

Arrange the taco shells open side up on a serving dish and fill with the beef mixture. Sprinkle the grated cheese over the meat and top with the pepper rings, before serving.

SERVES 3 TO 4

BEEF AND BACON CRUMBLE

METRIC/IMPERIAL	AMERICAN
4 lean bacon rashers, derinded and finely chopped	4 lean bacon slices, derinded and finely chopped
500 g/1 lb lean minced beef	1 lb lean ground beef
1 beef stock cube	1 beef bouillon cube
150 ml/¼ pint hot water	⅔ cup hot water
1 teaspoon turmeric	1 teaspoon turmeric
1 teaspoon cornflour	1 teaspoon cornstarch
150 ml/¼ pint cold water	⅔ cup cold water
Topping:	**Topping:**
175 g/6 oz self-raising flour	1½ cups self-rising flour
pinch of salt	pinch of salt
1 teaspoon baking powder	1 teaspoon baking powder
75 g/3 oz butter	⅓ cup butter

Put the bacon into a large shallow dish. MICROWAVE ON HIGH FOR 5 MINUTES, stirring occasionally. Add the beef and MICROWAVE ON HIGH FOR 5 MINUTES, breaking up the meat with a fork half-way through cooking.

Crumble the stock (bouillon) cube into the hot water and stir in the turmeric. Pour over the meat and stir well. Blend the cornflour (cornstarch) with the cold water and stir into the meat mixture. Cover and MICROWAVE ON HIGH FOR 2 MINUTES.

To prepare the topping, sift the flour, salt and baking powder into a mixing bowl. Rub in the butter until the mixture resembles coarse breadcrumbs.

Uncover the meat, stir, then spread the crumble evenly on top. MICROWAVE ON HIGH FOR 8 MINUTES. Place under a preheated grill (broiler) to brown the top, before serving.

SERVES 4 TO 6

Beef à la mexicaine

Beef moussaka

BEEF MOUSSAKA

METRIC/IMPERIAL
500 g/1 lb potatoes, cut into
  even-sized pieces
2 aubergines, sliced and
  par-boiled (optional)
2 onions, chopped
2 tablespoons vegetable oil
½ teaspoon garlic powder
500 g/1 lb lean minced beef
1 × 150 g/5 oz can tomato
  purée
1 teaspoon salt
½ teaspoon black pepper
1 teaspoon dried oregano
1 tablespoon chopped fresh
  parsley
2 eggs
5 tablespoons soured cream
5 tablespoons milk
4 tablespoons grated
  Parmesan cheese
50 g/2 oz Cheddar cheese,
  grated

AMERICAN
1 lb potatoes, cut into
  even-sized pieces
2 eggplants, sliced and
  par-boiled (optional)
2 onions, chopped
2 tablespoons vegetable oil
½ teaspoon garlic powder
1 lb lean ground beef
1 × 5 oz can tomato paste
1 teaspoon salt
½ teaspoon black pepper
1 teaspoon dried oregano
1 tablespoon chopped fresh
  parsley
2 eggs
⅓ cup sour cream
⅓ cup milk
⅓ cup grated Parmesan
  cheese
½ cup grated Cheddar
  cheese

Put the potatoes into a large roaster bag and lay flat on the oven shelf, tucking the open end loosely underneath. MICROWAVE ON HIGH FOR 10 MINUTES. Leave to stand for 5 minutes.

Combine the onions, oil and garlic powder in a large round dish and MICROWAVE ON HIGH FOR 3 MINUTES until the onions are soft. Add the beef, stir and MICROWAVE ON HIGH FOR 5 MINUTES, breaking up the meat with a fork half-way through cooking. Stir in the tomato purée (paste), salt, pepper and herbs and MICROWAVE ON HIGH FOR 2 MINUTES.

Place the aubergine (eggplant) slices on top, if using. Slice the potatoes thinly and arrange overlapping on top. Beat the eggs, soured cream, milk and Parmesan cheese together and pour over the potatoes. MICROWAVE ON HIGH FOR 4 MINUTES, giving the dish a half-turn once during cooking.

Sprinkle the top with grated Cheddar cheese and place under a preheated grill (broiler) to brown, before serving.

SERVES 6

Note: If preferred, the aubergines (eggplants) and meat may be layered in the casserole dish.

CORN ON THE COB

METRIC/IMPERIAL	AMERICAN
50 g/2 oz butter	*¼ cup butter*
4 fresh or frozen corn on the cob	*4 fresh or frozen corn on the cob*
salt	*salt*
freshly ground black pepper	*freshly ground black pepper*

Place the butter in a large deep dish and MICROWAVE ON HIGH FOR 30 SECONDS until softened. Add the corn and turn to coat with the butter. Cover tightly and MICROWAVE ON HIGH FOR 12 TO 16 MINUTES, rearranging the corn half-way through cooking. Season with salt and pepper to taste and serve hot.

SERVES 4

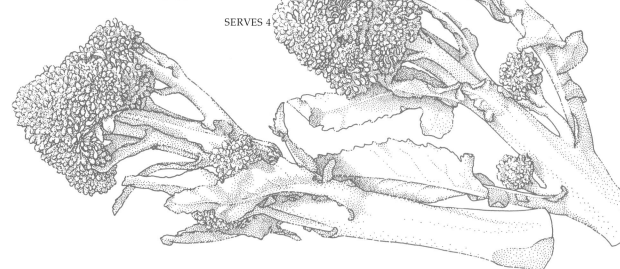

BROCCOLI SPEARS

METRIC/IMPERIAL	AMERICAN
350 g/12 oz broccoli spears	*¾ lb broccoli spears*
½ teaspoon salt	*½ teaspoon salt*
4 tablespoons water	*¼ cup water*
freshly ground black pepper	*freshly ground black pepper*

Arrange the broccoli spears with the stalks towards the outside edges, in a large shallow dish. Add the salt to the water and pour over the broccoli. Cover loosely with plastic cling film and MICROWAVE ON HIGH FOR 7 MINUTES.

Leave to stand, covered, for 5 minutes. Correct the seasoning, adding pepper to taste, before serving.

SERVES 4

JADE SPINACH

METRIC/IMPERIAL	AMERICAN
750 g/1 ½ lb fresh leaf spinach	*1 ½ lb fresh leaf spinach*
salt	*salt*
freshly ground black pepper	*freshly ground black pepper*
15 g/½ oz butter	*1 tablespoon butter*

Wash the spinach and shake off surplus water. Discard the thick stems. Put the leaves into a roasting bag, folding the open end underneath. Lay flat on a double sheet of absorbent kitchen paper and MICROWAVE ON HIGH FOR 5 MINUTES. Transfer to a heated serving dish, sprinkle with salt and pepper to taste, and dot with butter.

SERVES 4

FRENCH BEANS

METRIC/IMPERIAL	AMERICAN
500 g/1 lb French beans	1 lb green beans
6 tablespoons water	6 tablespoons water
½ teaspoon salt	½ teaspoon salt
freshly ground black pepper	freshly ground black pepper

Slice the beans lengthways, as finely as possible. Combine the water and salt in a large shallow dish and add the beans. Make a well in the centre of the beans, then cover the dish loosely with plastic cling film. MICROWAVE ON HIGH FOR 5 MINUTES, giving the dish a half-turn once or twice during cooking.

Leave to stand, covered, for 5 minutes, then carefully pull back one corner of the plastic cling film and pour off the liquid. Correct the seasoning, adding pepper to taste, before serving.

SERVES 4

SPICED RED CABBAGE

METRIC/IMPERIAL	AMERICAN
500 g/1 lb red cabbage, trimmed, cored and shredded	1 lb red cabbage, trimmed, cored and shredded
1 small onion, finely chopped	1 small onion, finely chopped
1 dessert apple, cored and chopped	1 dessert apple, cored and chopped
25 g/1 oz butter	2 tablespoons butter
2 tablespoons wine vinegar	2 tablespoons wine vinegar
2 tablespoons brown sugar	2 tablespoons brown sugar
1 teaspoon salt	1 teaspoon salt
½ teaspoon ground allspice	½ teaspoon ground allspice
½ teaspoon ground nutmeg	½ teaspoon ground nutmeg
1 teaspoon caraway seeds (optional)	1 teaspoon caraway seeds (optional)
freshly ground black pepper	freshly ground black pepper
150 ml/¼ pint boiling water	⅔ cup boiling water

Combine all the ingredients in a deep dish and mix thoroughly. Cover the dish with plastic cling film and MICROWAVE ON HIGH FOR 9 TO 11 MINUTES, until the cabbage is tender, stirring occasionally during cooking.

Leave to stand, covered, for 3 minutes, then drain off excess liquid. Check the seasoning and serve hot.

SERVES 4

LEMON GLAZED LEEKS WITH CHEESE

METRIC/IMPERIAL	AMERICAN
500 g/1 lb leeks, trimmed	1 lb leeks, trimmed
25 g/1 oz butter	2 tablespoons butter
½ teaspoon salt	½ teaspoon salt
1 tablespoon lemon juice	1 tablespoon lemon juice
1 tablespoon grated Parmesan cheese	1 tablespoon grated Parmesan cheese
freshly ground black pepper	freshly ground black pepper

Cut the leeks into 2.5 cm/1 inch slices and place in a shallow dish. Dot with the butter and sprinkle with the salt. Cover the dish with plastic cling film and MICROWAVE ON HIGH FOR 8 MINUTES, stirring once halfway through cooking.

Add the lemon juice, stir well, cover and MICROWAVE ON HIGH FOR 3 MINUTES, or until the leeks are tender. Sprinkle with the cheese and pepper to taste. Leave to stand, covered, for 3 minutes before serving.

SERVES 4

BUTTERED GINGER MARROW

METRIC/IMPERIAL	AMERICAN
1 × 750 g/1 ½ lb marrow, peeled	1 × 1 ½ lb squash, peeled
25 g/1 oz butter	2 tablespoons butter
1 teaspoon salt	1 teaspoon salt
½ teaspoon black pepper	½ teaspoon black pepper
½ teaspoon ground ginger	½ teaspoon ground ginger

Cut the marrow in half lengthways and scoop out the seeds. Cut into even-sized chunks. Put the butter in a large shallow dish and MICROWAVE ON HIGH FOR 1 MINUTE. Stir in the salt, pepper and ginger.

Add the marrow and toss to coat with the melted butter. Cover loosely with plastic cling film and MICROWAVE ON HIGH FOR 8 TO 10 MINUTES, giving the dish a thorough shake twice during cooking. Leave to stand for 3 or 4 minutes before serving.

SERVES 4

STEAMED BRUSSEL SPROUTS

METRIC/IMPERIAL	AMERICAN
750 g/1 ½ lb even-sized Brussel sprouts, trimmed	1 ½ lb even-sized Brussel sprouts, trimmed
6 tablespoons water	6 tablespoons water
salt	salt

Place the sprouts in a large deep casserole. Add the salt to the water and pour over the sprouts. Cover the dish loosely with plastic cling film. MICROWAVE ON HIGH FOR 8 TO 9 MINUTES, giving the dish a vigorous shake twice during cooking.

Leave to stand for 5 minutes. Carefully remove the plastic cling film, then test for tenderness, drain and serve hot.

SERVES 4 TO 6

Buttered ginger marrow; Steamed Brussel sprouts; Baked celery; Courgette (zucchini) casserole

BAKED CELERY

METRIC/IMPERIAL	AMERICAN
1 head of celery	1 bunch celery
250 ml/8 fl oz boiling water	1 cup boiling water
25 g/1 oz butter	2 tablespoons butter
1 chicken stock cube, crumbled	1 chicken bouillon cube, crumbled
freshly ground black pepper	freshly ground black pepper
salt	salt
chopped parsley to garnish	chopped parsley to garnish

Break the celery into stalks and cut each stalk in half. Place in a large deep dish with the water, butter, stock (bouillon) cube and pepper. Cover with a lid and MICROWAVE ON HIGH FOR 6 MINUTES.

Add salt to taste, then stir and MICROWAVE ON HIGH FOR 6 TO 10 MINUTES until tender. Drain, sprinkle with parsley and serve hot.

SERVES 4

COURGETTE (ZUCCHINI) AND TOMATO CASSEROLE

METRIC/IMPERIAL	AMERICAN
500 g/1 lb courgettes, sliced	1 lb zucchini, sliced
225 g/8 oz tomatoes, quartered	½ lb tomatoes, quartered
1 teaspoon dried basil	1 teaspoon dried basil
½ beef stock cube, crumbled	½ beef bouillon cube, crumbled
¼ teaspoon salt	¼ teaspoon salt
¼ teaspoon pepper	¼ teaspoon pepper

Combine all the ingredients in a large deep dish. Cover with a lid and MICROWAVE ON HIGH FOR 10 MINUTES, stirring occasionally until the courgettes (zucchini) are tender.

SERVES 4

DUMPLINGS

METRIC/IMPERIAL	AMERICAN
100 g/4 oz plain flour	*1 cup all-purpose flour*
1½ teaspoons baking powder	*1½ teaspoons baking powder*
½ teaspoon salt	*½ teaspoon salt*
50 g/2 oz soft margarine	*¼ cup soft margarine*
4–5 tablespoons milk	*4–5 tablespoons milk*
600 ml/1 pint boiling water	*2½ cups boiling water*
1 chicken stock cube	*1 chicken bouillon cube*

Sift the flour, baking powder and salt into a mixing bowl. Add the margarine and mix with a fork until thoroughly blended. Stir in just enough of the milk to form a very soft dough.

Pour the water into a large shallow dish and crumble in the stock (bouillon) cube. MICROWAVE ON HIGH FOR 2 MINUTES until the stock is boiling rapidly. Drop heaped teaspoonfuls of the dumpling dough into the boiling stock, spacing them well apart. MICROWAVE ON HIGH FOR 2 MINUTES. Give the dish a half-turn, cover and MICROWAVE ON HIGH FOR 2 MINUTES.

Lift out the dumplings with a slotted spoon, and drain well. Serve with Irish Stew (page 85) or other meat or vegetable casseroles.

SERVES 4

Note: Strain the stock and use as required for other dishes. A double quantity of dough may be cooked in batches, in the stock. The stock should be reheated to boiling point before cooking the second batch.

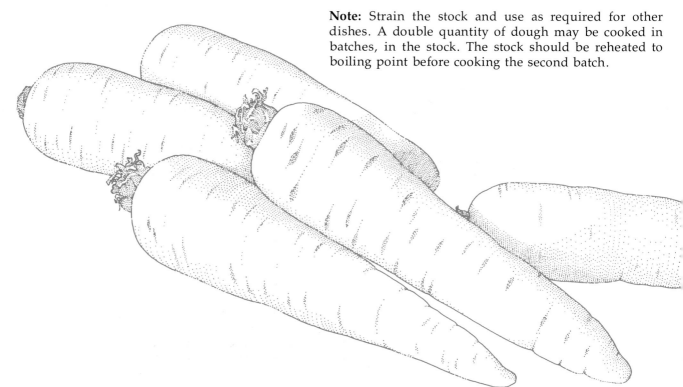

BRAISED ONIONS

METRIC/IMPERIAL	AMERICAN
500 g/1 lb small even-sized onions	*1 lb small even-sized onions*
15 g/½ oz butter	*1 tablespoon butter*
1 teaspoon yeast extract	*1 teaspoon yeast extract*
salt	*salt*
freshly ground black pepper	*freshly ground black pepper*

Score the onions round the middle with a sharp knife. Put the butter and yeast extract in a large shallow dish and MICROWAVE ON HIGH FOR 1 MINUTE. Add the onions and toss to coat with the savoury butter, then arrange round the sides of the dish.

Cover the dish loosely with plastic cling film and MICROWAVE ON HIGH FOR 7 TO 9 MINUTES until just tender, giving the dish a half-turn after 4 minutes. Leave to stand for 3 minutes, then carefully remove the plastic cling film.

Season the onions with salt and pepper to taste, just before serving.

SERVES 4

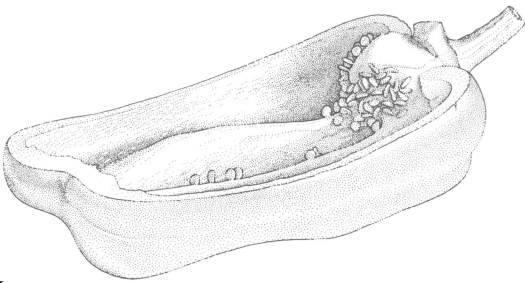

PEPERONI

METRIC/IMPERIAL	AMERICAN
15 g/½ oz butter	1 tablespoon butter
1 onion, chopped	1 onion, chopped
¼ teaspoon garlic salt	¼ teaspoon garlic salt
2 large green peppers, cored seeded and sliced	2 large green peppers, cored, seeded and sliced
2 red peppers, cored, seeded and sliced	2 red peppers, cored, seeded and sliced
freshly ground black pepper	freshly ground black pepper

Combine the butter, onion and garlic salt in a large deep dish and MICROWAVE ON HIGH FOR 3 MINUTES. Add the pepper slices and season with black pepper to taste. Stir thoroughly, then cover loosely with plastic cling film.

MICROWAVE ON HIGH FOR 8 TO 10 MINUTES until the peppers are just tender, giving the dish a vigorous shake once or twice during cooking. Carefully remove the plastic cling film and serve hot or cold.

SERVES 4

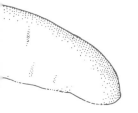

GLAZED CARROTS

METRIC/IMPERIAL	AMERICAN
½ teaspoon salt	½ teaspoon salt
4 tablespoons water	¼ cup water
750 g/1½ lb carrots, sliced	4½ cups sliced carrots
25 g/1 oz butter	2 tablespoons butter
1 tablespoon brown sugar	1 tablespoon brown sugar

Dissolve the salt in the water in a large shallow dish. Add the carrots, butter and sugar. Cover loosely with plastic cling film and MICROWAVE ON HIGH FOR 12 TO 15 MINUTES, giving the dish a vigorous shake twice during cooking. Leave covered for 5 minutes, then test for tenderness. Drain and serve hot.

SERVES 4 TO 6

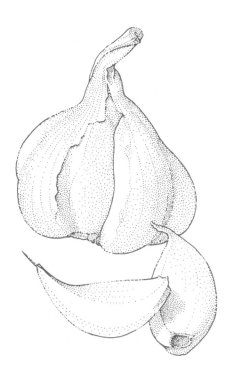

DICED POTATO MAYONNAISE

METRIC/IMPERIAL	AMERICAN
500 g/1 lb new potatoes, scraped and diced	1 lb young potatoes, scraped and diced
1 small onion, finely chopped	1 small onion, finely chopped
4 tablespoons water	¼ cup water
½ teaspoon salt	½ teaspoon salt
4 tablespoons mayonnaise	¼ cup mayonnaise
1 tablespoon double cream	1 tablespoon heavy cream
6 green olives, stoned and finely chopped	6 green olives, pitted and finely chopped
1 tablespoon chopped parsley	1 tablespoon chopped parsley

Combine the potatoes, onion, water and salt in a large shallow dish. Cover loosely with plastic cling film and MICROWAVE ON HIGH FOR 8 MINUTES, giving the dish a vigorous shake two or three times during cooking. Leave to stand for 3 minutes, then carefully remove the plastic cling film and drain the potatoes in a colander.

Mix the mayonnaise, cream and olives together in the dish. Replace the cooked potatoes and toss gently to coat with the sauce. Garnish with the chopped parsley and serve hot or cold.

SERVES 3 TO 4

BAKED POTATOES

METRIC/IMPERIAL	AMERICAN
4 large even-sized potatoes	4 large even-sized potatoes
15 g/½ oz butter	1 tablespoon butter
salt	salt
freshly ground black pepper	freshly ground black pepper

Scrub, dry and prick the potatoes thoroughly. Arrange well-spaced out on a double sheet of absorbent kitchen paper on the oven shelf. MICROWAVE ON HIGH FOR 6 MINUTES. Turn the potatoes over and MICROWAVE ON HIGH FOR 6 TO 10 MINUTES until tender but not soft.

Leave to stand for 5 minutes, then the potatoes should be completely cooked. Split in half lengthways and top each half with butter, salt and pepper. Serve immediately.

SERVES 4

Diced potato mayonnaise; Baked potatoes

NOODLES

METRIC/IMPERIAL
225 g/8 oz noodles
750–900 ml/1 1/4–1 1/2 pints
  boiling water
1 teaspoon salt
1 teaspoon vegetable oil

AMERICAN
1/2 lb noodles
3–3 3/4 cups boiling water
1 teaspoon salt
1 teaspoon vegetable oil

Place the noodles in a large deep dish. Add the water and salt, stir in the oil and without covering, MICROWAVE ON HIGH FOR 6 TO 7 MINUTES. Cover tightly and leave to stand for 8 to 10 minutes until the noodles are just tender. Drain and serve at once.

SERVES 4 TO 6

Note: Other varieties of pasta can also be cooked in this way.

BOILED RICE

METRIC/IMPERIAL
225 g/8 oz long-grain rice
1 1/2–2 teaspoons salt
750–900 ml/1 1/4–1 1/2 pints
  boiling water

AMERICAN
1 cup long-grain rice
1 1/2–2 teaspoons salt
3–3 3/4 cups boiling water

Rinse the rice in a sieve under cold running water, drain and place in a large deep dish. Add the salt and boiling water. Without covering, MICROWAVE ON HIGH FOR 15 MINUTES, stirring once during cooking.
  Test for tenderness, then drain the rice in a sieve and serve at once.

SERVES 4

Note: For better results, after cooking, pour cold water through the rice until the grains separate. Make holes in the rice with the handle of a wooden spoon and leave to drain. To reheat, MICROWAVE ON HIGH FOR 1 TO 4 MINUTES in the quantities required.

BROWN RICE

METRIC/IMPERIAL
225 g/8 oz brown rice
pinch of salt
600 ml/1 pint boiling water

AMERICAN
1 cup brown rice
pinch of salt
2 1/2 cups boiling water

Combine the rice, salt and water in a large bowl. MICROWAVE ON HIGH FOR 20 MINUTES, stirring occasionally. Cover and leave to stand for 5 minutes, then drain away any residual water.

SERVES 4

BAKED BANANAS WITH MARMALADE SAUCE

METRIC/IMPERIAL	AMERICAN
1 teaspoon lemon juice	1 teaspoon lemon juice
4 tablespoons cold water	¼ cup cold water
½ teaspoon cornflour	½ teaspoon cornstarch
6 tablespoons orange marmalade	6 tablespoons orange preserve
25 g/1 oz unsalted butter	2 tablespoons sweet butter
4 firm bananas, peeled	4 firm bananas, peeled

Combine the lemon juice, water and cornflour (cornstarch) in a large shallow dish and MICROWAVE ON HIGH FOR 1 MINUTE. Stir in the orange marmalade (preserve) and MICROWAVE ON HIGH FOR 2 TO 3 MINUTES until the mixture boils. Stir in the butter.

Place the bananas in the dish and spoon the sauce over them. MICROWAVE ON HIGH FOR 1 TO 2 MINUTES, moving the outside bananas to the centre after 45 seconds.

SERVES 4

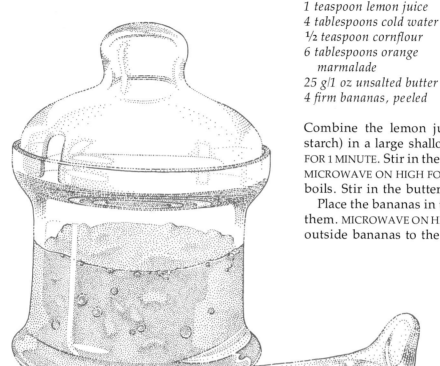

APRICOT SPONGE PUDDING

METRIC/IMPERIAL	AMERICAN
1 × 575 g/1 lb 4 oz can apricot halves	1 × 1¼ lb can apricot halves
1 teaspoon cornflour	1 teaspoon cornstarch
1 tablespoon cold water	1 tablespoon cold water
2 eggs, beaten	2 eggs, beaten
4 tablespoons sugar	¼ cup sugar
½ teaspoon vanilla essence	½ teaspoon vanilla extract
50 g/2 oz plain flour, sifted	½ cup all-purpose flour, sifted
2 tablespoons vegetable oil	2 tablespoons vegetable oil

Drain the apricots, reserving the juice, and place in the centre of a large shallow dish. Pour the apricot juice into a large jug and MICROWAVE ON HIGH FOR 5 MINUTES. Blend the cornflour (cornstarch) with the water, then stir in the apricot syrup and MICROWAVE ON HIGH FOR 2 MINUTES. Set aside.

Beat the eggs, sugar and vanilla essence (extract) together until thick and creamy. Fold in the flour, a little at a time, then gradually fold in the oil.

Place spoonsful of the mixture around the apricots to form a border. MICROWAVE ON LOW FOR 3 MINUTES, then MICROWAVE ON HIGH FOR 5 MINUTES or until the sponge is just dry on top. Place under a preheated medium grill (broiler) to brown the top.

Serve hot, accompanied by the sauce which can be reheated on HIGH FOR 1 MINUTE if necessary.

SERVES 4

DATE AND HAZELNUT PUDDING

METRIC/IMPERIAL	AMERICAN
4 eggs, separated	4 eggs, separated
50 g/2 oz brown sugar	⅓ cup brown sugar
50 g/2 oz fresh soft breadcrumbs	½ cup fresh soft breadcrumbs
50 g/2 oz hazelnuts, grated	½ cup grated hazelnuts
100 g/4 oz block cooking dates	¼ lb block cooking dates

Thoroughly grease a 2.25 litre/4 pint/2½ quart ring mould. In a mixing bowl, beat the egg yolks until frothy, add the sugar and continue beating until the mixture is very thick. Mix in the breadcrumbs and hazelnuts.

Put the block of dates in the oven and MICROWAVE ON HIGH FOR 20 TO 30 SECONDS until soft. Mash the dates and stir into the pudding mixture. Beat the egg whites until stiff, then fold into the mixture until completely incorporated.

Turn into the greased mould and MICROWAVE ON HIGH FOR 4 MINUTES, giving the dish a quarter-turn every minute, until just dry on top. Turn out on to a heated plate and serve at once.

SERVES 6 TO 8

Note: This pudding tends to sink slightly in the centre on turning out.

PINEAPPLE UPSIDE DOWN PUDDING

METRIC/IMPERIAL	AMERICAN
175 g/6 oz butter	¾ cup butter
75 g/3 oz dark brown sugar	½ cup dark brown sugar
1 × 567 g/1 lb 4 oz can pineapple rings	1¼ lb can pineapple rings
6–8 glacé cherries halved	6–8 candied cherries, halved
100 g/4 oz sugar	½ cup sugar
150 g/5 oz plain flour	1¼ cups all-purpose flour
2 teaspoons baking powder	2 teaspoons baking powder
pinch of salt	pinch of salt
2 eggs, beaten	2 eggs, beaten

Place one-third of the butter in a 20 cm/8 inch deep round dish and MICROWAVE ON HIGH FOR 1 MINUTE until melted. Add the brown sugar, mix well and spread over the base of the dish.

Drain the pineapple, reserving 4 tablespoons of the syrup. Arrange whole pineapple rings on the base and press halved rings around the sides of the dish, setting aside 2 rings for the pudding mixture. Place the halved cherries, shiny sides down, in the centres of the rings.

Cream the remaining butter with the sugar in a mixing bowl until light and fluffy. Sift the flour, salt and baking powder over the top. Add the eggs and heat for 2 to 3 minutes, adding just enough of the reserved pineapple syrup to form a soft dropping consistency. Chop the reserved pineapple and fold into the mixture.

Spread the mixture evenly over the fruit. MICROWAVE ON HIGH FOR 8 TO 10 MINUTES until the pudding is just dry on top, giving the dish a quarter-turn every 2 minutes. Invert the pudding on to a serving plate and leave for 3 minutes before removing the baking dish. Serve hot or cold.

SERVES 6 TO 8

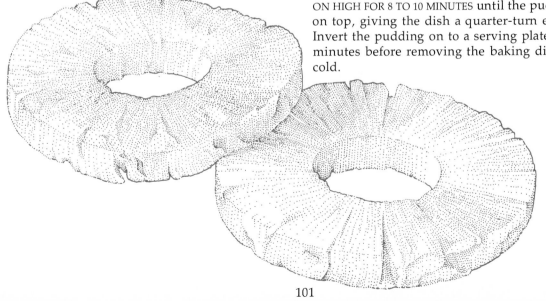

APPLE AND BLACKBERRY CRUMBLE

METRIC/IMPERIAL	AMERICAN
500 g/1 lb fresh or frozen blackberries	1 lb fresh or frozen blackberries
500 g/1 lb apples, peeled, cored and sliced	1 lb apples, peeled, cored and sliced
75 g/3 oz demerara sugar	6 tablespoons light brown sugar
Topping:	**Topping:**
175 g/6 oz plain flour	1½ cups all-purpose flour
½ teaspoon mixed spice	½ teaspoon mixed spice
40 g/1½ oz butter	3 tablespoons butter
40 g/1½ oz lard	3 tablespoons shortening
25 g/1 oz sugar	2 tablespoons sugar
50 g/2 oz fresh breadcrumbs	1 cup fresh breadcrumbs

Place the blackberries in a large deep dish and if frozen, MICROWAVE ON HIGH FOR 5 MINUTES. Add the sliced apples and two-thirds of the sugar; mix thoroughly.

To prepare the topping, sift the flour and spice into a bowl. Rub in the butter and lard (shortening) until mixture resembles coarse breadcrumbs. Stir in the sugar and breadcrumbs. Spread evenly over the fruit and flatten gently with a spatula. Sprinkle the remaining demerara (brown) sugar on top.

MICROWAVE ON HIGH FOR 7 MINUTES until a skewer inserted into the topping comes out clean. Leave to stand for 10 minutes before serving. If a crisp brown topping is preferred, place under a preheated grill (broiler) until lightly browned.

SERVES 6

Above: Apple curd pudding; Apple and blackberry crumble

Right: Peach crunch pie; Steamed treacle pudding

APPLE CURD PUDDING

METRIC/IMPERIAL	AMERICAN
3 large cooking apples, peeled, cored and quartered	3 large cooking apples, peeled, cored and quartered
lemon juice for sprinkling	lemon juice for sprinkling
1½ tablespoons cornflour	1½ tablespoons cornstarch
few drops of vanilla essence	few drops of vanilla extract
6 tablespoons soft brown sugar	6 tablespoons soft brown sugar
4 tablespoons undiluted orange squash	¼ cup undiluted orange concentrate
40 g/1½ oz butter	3 tablespoons butter
8 digestive biscuits, finely crushed	8 Graham crackers, finely crushed

Slice the apple thinly and sprinkle with lemon juice. Combine the cornflour (cornstarch), vanilla essence (extract), sugar and orange squash (concentrate) in a large shallow dish. Add the apples and mix thoroughly. MICROWAVE ON HIGH FOR 5 MINUTES, stirring once during cooking.

Put the butter in a bowl and MICROWAVE ON HIGH FOR 1 MINUTE until melted. Stir in the biscuit crumbs. Spread over the apples and MICROWAVE ON HIGH FOR 4 TO 5 MINUTES, giving the dish a half-turn half-way through cooking. Serve hot.

SERVES 4

STEAMED TREACLE PUDDING

METRIC/IMPERIAL
75 g/3 oz plain flour
75 g/3 oz fresh white
  breadcrumbs, sieved
50 g/2 oz sugar
50 g/2 oz shredded suet
1 egg
1 tablespoon golden syrup
1 tablespoon black treacle
3–4 tablespoons milk
¼ teaspoon bicarbonate of
  soda
3–4 tablespoons golden
  syrup, warmed

AMERICAN
¾ cup all-purpose flour
1½ cups fresh soft
  breadcrumbs, sieved
¼ cup sugar
½ cup shredded suet
1 egg
2 tablespoons light molasses
3–4 tablespoons milk
¼ teaspoon baking soda
3–4 tablespoons maple
  syrup, warmed

Combine the flour, breadcrumbs, sugar and suet in a mixing bowl and make a well in the centre. In another bowl beat the egg, syrup, treacle (light molasses), 3 tablespoons milk and the bicarbonate of soda together. Pour into the dry ingredients and mix thoroughly, adding more milk if necessary, to obtain a consistency which drops easily from a spoon.

Turn the mixture into a well-greased 1 litre/1¾ pint/ 1 quart glass pudding basin. Cover loosely with a large piece of plastic cling film, pleated across the middle. MIC-ROWAVE ON HIGH FOR 3½ TO 4 MINUTES until the pudding is just dry on top, giving a quarter-turn every minute.

Turn out on to a warm serving dish and pour the syrup over the top. Serve with custard, if desired.

SERVES 4 OR 5

PEACH CRUNCH PIE

METRIC/IMPERIAL
50 g/2 oz butter
175 g/6 oz sweet digestive
  biscuits (including some
  chocolate digestives),
  crushed
1 × 400 g/14 oz can sliced or
  halved peaches
25 g/1 oz icing sugar, sifted
2 teaspoons arrowroot
yellow food colouring

AMERICAN
¼ cup butter
1¼ cups fine cookie crumbs
  (including some
  chocolate-coated cookies),
  crushed
1 × 14 oz can sliced or
  halved peaches
¼ cup confectioners' sugar,
  sifted
2 teaspoons arrowroot flour
yellow food colouring

Put the butter in a 18 cm/7 inch round pie dish and MIC-ROWAVE ON HIGH FOR 1 TO 1½ MINUTES until melted. Add the biscuit crumbs, mix thoroughly, then press into the base and sides of the dish to form a flan case. MICROWAVE ON HIGH FOR 2 MINUTES, giving the dish a half-turn after 1 minute.

Drain the juice from the peaches and reserve 150 ml/¼ pint /⅔ cup. Arrange the peaches in the flan case. Combine the icing (confectioners') sugar, arrowroot and a few drops of yellow colouring in a jug. Gradually blend in the reserved peach juice. MICROWAVE ON HIGH FOR 2 MINUTES until the glaze thickens, stirring occasionally.

Pour the glaze over the fruit and leave to cool. Serve cold, with fresh cream, if liked.

SERVES 4

Note: To loosen the crust when cold, dip the base of the dish in hot water.

CREAMY RICE PUDDING

METRIC/IMPERIAL	AMERICAN
50 g/2 oz round-grained pudding rice	¼ cup Carolina rice
¼ teaspoon grated nutmeg	¼ teaspoon grated nutmeg
450 ml/¾ pint boiling water	2 cups boiling water
25 g/1 oz sugar	2 tablespoons sugar
1 × 175 g/6 fl oz can evaporated milk	¾ cup canned evaporated milk
knob of butter	1 teaspoon butter

Combine the rice, nutmeg and water in a large deep dish and MICROWAVE ON HIGH FOR 10 MINUTES, stirring occasionally. Add the sugar and the evaporated milk and MICROWAVE ON LOW FOR 20 TO 25 MINUTES, stirring occasionally, until the rice is just tender.

Stir in the butter. Cover and leave to stand for 5 minutes before serving.

SERVES 2 OR 3

Note: As rice pudding cools, it tends to thicken. Add a little fresh milk or cream to thin and reheat, if desired.

To serve 4 to 6, double the quantities. Combine the rice, nutmeg and water in a dish and MICROWAVE ON HIGH FOR 25 MINUTES, adding a little more water if necessary. Continue according to the recipe.

MANDARIN PUDDING

METRIC/IMPERIAL	AMERICAN
50 g/2 oz butter	¼ cup butter
3 slices bread, crusts removed	3 slices bread, crusts removed
50 g/2 oz brown sugar	⅓ cup brown sugar
1 × 225 g/8 oz can mandarin oranges, drained	1 × 8 oz can mandarin oranges, drained
25 g/1 oz sultanas	3 tablespoons golden raisins
2 eggs, beaten	2 eggs, beaten
300 ml/½ pint milk	1¼ cups milk

Put the butter in a deep round flameproof dish and MICROWAVE ON HIGH FOR 1 TO 1½ MINUTES, until melted. Cut the bread into triangles and place in the dish, turning the pieces over so that they are completely coated with butter, then arrange them neatly.

Sprinkle with all but 2 tablespoons of the brown sugar. Arrange the mandarin oranges and sultanas (golden raisins) on top.

Beat the eggs and milk together and pour over the fruit. MICROWAVE ON MEDIUM FOR 10 TO 12 MINUTES, until the custard has set at the edges but is still slightly damp in the centre; give the dish a quarter-turn every 4 minutes, during cooking.

Leave to stand for 5 minutes, then sprinkle with the remaining sugar and place under a preheated grill (broiler) to brown the top. Serve hot.

SERVES 4 TO 6

APPLE AND COCONUT CHARLOTTE

METRIC/IMPERIAL	AMERICAN
100 g/4 oz butter	½ cup butter
225 g/8 oz fresh soft bread crumbs	4 cups fresh breadcrumbs
50 g/2 oz desiccated coconut	⅔ cup desiccated coconut
150 g/5 oz brown sugar	¾ cup brown sugar
500 g/1 lb cooking apples	1 lb tart baking apples
grated rind and juice of 1 lemon	grated rind and juice of 1 lemon

Put the butter in a deep pie dish and MICROWAVE ON HIGH FOR 2 MINUTES until melted. Stir in the breadcrumbs and MICROWAVE ON HIGH FOR 3 MINUTES, then stir in the coconut and MICROWAVE ON HIGH FOR 1 MINUTE. Remove half of this mixture and set aside. Press the remainder into the base of the dish and sprinkle half of the sugar on top.

Peel, core and thinly slice the apples. Arrange them on top of the mixture. Sprinkle with the lemon rind, juice and the remaining sugar. Top with the rest of the coconut and crumbs. MICROWAVE ON HIGH FOR 4 TO 5 MINUTES until the apple is soft. Place under a preheated grill (broiler) to brown the top, if desired.

SERVES 4

JULY FRUIT MERINGUE PUDDING

METRIC/IMPERIAL	AMERICAN
1 banana, sliced	1 banana, sliced
1 sharp dessert apple, cored and sliced	1 sharp dessert apple, cored and sliced
1 large peach, stoned and sliced	1 large peach, pitted and sliced
1 tablespoon lemon juice	1 tablespoon lemon juice
3 egg whites	3 egg whites
175 g/6 oz caster sugar	¾ cup sugar

Combine the fruit in a large shallow dish and sprinkle with the lemon juice. Beat the egg whites until stiff. Add half of the sugar and continue beating until stiff peaks form.

Spread the meringue over the fruit with a spatula, making sure it reaches the edges of the dish. MICROWAVE ON MEDIUM FOR 8 MINUTES until the meringue is firm, giving the dish a half-turn after 4 minutes. Place under a pre-heated hot grill (broiler) for 30 seconds to brown the top. Serve hot or cold.

SERVES 6

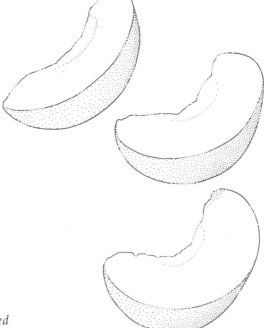

LEMON MERINGUE PIE

METRIC/IMPERIAL	AMERICAN
Filling:	**Filling:**
225 g/8 oz sugar	1 cup sugar
4 tablespoons cornflour	4 tablespoons cornstarch
pinch of salt	pinch of salt
250 ml/8 fl oz cold water	1 cup cold water
3 egg yolks	3 egg yolks
120 ml/4 fl oz lemon juice	½ cup lemon juice
2 teaspoons grated lemon rind	2 teaspoons grated lemon rind
40 g/1½ oz butter	3 tablespoons butter
Crumb Base:	**Crumb Base:**
50 g/2 oz butter	¼ cup butter
6 digestive biscuits, crushed	6 Graham crackers, crushed
25 g/1 oz sugar	2 tablespoons sugar
Meringue Topping:	**Meringue Topping:**
3 egg whites	3 egg whites
pinch of cream of tartar	pinch of cream of tartar
100 g/4 oz sugar	½ cup sugar
½ teaspoon vanilla essence	½ teaspoon vanilla extract

To prepare the filling, mix the sugar, cornflour (cornstarch) and salt together. Put the water in a large bowl and MICROWAVE ON HIGH FOR 3 MINUTES until boiling. Toss in the sugar mixture and beat vigorously until a smooth sauce is obtained. MICROWAVE ON HIGH FOR 3 MINUTES, stirring frequently.

Beat the egg yolks and lemon juice together and blend with a few spoonsful of the sauce. Add to the sauce and mix thoroughly. MICROWAVE ON HIGH FOR 1 MINUTE, then stir in the lemon rind and butter. Leave to cool.

For the crumb base, put the butter in a 20 cm /8 inch round pie dish and MICROWAVE ON HIGH FOR 1 MINUTE until melted. Add the biscuits (crackers) and sugar, mix thoroughly and press firmly into the base of the dish. Spoon the filling over the top.

To make the meringue topping, whisk the egg whites and cream of tartar together until stiff. Add half the sugar and the vanilla essence (extract) and whisk until the mixture is stiff once more, then fold in the remaining sugar. Spread the meringue evenly over the filling, to the edge of the dish.

MICROWAVE ON HIGH FOR 4 MINUTES, giving the dish a quarter-turn every minute. Flash briefly under a pre-heated grill (broiler) until lightly browned. Serve hot or cold.

SERVES 6

Note: If the meringue topping cracks during cooking, coax it back into position with a palette knife before browning.

OLDE ENGLISH CHRISTMAS PUDDING

METRIC/IMPERIAL	AMERICAN
50 g/2 oz currants	⅓ cup currants
75 g/3 oz raisins	½ cup raisins
75 g/3 oz sultanas	½ cup golden raisins
5 glacé cherries, chopped	5 candied cherries, chopped
1 small cooking apple, peeled, cored and chopped	1 small cooking apple, peeled, cored and chopped
25 g/1 oz candied peel, chopped	3 tablespoons chopped candied peel
40 g/1 ½ oz shelled almonds, skinned and chopped	⅓ cup shelled almonds, skinned and chopped
grated rind of 1 lemon	grated rind of 1 lemon
grated rind and juice of 1 small orange	grated rind and juice of 1 small orange
50 g/2 oz flour	½ cup all-purpose flour
¼ teaspoon salt	¼ teaspoon salt
¼ teaspoon mixed spice	¼ teaspoon mixed spice
¼ teaspoon ground cinnamon	¼ teaspoon ground cinnamon
¼ teaspoon grated nutmeg	¼ teaspoon grated nutmeg
50 g/2 oz dark brown sugar	⅓ cup dark brown sugar
25 g/1 oz fresh breadcrumbs	½ cup fresh breadcrumbs
50 g/2 oz shredded suet	½ cup shredded suet
3 tablespoons stout	3 tablespoons strong beer
2 tablespoons brandy	2 tablespoons brandy
1 tablespoon black treacle	1 tablespoon dark molasses
2 eggs, beaten	2 eggs, beaten
milk (as necessary)	milk (as necessary)

In a large bowl, mix together all of the fruit, peel, nuts, grated rind and juice. Sift the flour, salt and spices together. Add to the fruit with the sugar, breadcrumbs and suet. Mix well, then stir in the remaining ingredients, adding just enough milk to form a mixture which will easily drop from a spoon. Cover and leave in a cool place overnight.

Turn into a greased 1 litre/1¾ pint/2 quart pudding basin. Cover loosely with plastic cling film. MICROWAVE ON HIGH FOR 8 MINUTES. Leave to stand for a few hours, then MICROWAVE ON HIGH FOR 2 OR 3 MINUTES to reheat. Alternatively MICROWAVE ON LOW FOR 16 TO 24 MINUTES, then leave to stand for 10 minutes.

Serve with custard, cream or brandy butter.

SERVES 4 TO 6

SHERRY TRIFLE

METRIC/IMPERIAL	AMERICAN
750 ml/1 ¼ pints custard (see page 109)	3 cups custard (see page 109)
Cake base:	**Cake Base:**
½ teaspoon baking powder	½ teaspoon baking powder
50 g/2 oz self-raising flour	½ cup self-rising flour
50 g/2 oz sugar	¼ cup sugar
50 g/2 oz soft margarine	¼ cup soft margarine
1 large egg	1 large egg
½ teaspoon vanilla essence	½ teaspoon vanilla extract
Filling:	**Filling:**
1 × 400 g/14 oz can raspberries	1 × 14 oz can raspberries
2 tablespoons sweet sherry	2 tablespoons sweet sherry
Decoration:	**Decoration:**
150 ml/¼ pint double cream, whipped	⅔ cup heavy cream, whipped
few glacé cherries	few glacé cherries
few angelica leaves	few angelica leaves

Sherry trifle; Olde English Christmas pudding

Prepare the custard and allow to cool slightly. Beat together all the ingredients for the cake base in a large bowl for 1 to 2 minutes. MICROWAVE ON HIGH FOR 1 MINUTE. Give the bowl a half-turn and MICROWAVE ON HIGH FOR 1 MINUTE, until the cake base is just dry on top.

Break the cake into pieces, using a spoon, and turn into a serving bowl. Put the raspberries, together with their juice, on top and sprinkle with the sherry. Pour the custard over the top and chill until firm.

Decorate with whipped cream, glacé (candied) cherries and angelica leaves before serving.

SERVES 4 TO 6

Apricot fool

APRICOT FOOL

METRIC/IMPERIAL	AMERICAN
350 g/12 oz dried apricots	¾ lb dried apricots
350 ml/12 fl oz water	1½ cups water
350 ml/¾ pint custard (see page 109)	2 cups custard (see page 109)
2 tablespoons double cream	2 tablespoons heavy cream
sugar	sugar
1 egg white	1 egg white

Rinse the apricots and combine with the water in a large deep dish. Cover loosely with plastic cling film and MICROWAVE ON HIGH FOR 12 MINUTES. Allow to cool, then purée in an electric blender or press through a sieve (strainer).

Beat the custard and cream into the apricot purée and add sugar to taste. Beat the egg white until stiff, then fold into the mixture. Serve chilled, decorated with whipped cream.

SERVES 6

ORANGE CREAMS

METRIC/IMPERIAL
4 large firm oranges
300–450 ml/½–¾ pint milk
25 g/1 oz cornflour
50 g/2 oz sugar
50 g/2 oz chocolate chips
25 g/1 oz sweet biscuits,
  crushed

AMERICAN
4 large firm oranges
1¾–2 cups milk
¼ cup cornstarch
¼ cup sugar
2 tablespoons chocolate
  chips
⅓ cup crushed sweet
  cookies

Cut the oranges in half and carefully scoop out the flesh, without breaking the skins. Press the flesh through a strainer to squeeze out the juice. Make the juice up to 600 ml/1 pint/2½ cups with milk. Scrape away the pith from the orange shells and set them aside.

In a large bowl, blend the cornflour (cornstarch) and sugar with a little of the milk. Add the remaining milk and stir well. MICROWAVE ON HIGH FOR 4 TO 5 MINUTES until the mixture is smooth and thick, beating every minute.

Leave to cool for 10 minutes, then stir in the chocolate chips. Spoon into the reserved orange shells and sprinkle with the biscuit (cookie) crumbs.

SERVES 4 TO 6

APFELROMTOPF

METRIC/IMPERIAL
4 even-sized large cooking
  apples
1 banana
2 teaspoons lemon juice
25 g/1 oz blanched almonds,
  finely grated
1 teaspoon chopped angelica
6 glacé cherries, chopped
¼ teaspoon ground
  cinnamon
100 g/4 oz soft brown sugar
4 tablespoons double cream
1 tablespoon rum

AMERICAN
4 even-sized large baking
  apples
1 banana
2 teaspoons lemon juice
¼ cup finely grated
  blanched almonds
1 teaspoon chopped candied
  angelica
6 candied cherries, chopped
¼ teaspoon ground
  cinnamon
⅔ cup soft brown sugar
4 tablespoons heavy cream
1 tablespoon rum

Remove the cores from the apples, using a sharp knife or apple corer. Trim a thin slice from the top of each one. Arrange the apples in a shallow round dish and MICROWAVE ON HIGH FOR 3 TO 4 MINUTES until the sides yield under gentle pressure. Set aside for 2 to 3 minutes.

Mash the banana with the lemon juice, then stir in the almonds, angelica, cherries, cinnamon and half of the sugar. Scoop out about three-quarters of the pulp from the centre of each apple, leaving a thick shell. Stir the apple pulp into the banana mixture, then pile back into the apple shells.

In the same dish, MICROWAVE ON HIGH FOR 3½ TO 4 MINUTES until the stuffed apples are tender, giving the dish a half-turn once during cooking. Transfer the apples to individual serving dishes. Stir the cream, rum and remaining sugar into the residual juice in the dish and MICROWAVE ON HIGH FOR 1½ TO 2 MINUTES until the sauce boils. Spoon this syrup over the apples and serve hot.

SERVES 4

STEWED PLUMS

METRIC/IMPERIAL	AMERICAN
750 g/1½ lb firm dessert plums	1½ lb firm dessert plums
75–100 g/3–4 oz demerara sugar	½–⅔ cup light brown sugar
¼ teaspoon almond essence	¼ teaspoon almond extract

Combine the plums and sugar in a large deep dish. Cover loosely with plastic cling film and MICROWAVE ON HIGH FOR 3 MINUTES. Add the almond essence (extract) and stir well. Cover and MICROWAVE ON HIGH FOR 3 TO 4 MINUTES until the plums are soft. Leave to stand for 3 minutes before serving.

SERVES 4

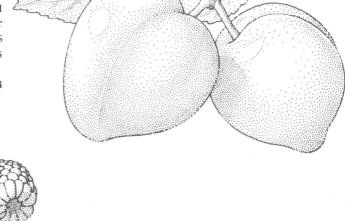

MARSHMALLOW AND ALMOND RASPBERRIES

METRIC/IMPERIAL	AMERICAN
175 g/6 oz plain cooking chocolate, broken up	6 squares semi-sweet cooking chocolate, broken up
100 g/4 oz packet marshmallows	18 marshmallows
3 tablespoons milk	3 tablespoons milk
6 tablespoons double cream	6 tablespoons heavy cream
350 g/12 oz fresh raspberries	¾ lb fresh raspberries
50 g/2 oz flaked almonds, toasted	½ cup slivered almonds, toasted

Line a 23 cm/9 inch shallow dish with plastic cling film. Add the broken chocolate and MICROWAVE ON HIGH FOR 3 TO 4 MINUTES until the chocolate has melted. Using a pastry brush, spread the chocolate evenly over the base and sides of the dish then chill in the refrigerator until set.

Combine the marshmallows and milk in a large bowl and MICROWAVE ON HIGH FOR 1½ TO 2 MINUTES until the marshmallows puff up. Stir until the mixture is smooth. Chill for 30 to 40 minutes, until just beginning to thicken.

Lightly whip the cream, then fold into the marshmallow mixture. Carefully transfer the chocolate case to a serving dish. Fill with the raspberries and pile the marshmallow cream on top. Sprinkle with the toasted almonds. Chill in the refrigerator for 5 hours, or until the topping has set, before serving.

SERVES 6

CUSTARD

METRIC/IMPERIAL	AMERICAN
1 large egg	1 large egg
40 g/1½ oz plain flour	¼ cup + 2 tablespoons all-purpose flour
25 g/1 oz soft brown sugar	3 tablespoons soft brown sugar
¼ teaspoon vanilla essence	¼ teaspoon vanilla extract
600 ml/1 pint milk	2½ cups milk

Beat the egg, flour, sugar and vanilla essence (extract) together. Put the milk in a large bowl and MICROWAVE ON HIGH FOR 4 MINUTES until steaming. Pour onto the egg mixture, whisking continuously.

Strain the custard back into the bowl and MICROWAVE ON LOW FOR 6 MINUTES until the sauce thickens, whisking 2 or 3 times during cooking.

MAKES 750 ml/1¼ pints/3 cups CUSTARD

ENTERTAINING

At one time, giving dinner parties inevitably involved days of preparation beforehand, but with the advent of modern labour-saving kitchen equipment this is no longer the case. The microwave oven is a tremendous asset for those who entertain. Most dishes can be prepared in advance and simply popped into the microwave oven at the last moment, with no adverse effect to the appearance or flavour of the finished dish. The comparative speed and efficiency of microwave cooking enables you to produce gourmet dishes with far less effort than the conventional cooker. So you can enjoy your dinner parties as much as the guests!

When planning a dinner party obtain all necessary dry ingredients and non-perishable goods well in advance. Perishable food cán either be purchased ahead and stored in the refrigerator for two or three days, or used from frozen. If cooked dishes are to be frozen complete, remember that aromatic ingredients, such as garlic, onion and herbs develop stronger flavour during freezing. Dishes should be garnished after defrosting and heating. It is better not to freeze dishes for longer than necessary, since long-term freezing affects both taste and texture.

When freezing cooked dishes make sure that the container you use is suitable for the microwave oven. Otherwise you will spoil the appearance of a dish such as *Mélange de fruits de mer honfleur (see page 120)*, if you have to transfer the food from one container to another. The best setting for defrosting in the microwave is LOW. The HIGH setting can be used, but you may find it necessary to break up lumps occasionally as the food softens.

Soups are ideal for advance preparation. Frozen soups should be allowed to defrost slowly in the refrigerator for 24 hours, so no valuable microwave time is lost on the night. Before reheating, the soup should be whisked to prevent it boiling over. Fish is best cooked on the day it will be eaten, but it can be reheated rapidly just before serving. Remember to shorten the initial cooking time if you intend to do this. Cold sweets can of course be prepared in advance. You may wish to round off the meal with cheese, or a savoury: perhaps Devils on horseback *(see page 112)* or Stuffed mushrooms *(see page 116)* which will only take moments to heat. Coffee can be reheated in the microwave oven more than once, providing it has been freshly strained – so your guests' second cup can be as hot as their first.

In this chapter you will find a variety of recipes, suitable for every kind of dinner party menu – from a relatively simple three course meal to a five course banquet. Every recipe is specially designed to make full use of the advantages the microwave oven offers.

SALTED ALMONDS

METRIC/IMPERIAL	AMERICAN
225 g/8 oz shelled almonds, skinned	1½ cups shelled almonds, skinned
50 g/2 oz butter	¼ cup butter
salt	salt

Put the almonds and butter in a large shallow dish and MICROWAVE ON HIGH FOR 5 MINUTES, stirring occasionally. Turn onto absorbent kitchen paper and sprinkle liberally with salt while still hot.

MAKES 225 g/½ lb SALTED ALMONDS

Note: These may be stored in a screwtop jar for up to 6 weeks.

Illustrated on pages 110–11: Salted almonds; Cheddar puffs; Sesame balls; Hot crab canapés; Devils on horseback

CHEDDAR PUFFS

METRIC/IMPERIAL	AMERICAN
25 g/1 oz softened butter	2 tablespoons softened butter
5 tablespoons water	⅓ cup water
pinch of salt	6 tablespoons all-purpose
40 g/1½ oz plain flour, sifted	flour, sifted
1 egg, beaten	pinch of salt
25 g/1 oz Cheddar cheese, grated	1 egg, beaten
	¼ cup grated Cheddar cheese

Place the butter, water and salt in a large measuring jug. MICROWAVE ON HIGH FOR 1½ TO 2 MINUTES until the water is boiling fast.

Remove from the oven, quickly toss in the flour and beat vigorously. Leave to cool for a few minutes, then add the egg gradually, beating thoroughly until the mixture is thick and shiny. Stir in the cheese.

Using two teaspoons, place small mounds of mixture on the oven shelf, lined with greaseproof (waxed) paper. MICROWAVE ON HIGH FOR 6 TO 8 MINUTES until crisp, giving the paper a half-turn after 3 minutes. Leave to cool then pile into a serving bowl.

MAKES 35 TO 45 PUFFS

DEVILS ON HORSEBACK

METRIC/IMPERIAL	AMERICAN
2 slices of bread, toasted and buttered	2 slices of bread, toasted and buttered
8 rashers streaky bacon	8 bacon slices
8 large prunes, soaked, drained and stoned	8 large prunes, soaked, drained and pitted
8 anchovies	8 anchovies
parsley sprigs to garnish	parsley sprigs to garnish

Cut the toast into 4 × 6 cm/2 × 3 inch fingers. Trim the bacon slices to fit the toast. Place between a folded sheet of absorbent kitchen paper. Stuff the prunes with the anchovies.

Cook the bacon and prunes simultaneously: MICROWAVE ON HIGH FOR 6 MINUTES until the bacon is crisp. Lay the bacon on the toast and arrange the prunes on top.

Place on individual plates and MICROWAVE ON HIGH FOR 2 MINUTES. Serve immediately, garnished with parsley.

SERVES 4

HOT CRAB CANAPÉS

METRIC/IMPERIAL	AMERICAN
1 small onion, finely chopped	1 small onion, finely chopped
15 g/½ oz butter	1 tablespoon butter
15 g/½ oz flour	2 tablespoons flour
2 tablespoons milk	2 tablespoons milk
4 tablespoons single cream	4 tablespoons light cream
175 g/6 oz cooked fresh, or canned crab meat, flaked	6 oz cooked fresh, or canned crab meat, flaked
½ teaspoon lemon juice	½ teaspoon lemon juice
salt	salt
freshly ground black pepper	freshly ground black pepper
24 small cracker biscuits	24 small cracker biscuits
Garnish:	**Garnish:**
paprika	paprika
mustard and cress	garden cress

Combine the onion and butter in a bowl and MICROWAVE ON HIGH FOR 1½ TO 2 MINUTES until the onion is soft. Stir in the flour, milk and cream and MICROWAVE ON HIGH FOR 2 MINUTES, stirring half-way through cooking.

Mix in the crab meat and lemon juice and season with salt and pepper to taste. MICROWAVE ON MEDIUM FOR 2 MINUTES, stirring after 1 minute.

Spread the crackers on the oven shelf and MICROWAVE ON HIGH FOR 1½ TO 2 MINUTES, rearranging the crackers twice during heating. Spread each cracker with a little of the hot crab paste and sprinkle with paprika and cress.

Arrange the canapés on a large serving platter and serve hot.

MAKES 24 CANAPÉS

SESAME BALLS

METRIC/IMPERIAL	AMERICAN
50 g/2 oz Cheddar cheese, grated	½ cup grated Cheddar cheese
1 small onion, finely chopped	1 small onion, finely chopped
1 small strip of green pepper, finely chopped	1 small strip of green pepper, finely chopped
2 tablespoons mayonnaise	2 tablespoons mayonnaise
2 drops Tabasco	2 drops Tabasco
100 g/4 oz fresh soft breadcrumbs	2 cups fresh soft breadcrumbs
1 egg, beaten	1 egg beaten
50 g/2 oz sesame seeds	½ cup sesame seeds
25 g/1 oz butter	2 tablespoons butter

Mix the cheese, onion, green pepper, mayonnaise, Tabasco and breadcrumbs together. Add the egg and stir with a fork, to form a stiff paste.

Put the sesame seeds in a small bowl. Form the mixture into 2 cm/¾ inch balls and toss, one at a time, in the sesame seeds.

PREHEAT A LARGE BROWNING SKILLET FOR 4 MINUTES. Add the butter and MICROWAVE ON HIGH FOR 1 MINUTE. Quickly add the sesame balls and MICROWAVE ON HIGH FOR 3 MINUTES, turning them over after 1½ minutes. Drain on absorbent kitchen paper, then transfer to a warm serving dish.

MAKES ABOUT 30 SESAME BALLS

SOURED CREAM AND CAVIAR TARTLETS

METRIC/IMPERIAL	AMERICAN
6 thin slices of bread	6 thin slices of bread
25 g/1 oz butter	2 tablespoons butter
4 tablespoons soured cream	¼ cup sour cream
1 × 50 g/2 oz jar caviar	1 × 2 oz jar caviar
Garnish:	**Garnish:**
parsley sprigs	parsley sprigs
lemon wedges	lemon wedges

Using an upturned cup or pastry cutter, cut out large rounds from each slice of bread. Butter each piece on both sides and press firmly into bun or muffin moulds. MICROWAVE ON HIGH FOR 2½ TO 3 MINUTES until crisp.

Put the cream in a jug and MICROWAVE ON LOW FOR 1 MINUTE. Arrange the tartlets on a heated serving platter, fill with the cream and top with caviar. Garnish with parsley sprigs and lemon wedges.

SERVES 4 TO 6

ASPÈRGES AU BEURRE MALTAISE

Fresh asparagus with orange-flavoured hollandaise sauce

METRIC/IMPERIAL	AMERICAN
750 g/1 ½ lb asparagus	1 ½ lb asparagus
3–4 tablespoons water	3–4 tablespoons water
Sauce:	**Sauce:**
100 g/4 oz butter	½ cup butter
4 tablespoons double cream	¼ cup heavy cream
3 egg yolks	3 egg yolks
juice of ½ lemon	juice of ½ lemon
juice and grated rind of 1 small sweet orange	juice and grated rind of 1 small sweet orange
¼ teaspoon salt	¼ teaspoon salt
¼ teaspoon black pepper	¼ teaspoon black pepper

Break off and discard the thick fibrous ends of the asparagus. Rinse under cold running water. Arrange in a large shallow dish with the asparagus tips towards the centre. Sprinkle the water over the top.

Cover the dish loosely with plastic cling film. MICROWAVE ON HIGH FOR 7 TO 9 MINUTES until the asparagus tips are just tender when pierced with the tip of a knife; give the dish a half-turn once during cooking. Leave to stand, covered, while preparing the sauce.

Put the butter in a bowl and MICROWAVE ON HIGH FOR 1 MINUTE until melted. Add all the remaining sauce ingredients and whisk until smooth. MICROWAVE ON LOW FOR 2 TO 3 MINUTES until the sauce thickens, beating vigorously every 30 seconds during cooking.

Carefully transfer the asparagus to a heated serving dish. Pour the sauce into a sauceboat and hand round separately.

SERVES 4

ARTICHAUTS AU BEURRE

Artichokes with peppered butter sauce

METRIC/IMPERIAL	AMERICAN
4 globe artichokes	4 globe artichokes
1 tablespoon lemon juice	1 tablespoon lemon juice
½ teaspoon salt	½ teaspoon salt
300 ml/½ pint water	1 ¼ cups water
small knob of butter	½ teaspoon butter
Sauce:	**Sauce:**
100 g/4 oz butter	½ cup butter
½ teaspoon salt	½ teaspoon salt
½ teaspoon black pepper	½ teaspoon black pepper

Artichauts au beurre

Aspèrges au beurre maltaise; Dolmades aux champignons; Soured cream and caviar tartlets (page 113)

Above right: Preparing Dolmades aux champignons

Trim the tips of the outer artichoke leaves, using kitchen scissors. Wash the artichokes under cold running water.

Combine the lemon juice, salt and water in a large dish and add the butter. MICROWAVE ON HIGH FOR 3 TO 4 MINUTES until boiling. Place the artichokes upright in the dish, cover the dish and MICROWAVE ON HIGH FOR 12 TO 15 MINUTES until the lower leaves can be pulled away from the stem easily. Leave to stand, covered, while preparing the sauce.

Place the butter, salt and pepper in a small serving jug and MICROWAVE ON HIGH FOR 1½ MINUTES, or until melted.

Transfer the artichokes to serving plates with a slotted spoon; serve each one on a small plate standing on a larger plate, so there is ample place for the discarded leaves. Hand the sauce round separately.

SERVES 4

DOLMADES AUX CHAMPIGNONS
Vine leaves with mushroom stuffing

METRIC/IMPERIAL	AMERICAN
12 fresh, packed or canned vine leaves	12 fresh, packed or canned vine leaves
50 g/2 oz butter	¼ cup butter
1 onion, chopped	1 onion, chopped
225 g/8 oz mushrooms, chopped	2 cups chopped mushrooms
175 g/6 oz cooked rice	1 cup cooked rice
1 tablespoon chopped parsley	1 tablespoon chopped parsley
salt	salt
freshly ground black pepper	freshly ground black pepper
1 × 350 g/12 oz can ready-to-use meat sauce	1 × ¾ lb can ready-to-use meat sauce

If using fresh vine leaves, place them in a deep dish. Add just sufficient cold water to cover and MICROWAVE ON HIGH FOR 10 MINUTES. Drain and set aside.

Place the butter in a large shallow dish and MICROWAVE ON HIGH FOR 1 MINUTE. Stir in the onion and MICROWAVE ON HIGH FOR 4 MINUTES. Add the mushrooms and MICROWAVE ON HIGH FOR 6 MINUTES, stirring occasionally.

Stir in the rice, parsley and a little salt and pepper. Mix thoroughly. Spread a little of the mixture along one edge of each vine leaf and roll up, enclosing the filling and tucking in the sides to form a packet.

Arrange the stuffed vine leaves, with the joins underneath, round the edge of the dish. Pour over the sauce. Cover and MICROWAVE ON HIGH FOR 8 MINUTES. Serve hot.

SERVES 4

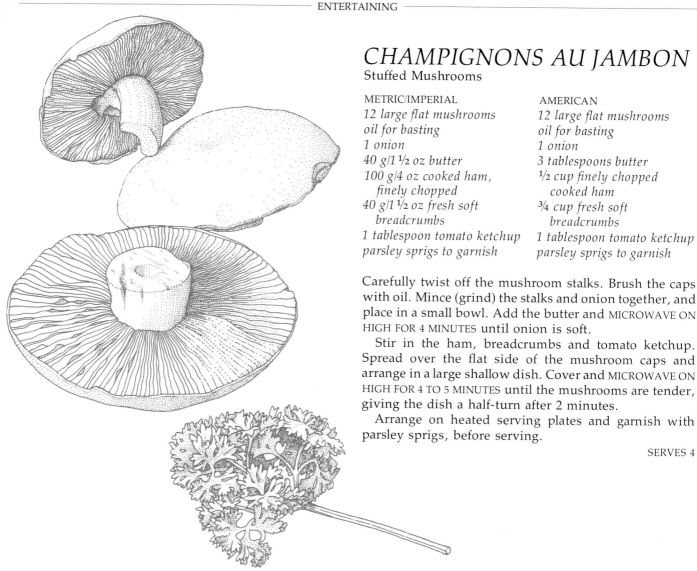

CHAMPIGNONS AU JAMBON
Stuffed Mushrooms

METRIC/IMPERIAL	AMERICAN
12 large flat mushrooms	12 large flat mushrooms
oil for basting	oil for basting
1 onion	1 onion
40 g/1½ oz butter	3 tablespoons butter
100 g/4 oz cooked ham, finely chopped	½ cup finely chopped cooked ham
40 g/1½ oz fresh soft breadcrumbs	¾ cup fresh soft breadcrumbs
1 tablespoon tomato ketchup	1 tablespoon tomato ketchup
parsley sprigs to garnish	parsley sprigs to garnish

Carefully twist off the mushroom stalks. Brush the caps with oil. Mince (grind) the stalks and onion together, and place in a small bowl. Add the butter and MICROWAVE ON HIGH FOR 4 MINUTES until onion is soft.

Stir in the ham, breadcrumbs and tomato ketchup. Spread over the flat side of the mushroom caps and arrange in a large shallow dish. Cover and MICROWAVE ON HIGH FOR 4 TO 5 MINUTES until the mushrooms are tender, giving the dish a half-turn after 2 minutes.

Arrange on heated serving plates and garnish with parsley sprigs, before serving.

SERVES 4

OEUFS BENEDICT
Poached eggs and ham on toast, topped with a creamy sauce

METRIC/IMPERIAL	AMERICAN
1 tablespoon vinegar	1 tablespoon vinegar
600 ml/1 pint water	2½ cups water
pinch of salt	pinch of salt
4 eggs	4 eggs
4 rounds of toast	4 rounds of toast
4 thin slices of cooked ham	4 thin slices of cooked ham
25 g/1 oz butter	2 tablespoons butter
175 ml/6 fl oz mayonnaise	¾ cup mayonnaise
3 tablespoons lemon juice	3 tablespoons lemon juice
4 tablespoons double cream, lightly whipped	4 tablespoons heavy cream, lightly whipped
1 teaspoon paprika	1 teaspoon paprika

Combine the vinegar, water and salt in a large deep dish and MICROWAVE ON HIGH FOR 3 TO 4 MINUTES until boiling. Break the eggs into the water. Cover the dish loosely with plastic cling film and MICROWAVE ON HIGH FOR 1¾ TO 2 MINUTES. Leave to stand, covered, for 2 minutes.

Arrange the toast rounds in a large shallow dish. Cover each round of toast with a slice of ham. Remove the poached eggs from the water, with a slotted spoon, drain well and place on the ham.

Put the butter in a bowl and MICROWAVE ON HIGH FOR 30 SECONDS until softened. Stir in the mayonnaise and lemon juice. MICROWAVE ON HIGH FOR 1 MINUTE until just hot, then fold in the cream. Spoon this sauce over the eggs and MICROWAVE ON HIGH FOR 45 SECONDS. Sprinkle with paprika and serve immediately.

SERVES 4

PÂTÉ DE FOIE
Smooth Liver Pâté

METRIC/IMPERIAL	AMERICAN
15 g/½ oz butter	1 tablespoon butter
1 small onion, chopped	1 small onion, chopped
1 rasher bacon, derinded and chopped	1 bacon slice, derinded and chopped
150 g/5 oz lambs' liver, chopped	5 oz lamb liver, chopped
2 hard-boiled eggs	2 hard-cooked eggs
4 tablespoons soured cream	¼ cup sour cream
3 tablespoons sherry	3 tablespoons sherry
salt	salt
freshly ground black pepper	freshly ground black pepper
1 lettuce heart, shredded	1 lettuce heart, shredded

Combine the butter, onion and bacon in a large shallow dish. MICROWAVE ON HIGH FOR 3 MINUTES. Stir in the liver and MICROWAVE ON HIGH FOR 4 TO 5 MINUTES until the liver is no longer pink, stirring occasionally.

Add the eggs to the liver mixture and blend in an electric blender or press through a sieve (strainer). Return to the dish and mix in the cream, sherry, and salt and pepper to taste. Cover loosely with plastic cling film and cool rapidly. Chill in the refrigerator for 3 to 4 hours.

Line individual serving plates with shredded lettuce, and pile the pâté on top. Serve, accompanied by thin slices of toast.

SERVES 4

ZUPPA RUSTICA
Chicken soup with shredded spinach, cheese and eggs

METRIC/IMPERIAL	AMERICAN
1.2 litres/2 pints chicken stock	5 cups chicken stock
1 chicken breast	1 chicken breast
100 g/4 oz fresh leaf spinach, washed and drained	¼ lb fresh leaf spinach, washed and drained
2 tablespoons grated Parmesan cheese	2 tablespoons grated Parmesan cheese
salt	salt
freshly ground black pepper	freshly ground black pepper
1 egg, beaten	1 egg, beaten

Pour the stock into a large bowl, add the chicken, then cover and MICROWAVE ON HIGH FOR 15 MINUTES. Take out the chicken, remove the skin and bone and shred the flesh. Discard the thick stem from the spinach, roll up the leaves and slice finely.

Add he shredded chicken and spinach to the stock and without covering, MICROWAVE ON HIGH FOR 5 MINUTES. Stir in the cheese and season to taste with salt and pepper. MICROWAVE ON HIGH FOR 2 MINUTES or until boiling.

Pour the soup into a hot serving tureen and quickly strain the beaten egg over the soup. Serve immediately.

SERVES 4

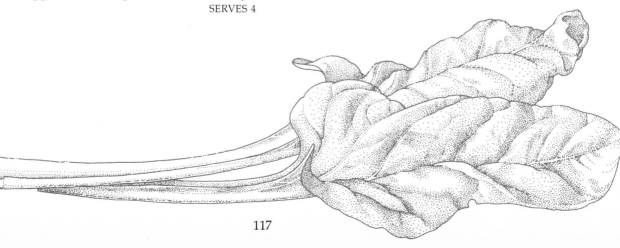

VICHYSOISSE
Chilled leek and potato soup

METRIC/IMPERIAL	AMERICAN
3 leeks, white part only, thinly sliced	3 leeks, white part only, thinly sliced
15 g/½ oz butter	1 tablespoon butter
500 g/1 lb potatoes, peeled and diced	1 lb potatoes, peeled and diced
1.2 litres/2 pints hot chicken stock	5 cups hot chicken stock
salt	salt
freshly ground black pepper	freshly ground black pepper
150 ml/¼ pint double cream	⅔ cup heavy cream
1 tablespoon chopped chives	1 tablespoon chopped chives

Combine the leeks and butter in a large deep dish and MICROWAVE ON HIGH FOR 4 MINUTES, stirring occasionally. Add the potatoes and stock. Cover and MICROWAVE ON HIGH FOR 10 MINUTES until the potatoes are soft, stirring twice during cooking.

Purée the soup in an electric blender or press through a sieve (strainer). Add salt and pepper. Chill in the refrigerator for at least 3 hours, before serving. Adjust the seasoning, stir in the cream and sprinkle with chopped chives to garnish.

SERVES 6

BOUILLABAISSE
Mediterranean mixed fish soup

METRIC/IMPERIAL	AMERICAN
500 g/1 ½ lb assorted filleted white fish, skinned	1 ½ lb assorted filleted saltwater fish, skinned
225 g/8 oz assorted cooked shellfish (shrimps, prawns, crab meat, lobster meat)	½ lb assorted cooked shellfish (shrimp, crab meat, lobster meat)
1 onion, finely chopped	1 onion, finely chopped
1 leek, thinly sliced	1 leek, thinly sliced
1 clove garlic, crushed	1 clove garlic, minced
2 tablespoons olive oil	2 tablespoons olive oil
2 tomatoes, skinned, seeded and chopped	2 tomatoes, skinned, seeded and chopped
1 tablespoon finely chopped parsley	1 tablespoon finely chopped parsley
¼ teaspoon powdered saffron	¼ teaspoon powdered saffron
1 bouquet garni	1 bouquet garni
1 teaspoon lemon juice	1 teaspoon lemon juice
1.2 litres/2 pints boiling water	5 cups boiling water
salt	salt
freshly ground black pepper	freshly ground black pepper
6 slices French bread	6 slices French bread

Cut the fish into 5 cm/2 inch slices. Shell the shrimps and prawns, if necessary; chop the crab and lobster meat.

Combine the onion, leek, garlic and olive oil in a large deep dish and MICROWAVE ON HIGH FOR 3 MINUTES. Add the fish, shellfish, tomatoes, parsley, saffron, bouquet garni and lemon juice. Pour in the water and add salt and pepper to taste.

Cover and MICROWAVE ON HIGH FOR 10 TO 12 MINUTES, until the fish is tender, stirring gently occasionally. Discard the bay leaf and the bouquet garni. Check the seasoning.

Place a slice of French bread in each warmed soup bowl and ladle the soup over the top. Serve immediately.

SERVES 6

CONSOMMÉ FROID DE MELON
Chilled melon soup

METRIC/IMPERIAL	AMERICAN
1 large canteloupe melon	1 large canteloupe melon
20 g/¾ oz butter	3 tablespoons butter
1 tablespoon sugar	1 tablespoon sugar
grated rind and juice of ½ lemon	grated rind and juice of ½ lemon
pinch of ground ginger	pinch of ground ginger
pinch of ground mace	pinch of ground mace
pinch of salt	pinch of salt
450 ml/¾ pint water	2 cups water
150 ml/¼ pint sweet white wine	⅔ cup sweet white wine
few sprigs of mint	few sprigs of mint

Cut the melon in half and discard the seeds. Scoop a few melon balls from the flesh, using a melon baller or teaspoon, and set aside for garnish.

Remove and dice all the remaining melon flesh, place in a large deep casserole with the butter, sugar, lemon rind and juice, ginger, mace and salt. MICROWAVE ON HIGH FOR 5 MINUTES.

Purée the mixture in an electric blender or pass through a sieve (strainer). Stir in the water and wine and chill in the refrigerator for 2 to 3 hours.

Adjust the seasoning, adding pepper to taste. Turn into a serving tureen or individual soup bowls. Serve chilled, garnished with the melon balls and sprigs of mint.

SERVES 4

Vichysoisse; Consommé froid de melon; Bouillabaisse

SOUPE AU CRABE ET MAIS
Corn and crab soup

METRIC/IMPERIAL	AMERICAN
1 small onion	1 small onion
1 stick celery	1 stalk celery
1 lean rasher bacon, derinded	1 lean bacon slice, derinded
15 g/½ oz butter	1 tablespoon butter
25 g/1 oz flour	¼ cup flour
600 ml/1 pint milk	2½ cups milk
450 ml/¾ pint water	2 cups water
1 bay leaf	1 bay leaf
1 × 225 g/8 oz can creamed sweetcorn	1 × ½ lb can creamed sweetcorn
225 g/8 oz fresh or canned crab meat	½ lb fresh or canned crab meat
salt	salt
freshly ground black pepper	freshly ground black pepper

Chop the onion, celery and bacon finely. Place in a large bowl and add the butter. MICROWAVE ON HIGH FOR 4 MINUTES, stirring once during cooking. Stir in the flour, then add the milk, water and bay leaf. MICROWAVE ON HIGH FOR 8 MINUTES, stirring occasionally. Strain into another bowl.

Lightly mash the sweetcorn and flake the crab meat. Add to the sauce and MICROWAVE ON HIGH FOR 4 MINUTES until hot. Add salt and pepper to taste. Serve hot.

SERVES 4 TO 6

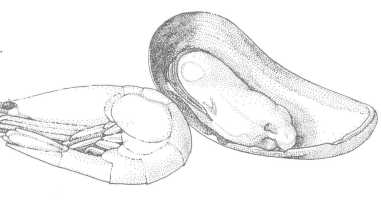

MÉLANGE DE FRUITS DE MER HONFLEUR
Mixed seafood in wine sauce, with crisp potato topping

METRIC/IMPERIAL	AMERICAN
1 small onion, chopped	1 small onion, chopped
40 g/1½ oz butter	3 tablespoons butter
4 scallops, shelled, cleaned and halved	4 scallops, shelled, cleaned and halved
225 g/½ lb filleted hake, skinned and cut into 2.5 cm/1 inch chunks	½ lb filleted hake, skinned and cut into 1 inch chunks
100 g/4 oz shelled scampi	¼ lb shelled jumbo shrimp
150 ml/¼ pint dry white wine	⅔ cup dry white wine
2 teaspoons lemon juice	2 teaspoons lemon juice
1 bay leaf	1 bay leaf
½–1 teaspoon salt	½–1 teaspoon salt
½ teaspoon black pepper	½ teaspoon black pepper
25 g/1 oz flour	¼ cup flour
150 ml/¼ pint water	⅔ cup water
100 g/4 oz button mushrooms	1 cup button mushrooms
100 g/4 oz shelled shrimps	¼ lb shelled shrimps
1 × 100 g/4 oz can tuna fish, flaked	1 × ¼ lb can tuna fish, flaked
1 × 150 g/5 oz jar mussels, drained	1 × 5 oz jar mussels, drained
500 g/1 lb potatoes, cooked and mashed	1 lb potatoes, cooked and mashed
Garnish:	**Garnish:**
50 g/2 oz black grapes, skinned and pipped	½ cup black grapes, skinned and seeded
lemon slices	lemon slices

Combine the onion and one third of the butter in a large deep dish and MICROWAVE ON HIGH FOR 3 MINUTES. Add the scallops, hake, scampi (jumbo shrimp), wine, lemon juice, bay leaf, salt and pepper. MICROWAVE ON HIGH FOR 5 MINUTES, basting occasionally. Carefully transfer the fish to a plate and set aside; strain the liquor into a small bowl.

Put the remaining butter in the dish, stir in the flour and MICROWAVE ON HIGH FOR 1 MINUTE. Stir in the reserved liquor and the water and MICROWAVE ON HIGH FOR 4 MINUTES, stirring occasionally.

Add the mushrooms to the sauce and MICROWAVE ON HIGH FOR 3 MINUTES. Fold in the shrimps, flaked tuna and mussels. Add the scallops, hake and scampi (jumbo shrimp). Cover and MICROWAVE ON LOW FOR 15 TO 18 MINUTES until all the fish is cooked; stir gently several times during cooking.

Pipe a deep border of mashed potato around the edges of a flameproof serving dish and place under a preheated hot grill (broiler) until crisp and lightly browned. Spoon the fish mixture into the centre. Put the grapes on a saucer and MICROWAVE ON HIGH FOR 30 SECONDS. Garnish the dish with the grapes and lemon slices, before serving.

SERVES 6

Note: If only 4 servings are required, reduce the amount of fish but leave the remaining quantities as stated above.

HALIBUT AUX CREVETTES
Halibut steaks, topped with a creamy prawn sauce

METRIC/IMPERIAL	AMERICAN
4 halibut steaks, about 2.5 cm /1 inch thick	4 halibut steaks, about 1 inch thick
15 g/½ oz butter, softened	1 tablespoon butter, softened
salt	salt
freshly ground pepper	freshly ground black pepper
100 g/4 oz shelled prawns	½ cup shelled shrimp
150 ml/¼ pint double cream	⅔ cup heavy cream
2 tablespoons tomato ketchup	2 tablespoons tomato ketchup

Arrange the halibut steaks in a large shallow dish, with the thickest part towards the edge of the dish. Spread with butter and season with salt and pepper. Cover and MICROWAVE ON HIGH FOR 4 MINUTES until the fish is opaque in colour.

Mix together the prawns (shrimps), cream and tomato ketchup. Spoon a little of the sauce over each fish steak. Cover and MICROWAVE ON LOW FOR 2 MINUTES. Serve immediately.

SERVES 4

DOVER SOLE AUX TOMATES ET CHAMPIGNONS
Sole in tomato and mushroom sauce

METRIC/IMPERIAL	AMERICAN
4 × 350 g/12 oz Dover sole, skinned and trimmed	4 ×¾ lb Dover sole, skinned and trimmed
Sauce:	**Sauce:**
1 small bunch spring onions, trimmed and thinly sliced	1 small bunch scallions, trimmed and thinly sliced
25 g/1 oz butter	2 tablespoons butter
225 g/8 oz mushrooms, sliced	2 cups sliced mushrooms
500 g/1 lb tomatoes, skinned and quartered	1 lb tomatoes, skinned and quartered
2 tablespoons chopped parsley	2 tablespoons chopped parsley
2 teaspoons basil	2 teaspoons basil
pinch of sugar	pinch of sugar
½ teaspoon salt	½ teaspoon salt
¼ teaspoon black pepper	¼ teaspoon black pepper

To prepare the sauce, combine the spring onions (scallions) and butter in a large shallow dish. MICROWAVE ON HIGH FOR 3 MINUTES, stirring once during cooking. Add the mushrooms and MICROWAVE ON HIGH FOR 3 MINUTES. Stir in the remaining ingredients, cover loosely with plastic cling film and MICROWAVE ON LOW FOR 15 MINUTES. Leave to stand while cooking the fish.

Place each fish on a suitable serving plate. Season with salt and pepper to taste and cover with plastic cling film. One at a time, MICROWAVE ON HIGH FOR 4 MINUTES.

Meanwhile, break up the vegetables in the sauce, with a potato masher. Spoon the sauce on top of the fish before serving.

SERVES 4

Note: Alternatively, to cook the fish, stack the plates and MICROWAVE ON HIGH FOR 12 MINUTES, altering the position of each plate occasionally during cooking.

SOLE XEREZ ROYALE

Sole in sherry sauce, topped with mushrooms and flambéed in brandy

METRIC/IMPERIAL	AMERICAN
750 g/1 ½ lb Dover sole, skinned and filleted	1 ½ lb Dover sole, skinned and filleted
120 ml/4 fl oz water	½ cup water
1 tablespoon vinegar	1 tablespoon vinegar
½ teaspoon salt	½ teaspoon salt
¼ teaspoon black pepper	¼ teaspoon black pepper
¼ onion, chopped	¼ onion, chopped
Sauce:	**Sauce:**
50 g/2 oz butter	¼ cup butter
40 g/1 ½ oz flour	6 tablespoons flour
400 ml/¾ pint milk	2 cups milk
½ teaspoon salt	½ teaspoon salt
¼ teaspoon black pepper	¼ teaspoon black pepper
100 g/4 oz Cheddar cheese, grated	1 cup grated Cheddar cheese
2 egg yolks	2 egg yolks
2 tablespoons single cream	2 tablespoons light cream
2 tablespoons dry sherry	2 tablespoons dry sherry
Topping:	**Topping:**
225 g/8 oz mushrooms, finely chopped	2 cups finely chopped mushrooms
7 g/¼ oz butter	1 teaspoon butter
To flambé:	**To flambé:**
2 tablespoons brandy	2 tablespoons brandy
Garnish:	**Garnish:**
parsley sprig	parsley sprig

Place the fish in a large shallow dish and pour over the water, vinegar, salt, pepper and onion. Cover and MIC-ROWAVE ON HIGH FOR 8 MINUTES until the fish is opaque; giving the dish a quarter-turn every 2 minutes. Leave to stand, covered, while preparing the sauce and topping.

To prepare the sauce, put the butter in a deep bowl and MICROWAVE ON HIGH FOR 1 MINUTE. Stir in the flour and MICROWAVE ON HIGH FOR 1 MINUTE. Add the milk, salt and pepper and whisk until smooth. MICROWAVE ON HIGH FOR 5 MINUTES, whisking every 1½ minutes. Beat in the cheese. Blend the egg yolks and cream together, stir into the sauce and MICROWAVE ON LOW FOR 2 MINUTES. Stir in the sherry, cover and leave to stand.

For the topping, place the mushrooms and butter in a bowl, cover and MICROWAVE ON HIGH FOR 3 MINUTES.

To assemble the dish, drain the fish and place in a serving dish. Spoon the sauce over the fish and arrange the mushrooms on top. Dot with the butter.

To reheat, MICROWAVE ON HIGH FOR 2 MINUTES. Pour the brandy into a small glass. MICROWAVE ON HIGH FOR 10 SECONDS, then ignite, pour over the mushrooms and serve immediately, garnished with parsley.

SERVES 4

SAUMON MEUNIÈRE

Salmon steaks with lemon

METRIC/IMPERIAL	AMERICAN
4 × 150 g/6 oz salmon steaks	4 × 6 oz salmon steaks
1 tablespoon lemon juice	1 tablespoon lemon juice
salt	salt
freshly ground black pepper	freshly ground black pepper
2 tablespoons flour	2 tablespoons flour
25 g/1 oz butter	2 tablespoons butter
lemon slices to garnish	lemon slices to garnish

PREHEAT A LARGE BROWNING SKILLET FOR 5 MINUTES (or according to the manufacturer's instructions). Rinse and dry the salmon steaks. Sprinkle with lemon juice and salt and pepper to taste. Coat with flour.

As soon as the skillet is hot, and without removing from the microwave oven, toss in the butter. Quickly put in the salmon slices, arranging them so that the thickest parts are towards the outside of the dish. MICROWAVE ON HIGH FOR 3 MINUTES. Turn the salmon over and MICROWAVE ON HIGH FOR 3 TO 4 MINUTES until the fish flakes easily, giving the dish a half-turn after 2 minutes. Cover and leave to stand for 5 minutes.

Garnish with lemon slices before serving.

SERVES 4

Sole xerez royale; Saumon meunière; Turbot aux huîtres

TURBOT AUX HUÎTRES
Turbot in sauce with oysters

METRIC/IMPERIAL	AMERICAN
4 × 175 g/6 oz turbot steaks	4 × 6 oz turbot steaks
salt	salt

Sauce:

METRIC/IMPERIAL	AMERICAN
40 g/1½ oz flour	6 tablespoons flour
3 tablespoons vegetable oil	3 tablespoons vegetable oil
450 ml/¾ pint milk	2 cups milk
1 egg yolk	1 egg yolk
2 tablespoons double cream	3 tablespoons heavy cream
freshly ground black pepper	freshly ground black pepper

Garnish:

METRIC/IMPERIAL	AMERICAN
12 oysters	12 oysters
50 g/2 oz grated Cheddar cheese	½ cup grated Cheddar cheese

Arrange the fish steaks in a single layer in a large shallow dish. Sprinkle with salt and cover loosely with plastic cling film. MICROWAVE ON HIGH FOR 5 MINUTES. Turn the fish slices over and give the dish a half-turn. Cover and MICROWAVE ON HIGH FOR 5 TO 6 MINUTES until the flesh is opaque. Leave to stand, covered, while preparing the sauce.

Combine the flour, oil and milk in a large bowl and stir thoroughly. MICROWAVE ON HIGH FOR 4 MINUTES, stirring every minute. Beat together the egg yolk and cream, then add a few spoonsful of the hot sauce and mix thoroughly. Stir this mixture into the sauce and MICROWAVE ON HIGH FOR 15 SECONDS. Add salt and pepper to taste.

Place the oysters on a plate, cover with a damp piece of absorbent kitchen paper and MICROWAVE ON HIGH FOR 2 TO 3 MINUTES until opaque, giving the dish a half-turn after 1 minute.

Transfer the turbot to a flameproof serving platter, coat with the sauce and arrange the oysters on top. Sprinkle with the cheese and place under a preheated hot grill (broiler) to brown the top. Serve immediately.

SERVES 4

QUENELLES
Fish quenelles in cheese sauce

METRIC/IMPERIAL	AMERICAN
500 g/1 lb filleted halibut, skinned	1 lb filleted halibut, skinned
2 tablespoons chopped parsley	2 tablespoons chopped parsley
25 g/1 oz flour	4 tablespoons flour
25 g/1 oz butter	2 tablespoons butter
5 tablespoons milk	⅓ cup milk
1 teaspoon salt	1 teaspoon salt
½ teaspoon black pepper	½ teaspoon black pepper
Court bouillon:	**Court bouillon:**
600 ml/1 pint boiling water	2½ cups boiling water
1 tablespoon wine vinegar	1 tablespoon wine vinegar
⅓ teaspoon powdered bay leaves	⅓ teaspoon powdered bay leaves
small piece of onion	small piece of onion
Sauce:	**Sauce:**
40 g/1½ oz butter	3 tablespoons butter
40 g/1½ oz flour	6 tablespoons flour
600 ml/1 pint milk	2½ cups milk
¼ teaspoon salt	¼ teaspoon salt
½ teaspoon black pepper	½ teaspoon black pepper
2 tablespoons anchovy essence	2 tablespoons anchovy essence
25 g/1 oz grated Cheddar cheese	¼ cup grated Cheddar cheese
Garnish:	**Garnish:**
8 canned anchovy fillets, drained and cut into thin strips	8 canned anchovy fillets, drained and cut into thin strips

Mince (grind) the fish and parsley together. Blend in the flour. Put the butter in a small bowl and MICROWAVE ON HIGH FOR 30 SECONDS or until melted. Add the milk, salt, pepper and melted butter to the fish and mix thoroughly until smooth.

To prepare the court bouillon, combine the boiling water, vinegar, powdered bay leaves and onion in a jug. MICROWAVE ON HIGH FOR 1 TO 2 MINUTES to bring back to the boil. Pour into a large shallow dish.

Divide the fish mixture into 12 equal pieces. Form each one into an oval-shaped quenelle, using two tablespoons. Arrange half the quenelles around the edge of the dish and MICROWAVE ON HIGH FOR 4 MINUTES. Move these into the centre of the dish and arrange the remaining quenelles round the edge. MICROWAVE ON HIGH FOR 2 MINUTES. Cover and set aside.

To prepare the sauce, put the butter in a deep bowl and MICROWAVE ON HIGH FOR 1 MINUTE. Blend in the flour and MICROWAVE ON HIGH FOR 1 MINUTE. Whisk in the milk, salt and pepper and MICROWAVE ON HIGH FOR 4 MINUTES, whisking thoroughly after each minute. Stir in the anchovy essence and the cheese. Taste and correct the seasoning if necessary.

Drain the quenelles, cover and MICROWAVE ON HIGH FOR 2 MINUTES to reheat, stirring once. Transfer to a heated serving platter and coat with the sauce. Arrange the anchovy strips in a lattice pattern on top. Serve immediately.

SERVES 4

Note: This dish also makes a tasty starter; the above quantities will serve 6 people as a first course.

SAUMON FROID POCHE
Cold poached salmon

METRIC/IMPERIAL	AMERICAN
500 g/1 lb piece of fresh salmon	1 lb piece of fresh salmon
300 ml/1½ pint water	1¼ cups water
2 tablespoons red wine	2 tablespoons red wine
1 small onion, quartered	1 small onion, quartered
¼ teaspoon black pepper	¼ teaspoon black pepper
1 teaspoon salt	1 teaspoon salt
6 white peppercorns, crushed	6 white peppercorns, crushed
1 bay leaf	1 bay leaf
pinch of dill, tarragon or dried mixed herbs	pinch of dried dill, tarragon or dried mixed herbs
¼ cucumber, peeled and thinly sliced	¼ cucumber, peeled and thinly sliced

Lay the salmon, cut side up, in a deep dish into which it fits snugly. Combine the water, wine, onion, seasoning and herbs. Pour over the fish. Cover the dish with a lid. MICROWAVE ON MEDIUM FOR 6 TO 8 MINUTES until the flesh can easily be separated from the bone; turn the salmon over half-way through cooking. Leave the fish to cool in the liquor.

Remove the skin from the salmon, by inserting the prongs of a fork between the skin and flesh and pulling it away from the sides of the fish. Carefully transfer the salmon to a serving dish, using a fish slice. Garnish with the cucumber slices and serve accompanied by mayonnaise.

SERVES 3 TO 4

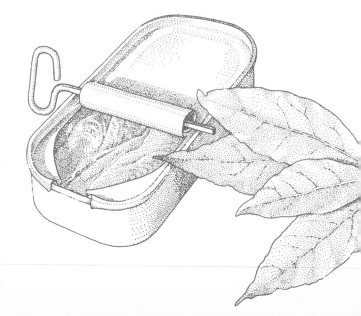

SUPRÊMES DE POULET MARENGO

Chicken breasts, cooked with tomatoes, mushrooms, white wine and fresh herbs and garnished with king prawns (giant shrimp)

METRIC/IMPERIAL	AMERICAN
4 chicken breasts, skinned and boned	4 chicken breasts, skinned and boned
2 tablespoons flour	2 tablespoons flour
6 to 8 spring onions, trimmed and chopped	½ cup chopped scallions
25 g/1 oz butter, softened	2 tablespoons softened butter
100 g/4 oz mushrooms, sliced	1 cup sliced mushrooms
1 × 400 g/14 oz can tomatoes	1 × 14 oz can tomatoes
1 teaspoon finely chopped basil	1 teaspoon finely chopped basil
½ teaspoon finely chopped thyme	½ teaspoon finely chopped thyme
2 bay leaves	2 bay leaves
½ teaspoon black pepper	½ teaspoon black pepper
1 teaspoon salt	1 teaspoon salt
1 lemon slice	1 lemon slice
150 ml/¼ pint medium white wine	⅔ cup medium white wine
Garnish:	**Garnish:**
4 cooked, unshelled king prawns (see note)	4 cooked, unshelled, giant shrimp (see note)

Beat the chicken to flatten, then dip in the flour and coat thoroughly. Blend the spring onions (scallions) and butter together.

PREHEAT A LARGE BROWNING SKILLET FOR 5 MINUTES (or according to the manufacturer's instructions). Quickly add the spring onions (scallions) and MICROWAVE ON HIGH FOR 2 MINUTES. Immediately add the chicken breasts and MICROWAVE ON HIGH FOR 2 MINUTES. Turn the chicken pieces over and MICROWAVE ON HIGH FOR 2 MINUTES.

Stir in the mushrooms and MICROWAVE ON HIGH FOR 1 MINUTE. Add all the remaining ingredients, crushing the tomatoes slightly. Cover with a lid and MICROWAVE ON LOW FOR 15 TO 20 MINUTES until the chicken is tender. Remove the lemon and bay leaves.

Serve garnished with the prawns (giant shrimp), curving their heads over the corners of the skillet.

SERVES 4

Note: To cook king prawns (giant shrimp), place in a dish and cover with water. Add a slice of lemon, a bay leaf and ½ teaspoon salt. Cover and MICROWAVE ON HIGH until boiling. Leave to stand for 5 minutes before serving.

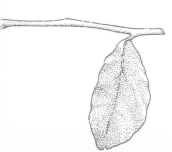

CANETON LYCHÉE
Duck with lychees

METRIC/IMPERIAL	AMERICAN
1 × 1.5 kg/3½ lb duckling	1 × 3½ lb duckling
1 teaspoon salt	1 teaspoon salt
1 × 400 g/14 oz can lychees	1 × 14 oz can lychees
100 g/4 oz petit pois	¼ lb petit pois
¼ teaspoon ground ginger	¼ teaspoon ground ginger
2 tablespoons chopped parsley	2 tablespoons chopped parsley

Rinse the duckling and pat dry with absorbent kitchen paper. Cover the leg and wing tips with small pieces of foil. Place, breast side down, on a trivet or upturned bowl in a large shallow dish. MICROWAVE ON HIGH FOR 15 MINUTES.

Remove the foil and turn the duck, breast side up. Prick the skin in several places to release the fat. Baste and MICROWAVE ON HIGH FOR 10 MINUTES until the juices from the cavity run clear.

Carefully lift the duck out of the dish and drain thoroughly. Remove all the flesh from the bone and cut into neat pieces. Sprinkle with salt.

Pour off the fat from the dish, leaving the residual duck juices. Add 150 ml/¼ pint/⅔ cup juice from the lychees, and the peas. Sprinkle with the ginger, then cover and MICROWAVE ON HIGH FOR 5 MINUTES. Stir in the duck and, without covering, MICROWAVE ON HIGH FOR 2 TO 3 MINUTES until thoroughly reheated.

Transfer to a hot serving dish, sprinkle with parsley and surround with the lychees.

SERVES 4

POULET AU KARI
Curried chicken

Poulet au kari; Saffron and paprika rice (page 136); Raita and Dahl (page 137)

METRIC/IMPERIAL
1 × 1.5 kg/3½ lb
  oven-ready chicken
4 tablespoons vegetable oil
4 onions, finely chopped
1 teaspoon ground coriander
1 teaspoon ground cumin
1 teaspoon ground turmeric
1 teaspoon ground
  cardamom
1 teaspoon salt
½ teaspoon black pepper
1 chicken stock cube
150 ml/¼ pint boiling water
2 tablespoons lemon juice
5 tablespoons tomato purée
4 tomatoes, quartered

AMERICAN
1 × 3½ lb ready-to-cook
  chicken
¼ cup vegetable oil
4 onions, finely chopped
1 teaspoon ground coriander
1 teaspoon ground cumin
1 teaspoon ground turmeric
1 teaspoon powdered
  cardamom
1 teaspoon salt
½ teaspoon black pepper
1 chicken bouillon cube
⅔ cup boiling water
2 tablespoons lemon juice
5 tablespoons tomato paste
4 tomatoes, quartered

Cut the chicken into 8 pieces. Combine the oil, onions, spices, salt and pepper in a large deep dish and MIC-ROWAVE ON HIGH FOR 10 MINUTES, stirring occasionally. Dissolve the stock (bouillon) cube in the water and add to the dish with the lemon juice and tomato purée (paste); stir well.

Arrange the chicken pieces in the sauce, with the boniest parts towards the centre. Add the tomatoes, cover tightly and MICROWAVE ON HIGH FOR 25 TO 30 MINUTES, stirring and turning the chicken pieces over two or three times during cooking. Leave to stand covered for 10 minutes before serving.

Serve with saffron and paprika rice (page 136) dahl (page 137) and raita (page 137).

SERVES 4

Note: Chicken curry may be prepared in advance and stored in the refrigerator or frozen. This will enhance the flavour. Reheat thoroughly before serving.

126

KEBABS À LA GRECQUE

METRIC/IMPERIAL	AMERICAN
4 lambs' kidneys	4 lamb kidneys
500 g/1¼ lbs lean boned leg of lamb	1¼ lb boneless lean leg of lamb
1 aubergine, peeled	1 eggplant, peeled
1 green pepper, cored and seeded	1 green pepper, cored and seeded
6 button mushrooms	6 button mushrooms
6 small firm tomatoes	6 small firm tomatoes
Marinade:	**Marinade:**
4 tablespoons vegetable oil	4 tablespoons vegetable oil
juice of ½ lemon	juice of ½ lemon
1 small onion, chopped	1 small onion, chopped
1 clove garlic, quartered	1 clove garlic, quartered
1 teaspoon salt	1 teaspoon salt
½ teaspoon black pepper	½ teaspoon black pepper
¼ teaspoon mustard powder	¼ teaspoon mustard powder
1 teaspoon dried oregano	1 teaspoon dried oregano
2 bay leaves	2 bay leaves

Slice the kidneys in half and remove the cores. Cut the lamb and aubergine (eggplant) into 2.5 cm/1 inch cubes and cut the green pepper into similar-sized squares.

Combine the marinade ingredients in a bowl. Add the kidneys, lamb, aubergine (eggplant) and green pepper, stir well. Cover and leave to marinate in the refrigerator for at least 12 hours, stirring occasionally.

Strain the marinade and reserve. Thread the lamb, kidneys and vegetables on to 6 kebab skewers, placing a tomato in the centre of each skewer. Arrange in a large shallow dish and spoon over the marinade. Without covering, MICROWAVE ON HIGH FOR 12 MINUTES, until the lamb is tender; baste and give the dish a half-turn occasionally during cooking.

Serve hot, on a bed of rice.

SERVES 4 TO 6

POULET CHASSEUR

Chicken pieces cooked with rosé wine, brandy, mushrooms, fresh herbs and onions

METRIC/IMPERIAL	AMERICAN
1 × 1.5 kg/3½ lb oven ready chicken, cut into 8 pieces	1 × 3½ lb ready to cook chicken, cut into 8 pieces
½ clove garlic	½ clove garlic
50 g/2 oz plain flour	½ cup all-purpose flour
50 g/2 oz butter	¼ cup butter
1 teaspoon salt	1 teaspoon salt
1 small onion, chopped	1 small onion, chopped
100 g/4 oz button mushrooms	1 cup button mushrooms
2 tablespoons tomato purée	2 tablespoons tomato paste
1 tablespoon chopped parsley	1 tablespoon chopped parsley
3 sprigs of thyme	3 sprigs of thyme
2 bay leaves	2 bay leaves
½ teaspoon freshly ground black pepper	½ teaspoons freshly ground black pepper
250 ml/8 fl oz brown stock	1 cup brown stock
5 tablespoons rosé wine	5 tablespoons rosé wine
2 tablespoons brandy	2 tablespoons brandy
Garnish:	**Garnish:**
4 to 6 parsley sprigs	4 to 6 parsley sprigs
8 triangles of toast (see page 21)	8 triangles of toast (see page 21)

Skin the chicken pieces, rub with the cut side of the garlic, then dust liberally with the flour. PREHEAT A LARGE BROWNING SKILLET FOR 5 MINUTES (or according to manufacturer's instructions). Toss in 40 g/1½ oz of the butter and the salt and quickly put in four of the chicken pieces. MICROWAVE ON HIGH FOR 2 MINUTES.

Add the remaining chicken and MICROWAVE ON HIGH FOR 10 MINUTES, turning the pieces over once or twice during cooking. Remove the skillet from the microwave oven and spoon away any surplus fat. Cover with the lid and leave to stand whilst preparing the sauce.

Place the onion and the remaining butter in a large shallow dish and MICROWAVE ON HIGH FOR 3 TO 4 MINUTES until the onion is lightly browned. Stir in the mushrooms and MICROWAVE ON HIGH FOR 4 MINUTES. Add the tomato purée (paste), herbs, pepper, stock, wine and brandy. MICROWAVE ON HIGH FOR 3 MINUTES. Taste and add salt if necessary.

Pour the sauce over the chicken, cover with the skillet lid and MICROWAVE ON LOW FOR 20 MINUTES. Remove the thyme and bay leaves.

Garnish with parsley sprigs and triangles of toast before serving.

SERVES 4

LAMB DÉLICE
Lamb casserole with aubergine (eggplant) and artichokes

METRIC/IMPERIAL	AMERICAN
1 large aubergine, peeled and cut into cubes	1 large eggplant, peeled and cut into cubes
salt	salt
2 tablespoons vegetable oil	2 tablespoons vegetable oil
750 g/1 ½ lb boned leg of lamb, cut into cubes	1 ½ lb boneless leg of lamb, cut into cubes
4 tablespoons plum jam	¼ cup plum jam
8 tablespoons red wine	½ cup red wine
1 × 400 g/14 oz can artichoke hearts, drained	1 × 14 oz can artichoke hearts, drained
2 tablespoons chopped gherkins	2 tablespoons chopped gherkins
2 teaspoons cornflour	2 teaspoons cornstarch
4 tablespoons cold water	¼ cup cold water

Sprinkle the aubergine (eggplant) with salt and set aside for at least 30 minutes. Rinse and pat dry with absorbent kitchen paper.

PREHEAT A LARGE BROWNING SKILLET FOR 5 MINUTES (or according to the manufacturer's instructions). Quickly add the oil, then rapidly stir in the lamb. MICROWAVE ON HIGH FOR 5 MINUTES, stirring once during cooking.

Add the aubergine (eggplant), cover the dish with a lid and MICROWAVE ON HIGH FOR 5 MINUTES. Stir in the jam, wine and 1 teaspoon salt, then add the artichoke hearts and chopped gherkins. Cover and MICROWAVE ON LOW FOR 35 MINUTES. Leave to stand for 10 minutes.

Blend the cornflour (cornstarch) with the water, stir into the skillet and MICROWAVE ON HIGH FOR 3 MINUTES, stirring occasionally, until the sauce thickens. Serve hot.

SERVES 4

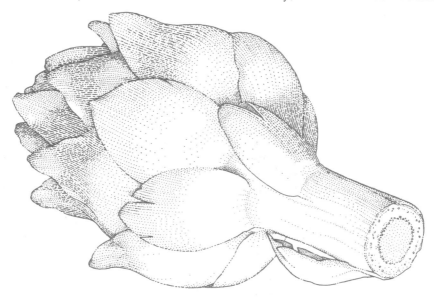

CARRÉ D'AGNEAU AU MIEL
Lamb chops stuffed with orange slices

METRIC/IMPERIAL	AMERICAN
4 thick lamb cutlets (with 2 rib bones)	4 double rib lamb chops
2 teaspoons vegetable oil	2 teaspoons vegetable oil
2 tablespoons flour	2 tablespoons all-purpose flour
2 tablespoons demerara sugar	2 tablespoons light brown sugar
4 orange slices	4 orange slices
7 tablespoons hot chicken stock	7 tablespoons hot chicken stock
2 tablespoons clear honey	2 tablespoons clear honey
½ teaspoon salt	½ teaspoon salt
freshly ground black pepper	freshly ground black pepper
sprigs of mint to garnish	sprigs of mint to garnish

With a sharp knife make two horizontal slits through the meat to the bone, but do not completely cut through. Brush both sides of the chops with oil and coat with flour. Sprinkle with the sugar, then insert an orange slice into each 'slit'.

PREHEAT A BROWNING SKILLET FOR 5 MINUTES (or according to the manufacturer's instructions). Quickly put the chops into the skillet, arranging the thicker parts towards the outside. MICROWAVE ON HIGH FOR 4 MINUTES, turning the chops over after 2 minutes.

Mix together the stock, honey, salt and pepper to taste, then pour into the skillet. Cover with a lid and MICROWAVE ON LOW FOR 8 TO 10 MINUTES until the meat is tender, giving the dish a half-turn once or twice during cooking.

Leave to stand, covered, for 5 minutes before serving. Garnish with sprigs of fresh mint and serve hot.

SERVES 4

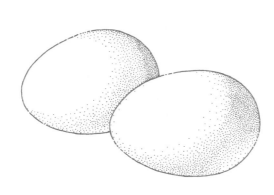

JULIENNES DE VEAU AUX PIMENTS À LA CRÈME
Veal and pimentos in a rich creamy sauce

METRIC/IMPERIAL	AMERICAN
500 g/1 lb fillet of veal	1 lb fillet of veal
1 × 225 g/8 oz can sweet pimentos, drained	1 × ½ lb can sweet pimentos, drained
2 tablespoons flour	2 tablespoons flour
2 tablespoons vegetable oil	2 tablespoons vegetable oil
1 small onion, chopped	1 small onion, chopped
300 ml/½ pint hot chicken stock	1¼ cups hot chicken stock
salt	salt
freshly ground black pepper	freshly ground black pepper
1 egg yolk	1 egg yolk
150 ml/¼ pint soured cream	⅔ cup sour cream

Slice the veal thinly and cut the veal and pimentos into strips, 1 × 7.5 cm/½ × 3 inches. Combine the flour and oil in a large deep dish and MICROWAVE ON HIGH FOR 3 MINUTES. Stir in the onion and MICROWAVE ON HIGH FOR 4 MINUTES, stirring occasionally. Add the veal strips and MICROWAVE ON HIGH FOR 2 MINUTES, stirring after 1 minute.

Pour the chicken stock over the veal and sprinkle with salt and pepper to taste. Gently stir in the pimentos and cover. MICROWAVE ON HIGH FOR 5 MINUTES. Stir, then MICROWAVE ON LOW FOR 10 MINUTES until the veal is tender.

Beat the egg yolk and soured cream together, then blend in 2 or 3 tablespoons of the hot sauce. Stir this mixture into the dish, then MICROWAVE ON LOW FOR 2 TO 3 MINUTES until the sauce has thickened. Leave to stand, covered, for 5 minutes before serving.

No additional garnish is required for this dish, although it may be served on a heated platter surrounded by a border of boiled rice.

SERVES 4

ESCALOPES AUTRICHE
Veal fillets in egg and breadcrumbs

METRIC/IMPERIAL	AMERICAN
500 g/1 lb veal fillet	1 lb fillet of veal
1 large egg, beaten	1 large egg, beaten
7 tablespoons golden crumbs or dark toasted breadcrumbs	7 tablespoons golden crumbs or dark toasted breadcrumbs
1 tablespoon flour	1 tablespoon flour
salt	salt
freshly ground black pepper	freshly ground black pepper
5 tablespoons vegetable oil	5 tablespoons vegetable oil
Garnish:	**Garnish:**
1 tablespoon chopped parsley	1 tablespoon chopped parsley
6 lemon slices	6 lemon slices

Cut the veal into slices, about 5 × 10 cm/2 × 4 inches, and beat to flatten with a mallet or rolling pin. Dip the veal slices into beaten egg and coat with the crumbs, pressing them on with a palette knife. Dust with flour and sprinkle with salt and pepper.

PREHEAT A LARGE BROWNING SKILLET FOR 5 MINUTES (or according to the manufacturer's instructions). Add the oil and MICROWAVE ON HIGH FOR 2 MINUTES. Quickly lay the veal in the dish and MICROWAVE ON HIGH FOR 5 MINUTES, turning the slices over after 2 minutes.

Drain on absorbent kitchen paper, then arrange on a heated serving dish and garnish with chopped parsley and twists of lemon.

SERVES 3 TO 4

ESCALOPES DE VEAU CORDON BLEU

Veal stuffed with ham and cheese

METRIC/IMPERIAL	AMERICAN
4 × 100 g/4 oz slices veal escalope	4 × ¼ lb slices veal fillet
100 g/4 oz cooked ham, thinly sliced	¼ lb cooked ham, thinly sliced
50 g/2 oz Edam cheese, thinly sliced	4 thin slices Edam cheese
1 egg, beaten	1 egg, beaten
40 g/1½ oz dried breadcrumbs	⅓ cup dry breadcrumbs
4 tablespoons vegetable oil	¼ cup vegetable oil
Garnish:	**Garnish:**
1 hard-boiled egg, chopped	1 hard-cooked egg, chopped
few sprigs of parsley	few sprigs of parsley
lemon wedges	lemon wedges

Beat the veal to flatten, with a mallet or rolling pin. Place a slice of ham and cheese on the centre of each. Fold up, completely enclosing the cheese and ham, to form a parcel. Dip into the beaten egg and coat with the crumbs.

PREHEAT A LARGE BROWNING SKILLET FOR 5 MINUTES (or according to the manufacturer's instructions). Quickly add the oil, then the veal and MICROWAVE ON HIGH FOR 1 MINUTE. Turn over and MICROWAVE ON HIGH FOR 5 MINUTES, giving the dish a half-turn after 2½ minutes. Drain on absorbent kitchen paper.

Transfer the veal to a heated serving dish. Garnish with chopped egg, parsley and lemon wedges.

SERVES 4

MEDAILLONS DE BOEUF SAUTÉ VIN BLANC

Fillet of beef, mushrooms, paprika, white wine, cream and brandy

METRIC/IMPERIAL	AMERICAN
500 g/1 lb fillet steak	1 lb beef fillet
2 tablespoons vegetable oil	2 tablespoons vegetable oil
25 g/1 oz butter	2 tablespoons butter
1 small onion, chopped	1 small onion, chopped
225 g/8 oz button mushrooms	2 cups button mushrooms
2 tablespoons flour	2 tablespoons flour
150 ml/¼ pint medium dry white wine	⅔ cup medium dry white wine
150 ml/¼ pint condensed beef consommé	⅔ cup condensed beef consommé
5 tablespoons water	⅓ cup water
1 teaspoon lemon thyme	1 teaspoon lemon thyme
1 teaspoon salt	1 teaspoon salt
¼ teaspoon black pepper	¼ teaspoon black pepper
1 teaspoon paprika	1 teaspoon paprika
½ teaspoon sugar	½ teaspoon sugar
3 tablespoons double cream	3 tablespoons heavy cream
Garnish:	**Garnish:**
sprigs of lemon thyme	sprigs of lemon thyme
Pommes de terre à la parisienne (see page 138)	Pommes de terre à la parisienne (see page 138)

Slice the fillet steak thinly and brush with the oil. Combine the butter and onion in a large shallow dish and MICROWAVE ON HIGH FOR 5 MINUTES until the onion begins to brown. Stir in the mushrooms and MICROWAVE ON HIGH FOR 3 MINUTES.

Sprinkle the flour over the mushrooms, turning them with a spoon to coat evenly. Stir in the wine, consommé, water, thyme, salt, pepper, paprika and sugar. MICROWAVE ON HIGH FOR 7 MINUTES. Stir in the cream, cover and set aside.

PREHEAT A LARGE BROWNING SKILLET FOR 5 MINUTES (or according to the manufacturer's instructions). Add the steak and toss quickly. MICROWAVE ON HIGH FOR 3 TO 4 MINUTES, stirring occasionally.

Add the steak to the sauce, stir well, MICROWAVE ON LOW FOR 2 TO 3 MINUTES until thoroughly reheated. Transfer to a large serving platter and garnish with sprigs of lemon thyme, and clusters of Pommes de terre à la parisienne.

SERVES 4

Left: Medaillons de boeuf sauté vin blanc

Right: Escalopes de veau cordon bleu; Escalopes de veau suedoise

ESCALOPES DE VEAU SUEDOISE
Veal cooked with button mushrooms, red wine and cream

METRIC/IMPERIAL	AMERICAN
500 g/1 lb veal escalope, thinly sliced	1 lb veal fillet, thinly sliced
25 g/1 oz plain flour	¼ cup all-purpose flour
1 teaspoon salt	1 teaspoon salt
½ teaspoon black pepper	½ teaspoon black pepper
50 g/2 oz butter	¼ cup butter
1 onion, chopped	1 onion, chopped
1 × 225 g/8 oz can button mushrooms	1 × 8 oz can button mushrooms
1 teaspoon dried oregano	1 teaspoon dried oregano
120 ml/4 fl oz dry red wine	½ cup dry red wine
5 tablespoons double cream	⅓ cup heavy cream
chopped parsley to garnish	chopped parsley to garnish

Beat the veal slices to flatten, with a mallet or rolling pin. Coat with flour, then season with salt and pepper.

Place half of the butter in a large shallow dish and MICROWAVE ON HIGH FOR 1 MINUTE until melted. Stir in the onion and MICROWAVE ON HIGH FOR 4 TO 5 MINUTES until soft and lightly browned, stirring occasionally.

Place the veal slices on top and dot with the remaining butter. MICROWAVE ON HIGH FOR 4 MINUTES then turn the veal over and add the mushrooms, together with their juice, the oregano and wine. Move the veal towards the sides of the dish, leaving a well in the centre. Cover with a lid or plastic cling film and MICROWAVE ON LOW FOR 30 MINUTES, stirring once or twice during cooking.

Add the cream, stir and MICROWAVE ON LOW or DEFROST FOR 5 MINUTES. Serve immediately, garnished with parsley and accompanied by carrots, if liked.

SERVES 4

131

FILETS DE BOEUF BORDELAISE
Fillet steak in a red wine sauce

METRIC/IMPERIAL	AMERICAN
4 × 150 g/6 oz fillet steaks	4 × 6 oz fillet steaks
25 g/1 oz butter	2 tablespoons butter
2 teaspoons Worcestershire sauce	2 teaspoons Worcestershire sauce
Sauce:	**Sauce:**
1 small onion, chopped	1 small onion, chopped
2 tablespoons vegetable oil	2 tablespoons vegetable oil
1 tablespoon flour	1 tablespoon flour
5 tablespoons canned beef consommé	⅓ cup canned beef consommé
5 tablespoons water	⅓ cup water
150 ml/¼ pint red wine	⅔ cup red wine
1 tablespoon brandy	1 tablespoon brandy

Spread the steaks with butter and brush with the Worcestershire sauce; cover and set aside.

To prepare the sauce, combine the onion and oil in a large shallow dish and MICROWAVE ON HIGH FOR 3 MINUTES until the onion turns brown. Stir in the flour and MICROWAVE ON HIGH FOR 2 MINUTES. Add the consommé, water, wine and brandy and MICROWAVE ON HIGH FOR 3 MINUTES, stirring occasionally. Cover and set aside.

PREHEAT A LARGE BROWNING SKILLET FOR 5 MINUTES (or according to the manufacturer's instructions). Quickly add two steaks, turning them over almost immediately. MICROWAVE ON HIGH FOR 2 MINUTES, turn the steaks over then MICROWAVE ON HIGH FOR 2 TO 3 MINUTES until cooked according to taste. Add to the sauce.

Wipe out the browning skillet with absorbent kitchen paper. REHEAT FOR 4 MINUTES, then MICROWAVE the remaining steaks. Add to the sauce and MICROWAVE ON HIGH FOR 3 MINUTES to reheat. Serve immediately.

SERVES 4

Note: Alternatively, cook the steaks simultaneously: MICROWAVE ON HIGH FOR 6 TO 10 MINUTES, until cooked according to taste. This method will not give the same crisp finish to the steaks.

CASSEROLE DE BOEUF SANTAUBUN
Beef with walnuts and celery cooked in beer

METRIC/IMPERIAL	AMERICAN
750 g/1 ½ lb chuck steak	1 ½ lb chuck steak
25 g/1 oz butter	2 tablespoons butter
2 tablespoons flour	2 tablespoons flour
1 onion, finely chopped	1 onion, finely chopped
4 sticks celery, thinly sliced	4 celery stalks, thinly sliced
100 g/4 oz shelled walnuts chopped	1 cup chopped walnuts
300 ml/½ pint hot water	1 ¼ cups hot water
1 beef stock cube, crumbled	1 beef bouillon cube, crumbled
300 ml/½ pint brown ale	1¼ cups brown ale
1 teaspoon salt	1 teaspoon salt
freshly ground black pepper	freshly ground black pepper

Trim the meat and cut into 2.5 cm/1 inch cubes. Put the butter in a large deep dish and MICROWAVE ON HIGH FOR 30 SECONDS. Blend in the flour and MICROWAVE ON HIGH FOR 5 MINUTES until beige in colour.

Add the meat, onion, celery and walnuts. Stir in the water and stock (bouillon) cube. MICROWAVE ON LOW FOR 30 MINUTES, stirring occasionally.

Add the brown ale, salt and pepper to taste. MICROWAVE ON LOW OR MEDIUM FOR 20 TO 30 MINUTES, stirring occasionally, then MICROWAVE ON HIGH FOR 15 MINUTES. Leave to stand, covered, for 10 minutes before serving.

SERVES 4

CARIBBEAN PORK

METRIC/IMPERIAL	AMERICAN
4 thick pork chops	4 thick pork chops
1 tablespoon flour	1 tablespoon flour
salt	salt
freshly ground black pepper	freshly ground black pepper
25 g/1 oz butter	2 tablespoons butter
1 small onion, finely chopped	1 small onion, finely chopped
150 ml/¼ pint soured cream	⅔ cup sour cream
2 bananas, sliced in half lengthways	2 bananas, sliced in half lengthways
1 teaspoon paprika	1 teaspoon paprika

Trim the surplus fat from the chops and coat with flour. Season with salt and pepper. Put the butter in a large browning skillet and MICROWAVE ON HIGH FOR 4 MINUTES. Quickly add the chops, turning them to brown on both sides. Remove the chops and set aside.

Return the browning skillet to the oven and MICROWAVE ON HIGH FOR 3 MINUTES. Add the onion and MICROWAVE ON HIGH FOR 3 MINUTES. Replace the chops, cover and MICROWAVE ON HIGH FOR 10 MINUTES, giving the dish a quarter-turn every 2 minutes.

Spoon off all surplus fat from the skillet. Stir in all but 2 tablespoons of the soured cream. Place a banana half on each chop and baste with the sour cream. Cover and MICROWAVE ON LOW FOR 5 MINUTES, giving the skillet a quarter-turn every minute.

Arrange the chops and creamy sauce on a hot serving platter. Spoon the remaining cream over the top and sprinkle with the paprika. Serve immediately.

SERVES 4

AUBERGINE (EGGPLANT) AND POTATO TIMBALE

METRIC/IMPERIAL	AMERICAN
500 g/1 lb aubergines, thinly sliced	1 lb eggplants, thinly sliced
salt	salt
225 g/8 oz potatoes	½ lb potatoes
2 large eggs	2 large eggs
300 ml/½ pint milk	1¼ cups milk
¼ teaspoon mustard powder	¼ teaspoon mustard powder
freshly ground black pepper	freshly ground black pepper

Place the aubergine (eggplant) slices in a colander and sprinkle generously with salt. Cover with a plate and leave for 1 hour. Rinse in cold water and pat dry with absorbent kitchen paper.

Meanwhile cook the potatoes in boiling salted water until just tender, drain and slice thinly. To prepare the sauce, beat together the eggs, milk, mustard, ½ teaspoon salt and pepper to taste.

PREHEAT A LARGE BROWNING SKILLET FOR 5 MINUTES (or according to the manufacturer's instructions). Add the butter and quickly toss in the aubergines (eggplant). Immediately MICROWAVE ON HIGH FOR 6 MINUTES, stirring briefly after 3 minutes. Arrange a layer of sliced potato on top, strain the sauce over the MICROWAVE ON LOW FOR 4 MINUTES. Draw the mixture away from the edges of the dish and MICROWAVE ON LOW FOR 6 MINUTES until the sauce is nearly set. Cover and leave to stand for 5 minutes before serving.

SERVES 4 TO 6

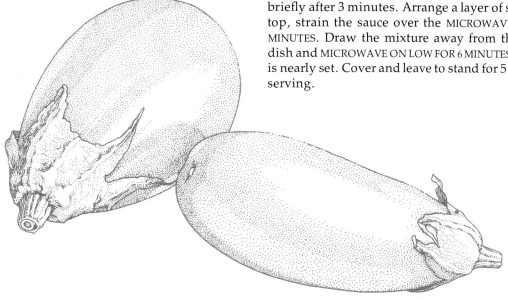

SALSIFIS EN SAUCE BLONDE
Salsify in piquant sauce

METRIC/IMPERIAL	AMERICAN
500 g/1 lb salsify	*1 lb salsify*
juice of ½ lemon	*juice of ½ lemon*
25 g/1 oz butter	*2 tablespoons butter*
salt	*salt*
1 tablespoon flour	*1 tablespoon flour*
1 tablespoon white wine	*1 tablespoon white wine*
freshly ground black pepper	*freshly ground black pepper*
1 tablespoon soured cream	*1 tablespoon sour cream*

Salsifis en sauce blonde; Courgettes entières; Mange-tout

Cut the salsify into 2.5 cm/½ inch pieces and place in a small deep dish. Immediately sprinkle with the lemon juice and stir well. Set aside for 10 minutes. Cover with cold water, then drain.

Add half of the butter and just enough salted water to cover the salsify. Cover the dish tightly with plastic cling film and MICROWAVE ON HIGH FOR 10 MINUTES, shaking occasionally. Drain the salsify, reserving 150 ml/¼ pint/⅔ cup of the liquor. Arrange the salsify in a hot serving dish. Cover and keep warm.

To make the sauce, blend the remaining butter with the flour. Whisk into the reserved liquor, a little at a time until thoroughly incorporated. Add the wine, season with pepper, then MICROWAVE ON HIGH FOR 2½ TO 3 MINUTES until the sauce thickens. Stir in the soured cream.

Pour the sauce over the salsify and serve at once.

SERVES 4

COURGETTES ENTIÈRES
Glazed whole courgettes (zucchini) with fresh nutmeg

METRIC/IMPERIAL	AMERICAN
12 small even-shaped firm courgettes	12 small even-shaped firm zucchini
25 g/1 oz unsalted butter	2 tablespoons sweet butter
1 teaspoon grated nutmeg	1 teaspoon grated nutmeg
salt	salt
freshly ground black pepper	freshly ground black pepper

Trim the courgettes (zucchini) and pierce each one in two or three places with the tip of a sharp knife. Put the butter and nutmeg in a large shallow dish and MICROWAVE ON HIGH FOR 30 SECONDS. Arrange the courgettes (zucchini) in a single layer in the dish and MICROWAVE ON HIGH FOR 3 MINUTES.

Transfer the courgettes (zucchini) in the centre of the dish to the edges. Baste with the butter. Cover loosely with plastic cling film and MICROWAVE ON HIGH FOR 4 MINUTES, giving the dish a half-turn after 2 minutes.

Leave to stand, covered, for 5 minutes; then without removing the plastic cling film, lightly press each courgette (zucchini) with a finger. Those which just yield to this pressure are cooked. Transfer any undercooked courgettes (zucchini) to a small dish and MICROWAVE ON HIGH FOR A FURTHER 30 SECONDS.

Transfer the courgettes (zucchini) to a heated serving dish, season with salt and pepper to taste and pour over the melted butter before serving.

SERVES 4

MANGE-TOUT
Sweet young (snow) peas in the pod

METRIC/IMPERIAL	AMERICAN
350 g/12 oz fresh mange-tout	¾ lb fresh snow peas
6 tablespoons water	6 tablespoons water
½ teaspoon salt	½ teaspoon salt
15 g/½ oz butter	1 tablespoon butter
sprigs of fresh mint to garnish	sprigs of fresh mint to garnish

Top and tail the mange-tout and discard any stringy spines. Combine the water and salt in a large shallow dish. Add the mange-tout (snow-peas), cover and MICROWAVE ON HIGH FOR 8 MINUTES, stirring occasionally. Leave to stand, covered, for 5 minutes. Drain, add the butter and toss well.

Serve garnished with sprigs of fresh mint.

SERVES 4

Note: Frozen mange-tout may be used if fresh ones are unobtainable. They will take approximately half the above cooking time (see chart on page 155).

SAFFRON AND PAPRIKA RICE

METRIC/IMPERIAL	AMERICAN
3 tablespoons dry white wine	3 tablespoons dry white wine
¼ teaspoon ground cumin	¼ teaspoon ground cumin
¼ teaspoon saffron powder	¼ teaspoon saffron powder
150 g/6 oz long-grain rice	1 cup long-grain rice
1 onion, finely chopped	1 onion, finely chopped
1 small green pepper, cored, seeded and chopped	1 small green pepper, cored, seeded and chopped
½ teaspoon salt	½ teaspoon salt
450 ml/¾ pint hot chicken stock	2 cups hot chicken stock
½ teaspoon paprika	½ teaspoon paprika
few drops red food colouring	few drops red food colouring
2 teaspoons water	2 teaspoons water

Combine the wine, cumin, and saffron in a large deep dish. MICROWAVE ON HIGH FOR 2 MINUTES until boiling. Stir in the rice, onion, green pepper, salt and stock. Cover and MICROWAVE ON HIGH FOR 10 TO 12 MINUTES until the rice is tender and the stock has been absorbed, stirring 2 or 3 times during cooking.

Leave to stand covered for 5 minutes. Transfer 3 to 4 tablespoons of the rice mixture to a separate dish and mix in the paprika, food colouring and water. Continue stirring until all the rice grains are red. Return to the saffron rice mixture and fold in gently. Serve hot.

SERVES 3 TO 4

Note: It may be necessary to add a little hot water during cooking if the rice absorbs all the stock before it is tender.

JULIENNES DE POMMES NOUVELLE

Grated new potatoes flavoured with Parmesan cheese

METRIC/IMPERIAL	AMERICAN
500 g/1 lb new potatoes	1 lb new potatoes
50 g/2 oz butter	¼ cup butter
1 teaspoon salt	1 teaspoon salt
freshly ground black pepper	freshly ground black pepper
50 g/2 oz Parmesan cheese, grated	½ cup grated Parmesan cheese
1 tablespoon chopped parsley	1 tablespoon chopped parsley

Wash and dry but do not scrape the potatoes. Place the butter in a large shallow dish and MICROWAVE ON HIGH FOR 1 MINUTE until melted. Stir in the salt, pepper to taste and Parmesan cheese. Using a fine cutter, grate the potato into the mixture and mix thoroughly. MICROWAVE ON HIGH FOR 10 MINUTES, stirring occasionally. Garnish with the chopped parsley and serve hot.

SERVES 4

PERSIAN RICE PILAFF

METRIC/IMPERIAL	AMERICAN
225 g/8 oz long-grain rice	½ cup + 2 tablespoons long-grain rice
50 g/2 oz butter	¼ cup butter
50 g/2 oz hazelnuts, finely chopped	½ cup finely chopped hazelnuts or filberts
600 ml/1 pint hot chicken or beef stock	2½ cups hot chicken or beef stock
1 teaspoon salt	1 teaspoon salt
1 teaspoon powdered cardamoms	1 teaspoon powdered cardamoms
½ teaspoon turmeric	½ teaspoon turmeric
25 g/1 oz sultanas	3 tablespoons golden raisins

Rinse the rice and drain thoroughly. Put the butter in a large deep casserole and MICROWAVE ON HIGH FOR 1 MINUTE. Stir in the rice. MICROWAVE ON HIGH FOR 3 MINUTES, stirring once during cooking. Add the hazelnuts and MICROWAVE ON HIGH FOR 2 MINUTES.

Stir in the stock, salt, cardamoms, turmeric and sultanas. MICROWAVE ON HIGH FOR 15 MINUTES, stirring once during cooking. Stir, then cover tightly and leave to stand for 5 minutes before serving.

SERVES 4 TO 6

Serve as a curry accompaniment, or simply with a mixed salad, or sprinkled with chopped hard-boiled (hard-cooked) egg.

DAHL

METRIC/IMPERIAL	AMERICAN
150 g/6 oz dried lentils	⅔ cup dried lentils
2 tablespoons vegetable oil	2 tablespoons vegetable oil
1 small onion, chopped	1 small onion, chopped
1 clove garlic, crushed	1 clove garlic, minced
1 teaspoon curry powder	1 teaspoon curry powder
¼ teaspoon ground ginger	¼ teaspoon ground ginger
¼ teaspoon chilli powder	¼ teaspoon chili powder
1 teaspoon salt	1 teaspoon salt
1 litre/¾ pint boiling water	4¼ cups boiling water

Rinse and drain the lentils. Combine the oil, onion, garlic, curry powder, ginger and chilli powder in a large deep dish and MICROWAVE ON HIGH FOR 4 MINUTES until the onions are lightly browned. Stir in the lentils, salt and boiling water. MICROWAVE ON HIGH FOR 25 TO 30 MINUTES until the lentils are tender, stirring 2 or 3 times during cooking.

Mash the lentils thoroughly, using a potato masher, to form a thick purée. Continue cooking for a further 3 to 5 minutes if the lentils are not soft enough to mash. Serve as a curry accompaniment or vegetable.

SERVES 4

RAITA

METRIC/IMPERIAL	AMERICAN
150 ml/¼ pint natural yogurt	⅔ cup unflavored yogurt
1 tablespoon lemon juice	1 tablespoon lemon juice
¼ teaspoon salt	¼ teaspoon salt
freshly ground black pepper	freshly ground black pepper
¼ cucumber, peeled and diced	¼ cucumber, peeled and diced
¼ teaspoon paprika powder	¼ teaspoon paprika powder

Mix the yogurt with the lemon juice, salt and pepper to taste. Stir in the diced cucumber. Turn into a serving dish and sprinkle with paprika. Serve as a curry accompaniment.

SERVES 4

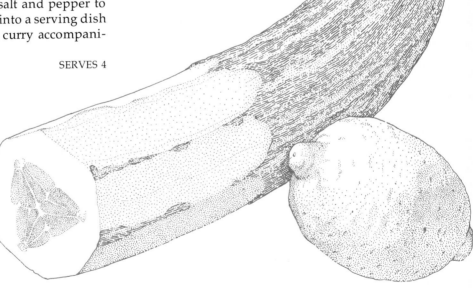
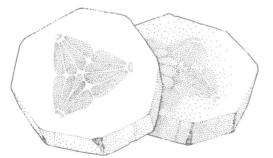

POTATO AND GREEN PEPPER RATATOUILLE

METRIC/IMPERIAL	AMERICAN
225 g/8 oz peeled potatoes	½ lb peeled potatoes
1 green pepper, cored and seeded	1 green pepper, cored and seeded
1 onion	1 onion
½ teaspoon salt	½ teaspoon salt
½ teaspoon pepper	½ teaspoon pepper
2 tablespoons vegetable oil	2 tablespoons vegetable oil
3 tablespoons soy sauce	3 tablespoons soy sauce
1 tablespoon water (approximately)	1 tablespoon water (approximately)

Slice the vegetables paper thin. (use a food processor or mandoline if you have one.) Combine all the ingredients in a large deep dish and make a well in the centre. Cover loosely with plastic cling film or a tight-fitting lid and MICROWAVE ON HIGH FOR 6 MINUTES.

Stir in a little more water if the ratatouille seems too dry. MICROWAVE ON HIGH FOR 6 TO 10 MINUTES until the potatoes are just tender. Leave to stand covered, for 5 minutes. Serve hot or cold.

SERVES 4

POMMES DE TERRE À LA PARISIENNE
Golden potato balls

METRIC/IMPERIAL	AMERICAN
500 g/1 lb large potatoes, peeled	1 lb large potatoes, peeled
1 tablespoon flour	1 tablespoon flour
1 teaspoon salt	1 teaspoon salt
1 teaspoon paprika	1 teaspoon paprika
50 g/2 oz butter	¼ cup butter
sprigs of parsley to garnish	sprigs of parsley to garnish

Using a potato baller or teaspoon, cut out small even-shaped balls from the potatoes. Shake in a cloth to dry, then coat with flour, salt and paprika.

Place the butter in a large browning skillet and MICROWAVE ON HIGH FOR 4 MINUTES. Quickly toss in the potato balls and stir once. MICROWAVE ON HIGH FOR 5 MINUTES until the potatoes are tender, stirring occasionally during cooking.

Transfer to a heated serving dish and garnish with parsley. Serve as an accompaniment, or as a garnish, for meat or fish dishes.

SERVES 4

JAMAICAN SAVARIN

Above: Jamaican savarin

Left: Preparing potato and green pepper ratatouille

METRIC/IMPERIAL
150 ml/¼ pint milk
2 teaspoons sugar
2 teaspoons dried yeast
225 g/8 oz plain flour
pinch of salt
150 g/5 oz butter
4 eggs, beaten
Syrup:
175 g/6 oz sugar
5 tablespoons water
2 tablespoons rum
Glaze:
6 tablespoons apricot jam
25 g/1 oz chopped mixed
    candied peel
To decorate:
fresh fruit to taste

AMERICAN
⅔ cup milk
2 teaspoons sugar
2 teaspoons active dry yeast
2 cups all-purpose flour
pinch of salt
½ cup + 2 tablespoons
    butter
4 eggs, beaten
Syrup:
⅔ cup + 2 tablespoons
    sugar
5 tablespoons water
2 tablespoons rum
Glaze:
6 tablespoons apricot
    conserve
3 tablespoons chopped
    mixed candied peel
To decorate:
fresh fruit to taste

Pour the milk into a jug and MICROWAVE ON HIGH FOR 30 SECONDS until warm. Whisk in the sugar and yeast with a fork. Set aside for 10 to 15 minutes until frothy.

Sift the flour and salt into a mixing bowl and MICROWAVE ON HIGH FOR 20 SECONDS. Make a well in the centre and pour in the yeast liquid. Draw some of the flour over the top. Cover and set aside for 40 minutes until the mixture is spongy.

Cut the butter into small pieces and add to the mixture with the beaten eggs. Beat thoroughly for at least 5 minutes until the mixture is smooth and elastic. Turn into a well-greased 2.2 litre/ 4 pint/2 quart ring mould. Cover with plastic cling film and leave in the microwave oven until doubled in bulk; MICROWAVE ON LOW FOR 15 SECONDS every 10 minutes to hasten rising.

When the mixture has risen half-way up the mould, MICROWAVE ON HIGH FOR 3 TO 3½ MINUTES, until just dry on top, giving the dish a quarter-turn every minute. Turn out on to a wire tray and allow to cool slightly.

To make the syrup, place the sugar and water in a large jug and MICROWAVE ON HIGH FOR 7 MINUTES. Stir in the rum. Spoon the syrup over the savarin and allow it to soak through.

Place the apricot jam (conserve) in a jug and MICROWAVE ON HIGH FOR 15 SECONDS. Spread over the top and sides of the savarin. Sprinkle the sides with chopped peel. Transfer carefully to a serving plate and allow to cool. Fill the centre of the savarin with chopped fresh fruit to taste and serve accompanied by fresh cream.

SERVES 8

Note: This cake may successfully be frozen. To defrost, MICROWAVE ON HIGH FOR 1 MINUTE, then leave to completely thaw at room temperature.

139

HONEY CHEESECAKE

METRIC/IMPERIAL	AMERICAN
75 g/3 oz butter	6 tablespoons butter
175 g/6 oz crunchy sweet biscuits, finely crushed	1¼ cups finely crushed cookie crumbs
500 g/1 lb cream cheese	2 × ½ lb packages cream cheese
100 g/4 oz caster sugar	½ cup sugar
3 eggs, beaten	3 eggs, beaten
2 teaspoons vanilla essence	2 teaspoons vanilla extract
¼ pint soured cream	⅔ cup sour cream
3 tablespoons clear honey	3 tablespoons clear honey
To decorate:	**To decorate:**
½ can cherry pie filling	1 cup cherry pie filling
150 ml/¼ pint double cream, whipped	⅔ cup heavy cream, whipped

Put the butter in a bowl and MICROWAVE ON HIGH FOR 1 MINUTE. Add the biscuit crumbs, stir well, then MICROWAVE ON HIGH FOR 1 MINUTE. Line the base of a 20 cm/8 in round flan dish with greaseproof paper or non-stick parchment. Press the crumbs into the base and the sides of the dish to form a flan case.

Beat the cheese, sugar, eggs and vanilla essence (extract) together until smooth. Pour this filling into the flan dish. MICROWAVE ON LOW FOR 20 TO 25 MINUTES until the centre is almost set, giving the dish a quarter-turn every 5 minutes during cooking.

Stir the soured cream into the honey, then pour over the top of the cheesecake. MICROWAVE ON HIGH FOR 1 MINUTE. Allow to cool, then chill in the refrigerator for 1 hour. Pile the cherry filling on top of the cake and decorate the edge with rosettes of whipped cream.

MAKES ONE 20 cm/8 inch CHEESECAKE

BAKEWELL TART

METRIC/IMPERIAL	AMERICAN
Pastry:	**Pastry:**
100 g/4 oz plain flour	1 cup all-purpose flour
50 g/2 oz butter	¼ cup butter
25 g/1 oz sugar	2 tablespoons sugar
2 egg yolks, beaten	2 egg yolks, beaten
Filling:	**Filling:**
50 g/2 oz butter	¼ cup butter
50 g/2 oz sugar	¼ cup sugar
1 egg, beaten	1 egg, beaten
25 g/1 oz ground almonds	¼ cup ground almonds
50 g/2 oz cake crumbs	1 cup cake crumbs
few drops of vanilla essence	few drops of vanilla extract
1 teaspoon lemon juice	1 teaspoon lemon juice
2 tablespoons raspberry jam	2 tablespoons raspberry jam
Topping:	**Topping:**
100 g/4 oz icing sugar, sifted	1 cup confectioners' sugar, sifted
1 tablespoon water	1 tablespoon water
red food colouring	red food colouring

Sift the flour into a bowl. Rub in the butter until the mixture resembles fine breadcrumbs, then stir in the sugar. Add the egg yolks and knead lightly until the mixture forms a ball. Put into a polythene (plastic) bag and chill in the refrigerator for at least 30 minutes.

Roll out the pastry thinly and use to line a 20 cm/8 inch fluted flan dish. Prick the base and sides of the pastry with a fork and MICROWAVE ON MEDIUM FOR 6 MINUTES until dry on top.

To prepare the filling, cream the butter and sugar together in a bowl until light and fluffy. Stir in the egg, almonds, cake crumbs, vanilla essence (extract) and lemon juice.

Spread a thin layer of jam over the base of the pastry, cover with the filling and MICROWAVE ON LOW FOR 6½ TO 7 MINUTES until the filling has set in the middle. Blend the icing (confectioners') sugar with the water to form a thin paste. Transfer 1 tablespoon of the icing to a separate bowl and beat in the red food colouring.

Pour the white icing over the flan, then quickly pipe thin straight lines of red icing, about 2.5 cm/1 inch apart; on top. Quickly draw a skewer across the lines, at right angles at similar intervals to create a feathered pattern.

MAKES ONE 20 cm/8 inch TART

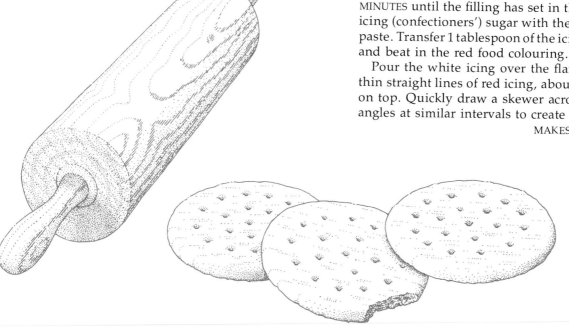

GÂTEAU ALLEMANDE
Raspberry gâteau with fresh cream

METRIC/IMPERIAL	AMERICAN
4 eggs, separated	4 eggs, separated
175 g/6 oz sugar	¾ cup sugar
grated rind and juice of 1 lemon	grated rind and juice of 1 lemon
75 g/3 oz fine semolina	½ cup semolina flour
1 tablespoon ground almonds	1 tablespoon ground almonds
2 tablespoons sweet sherry	2 tablespoons sweet sherry
500 g/1 lb raspberries	3 cups raspberries
sugar (optional)	sugar (optional)
300 ml/½ pint double cream, whipped	1¼ cups heavy cream, whipped
100 g/4 oz flaked almonds, toasted	1 cup slivered almonds, toasted

Place the egg yolks and sugar in a bowl and whisk together until thick and creamy. Add the lemon rind, juice, semolina and ground almonds. Stiffly beat the egg whites and fold them into the mixture.

Line two 18 cm/7 in flan dishes with plastic cling film. Spoon equal amounts of the mixture into each dish and spread evenly. Cook the cakes one at a time; MICROWAVE ON MEDIUM FOR 5 TO 6 MINUTES until dry on top, giving the dish a half-turn after 2½ minutes.

Leave the cakes in the dishes until cold, then invert one cake on to a serving plate. Sprinkle with the sherry, then cover with the raspberries, reserving a few for decoration. Add sugar to taste if desired.

Invert the other cake on top. Spread two-thirds of the cream over the sides and top of the cake. Press the almond around the sides and decorate the top with piped cream rosettes and the reserved raspberries.

MAKES ONE 18 cm/7 inch GÂTEAU

CRÈME BRULÉE

METRIC/IMPERIAL	AMERICAN
300 ml/½ pint double cream	1¼ cups heavy cream
300 ml/½ pint milk	1¼ cups milk
1 tablespoon granulated sugar	1 tablespoon granulated sugar
1 tablespoon vanilla essence	1 tablespoon vanilla extract
4 egg yolks, beaten	4 egg yolks, beaten
4 tablespoons brown sugar	⅓ cup brown sugar

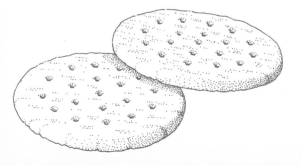

Combine the cream, milk, granulated sugar and vanilla essence (extract). Strain in the egg yolks and beat thoroughly. Divide the mixture between 4 or 6 individual ramekin dishes or custard cups.

Half-fill a 600 ml/1 pint /2½ cup measuring jug with cold water and put in the microwave oven. Arrange the ramekin dishes well-spaced out on the oven shelf. MICROWAVE ON HIGH FOR 5 TO 7 MINUTES, rearranging the dishes every 3 minutes and removing each one as soon as it is cooked. Test by inserting a knife into the centre; the crème is cooked when the knife comes out clean.

Leave to cool, then chill in the refrigerator for at least 4 hours before serving. Sprinkle the brown sugar over the chilled crème. Press lightly, then place under a preheated hot grill (broiler) until the sugar melts and caramelizes. Chill thoroughly in the refrigerator before serving.

SERVES 4 TO 6

STRAWBERRY SHORTCAKE

METRIC/IMPERIAL
225 g/8 oz plain flour
50 g/2 oz icing sugar
150 g/5 oz unsalted butter,
    softened
1/4 teaspoon vanilla essence
500 g/1 lb fresh strawberries
300 ml/1/2 pint double cream,
    whipped
25 g/1 oz granulated sugar

AMERICAN
2 cups all-purpose flour
1/2 cup confectioners' sugar
1/2 cup + 2 tablespoons
    sweet butter, softened
1/4 teaspoon vanilla extract
1 lb fresh strawberries
1 1/4 cups heavy cream,
    whipped
2 tablespoons granulated
    sugar

Sift the flour and icing sugar together in a bowl. Add the butter and vanilla essence (extract) and mix with a table knife until the butter is completely incorporated and the mixture resembles fine breadcrumbs.

Line the base of a 23 cm/9 inch round shallow dish with greaseproof paper or non-stick parchment. Spoon in the shortcake mixture and spread evenly. Press down with the back of a spoon to smooth the top. MICROWAVE ON LOW FOR 8 MINUTES or until a skewer, inserted into the centre of the shortcake, comes out clean; give the dish a quarter-turn every 2 minutes during cooking. Leave to cool in the dish for at least 1 hour.

Carefully turn out the shortcake onto a serving plate, or leave in the dish if preferred. Slice half the strawberries and arrange them, overlapping, over the shortcake. Cover with a thick layer of cream, then pile the remaining strawberries on top. Pipe the remaining whipped cream on top to decorate edges. Sprinkle generously with granulated sugar just before serving.

MAKES ONE 23 cm/9 inch CAKE

Note: Frozen strawberries are not recommended for this dessert but frozen blackberries, carefully thawed and drained, may be substituted if soft fruit is unobtainable.

CRÈME DE CHOCOLAT PRALINÉ

METRIC/IMPERIAL	AMERICAN
150 g/6 oz plain cooking chocolate	1 cup semi-sweet chocolate chips
4 tablespoons cold strong black coffee	¼ cup cold strong black coffee
25 g/1 oz butter softened	2 tablespoons butter, softened
1 tablespoon sugar	1 tablespoon sugar
1 teaspoon brandy	1 teaspoon brandy
75 g/3 oz finely crushed praline (see page 145)	½ cup (firmly packed) finely crushed praline (see page 145)
175 g/6 fl oz double cream	¾ cup heavy cream
little grated chocolate	little grated chocolate
To serve:	**To serve:**
few boudoir biscuits or ratafias	few boudoir biscuits or ratafias

Put the chocolate and coffee in a bowl and MICROWAVE ON HIGH FOR 3 MINUTES until the chocolate is melted. Beat thoroughly, then add the butter, sugar, brandy and praline. Leave to cool slightly.

Whip the cream until it forms soft peaks. Fold most of the cream into the chocolate mixture, reserving the remainder for decoration. Divide the crème between 4 to 6 ramekin dishes and chill in the refrigerator for at least 1 hour before serving.

Whip the remaining cream until stiff and use to pipe a rosette on each serving. Sprinkle with grated chocolate to decorate. Serve with boudoir biscuits or ratafias.

SERVES 4 TO 6

ZABAGLIONE

METRIC/IMPERIAL	AMERICAN
1 large egg	1 large egg
2 large egg yolks	2 large egg yolks
50 g/2 oz caster sugar	¼ cup sugar
150 ml/¼ pint sweet sherry	⅔ cup sweet sherry
To serve:	**To serve:**
4 sponge fingers	4 ladies fingers

Place the whole egg and egg yolks in a large bowl, remove the threads, then whisk until creamy. Add the sugar and continue whisking until the mixture is light and the consistency of half-whipped cream.

Pour the sherry into a jug and MICROWAVE ON HIGH FOR 1½ TO 2 MINUTES until just boiling. Pour onto the eggs, in a thin stream, whisking continuously. As soon as the mixture thickens, MICROWAVE ON LOW FOR 1 TO 1½ MINUTES until the sides of the bowl feel warm. Beat vigorously for 4 to 5 minutes until the zabaglione is thick. Spoon into warmed stemmed glasses and serve at once, decorated with sponge (ladies) fingers.

SERVES 4

Note: For best results use an electric mixer, on high speed, to whisk the zabaglione before serving to make the mixture as thick and frothy as possible. If obtainable, use Marsala or Madeira in place of sweet sherry for this Italian dessert.

Above left: Strawberry shortcake

Above right: Zabaglione; Crème de chocolat praliné

ORANGES ÉPICE
Caramelized oranges, flavoured with mint

METRIC/IMPERIAL	AMERICAN
4 large oranges	4 large oranges
25 g/1 oz unsalted butter	2 tablespoons sweet butter
50 g/2 oz demarara sugar	⅓ cup light brown sugar
1 tablespoon chopped mint	1 tablespoon chopped mint
20 cloves	20 cloves
Syrup:	**Syrup:**
100 g/4 oz sugar	½ cup sugar
4 tablespoons water	4 tablespoons water
To decorate:	**To decorate:**
4 sprigs of mint	4 sprigs of mint

Grate the rind from the oranges and set aside. Remove all of the pith with a sharp knife and cut each orange horizontally into 4 or 5 slices. Blend the butter, half of the sugar and chopped mint together.

Spread a little of the mixture over each orange slice, then re-assemble the slices to form whole oranges. Spread the rest of the mixture over the outside of the oranges and sprinkle with the remaining sugar and grated orange rind. Insert a wooden cocktail stick (toothpick) through the centre of each orange to secure. Press 5 or 6 cloves into each orange.

To prepare the syrup, spread the sugar in a large shallow dish and sprinkle with the water. MICROWAVE ON HIGH FOR 1 MINUTE until melted. Stir, then MICROWAVE ON HIGH FOR 1 MINUTE until a thick syrup is formed.

Place the oranges in the syrup and MICROWAVE ON HIGH FOR 1 MINUTE. Baste with the syrup and give the dish a half-turn. MICROWAVE ON HIGH FOR 3 MINUTES. Baste again. Leave until cold to allow the oranges to fully absorb the flavours of the spices.

To reheat for serving, MICROWAVE ON HIGH FOR 2 TO 3 MINUTES. Decorate with sprigs of mint.

SERVES 4

GLACÉ (CANDIED) GRAPES

METRIC/IMPERIAL	AMERICAN
175 g/6 oz bunch of large grapes	6 oz bunch of large grapes
100 g/4 oz granulated sugar	½ cup granulated sugar
1 teaspoon powdered glucose	1 teaspoon powdered glucose
5 tablespoons water	5 tablespoons water

Prepare glacé (candied) fruit no longer than 1 hour before serving. Wash and dry the grapes throughly and separate into pairs. Brush a baking tray with oil or line with non-stick parchment.

Place the sugar, glucose and water in a large jug. Stir once. MICROWAVE ON HIGH FOR 5 TO 6½ MINUTES until a sugar thermometer registers 155°C, 310°F, when the crack stage is reached and a little of the syrup poured into cold water forms brittle strands. Do not stir during cooking.

Using a fork, quickly dip the grapes, one pair at a time, into the syrup to coat completely. Place on the prepared tray and leave for 5 minutes until set.

MAKES ABOUT 12 PAIRS GRAPES

Note: Other fresh fruit such as cherries and orange segments may be glacéd (candied) in the same way with similar success, provided they are completely dry before dipping in the syrup.

CHOCOLATE MARZIPAN CHERRIES

METRIC/IMPERIAL	AMERICAN
1 × 225 g/8 oz packet marzipan	1 × ½ lb package marzipan
few drops of pink food colouring	few drops pink food colouring
16 to 20 glacé cherries	16 to 20 candied cherries
175 g/6 oz plain cooking chocolate	6 oz semi-sweet cooking chocolate

Knead the marzipan lightly, pour on the pink food colouring and knead until an even colour is obtained. Divide into 16 to 20 even-sized pieces. Roll each one into a ball, then flatten to form a circle. Place a cherry in the centre of each, draw up the sides and roll gently between the palms of the hands until no joins are visible.

Arrange the marzipan cherries on a tray and chill in the refrigerator for 30 minutes. Place the chocolate in a small bowl and MICROWAVE ON HIGH FOR 2 TO 3 MINUTES until melted but still holding its shape. Dip the cherry balls into the chocolate, one at a time, to coat thoroughly. Leave until the chocolate has set. Serve chilled, if preferred.

MAKES 16 TO 20 MARZIPAN CHERRIES

MARRONS GLACÉS
Chestnuts in syrup

METRIC/IMPERIAL	AMERICAN
750 g/1½ lb large chestnuts	1½ lb large chestnuts
350 g/12 oz granulated sugar	¾ lb granulated sugar
350 g/12 oz powdered glucose	¾ lb powdered glucose
300 ml/½ pint water	1⅓ cups water
1 teaspoon vanilla essence	1 teaspoon vanilla extract

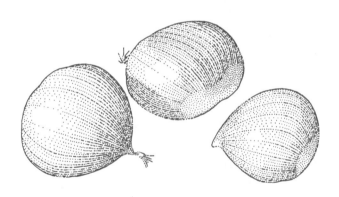

Start preparing marrons glacés at least 3 days before you intend to serve them.

Slit the chestnuts and place 10 on the oven shelf. MICROWAVE ON HIGH FOR 2 TO 3 MINUTES, stirring frequently, until the chestnuts are soft. Quickly remove the skins. Repeat with the remaining chestnuts.

Combine the sugar, glucose, water and vanilla essence (extract) in a large bowl. Mix thoroughly, then set aside for 15 minutes. Stir again, then MICROWAVE ON HIGH FOR 5 MINUTES or until the mixture is boiling. MICROWAVE ON HIGH FOR 2 MINUTES. Add the chestnuts and MICROWAVE ON HIGH FOR 2 MINUTES. Cover and set aside for 24 hours.

Without covering, MICROWAVE ON HIGH FOR 5 MINUTES or until boiling, then MICROWAVE ON HIGH FOR 2 MINUTES. Cover and set aside for a further 24 hours. Repeat the process once more.

Carefully remove the chestnuts from the syrup and leave on a wire rack to drain and cool. When cold, wrap each chestnut in waxed paper.

MAKES 20 TO 30 MARRONS GLACÉS

PRALINE

METRIC/IMPERIAL	AMERICAN
100 g/4 oz whole almonds	¾ cup whole almonds
225 g/8 oz granulated sugar	1 cup granulated sugar

Cut a double sheet of non-stick parchment to fit the oven shelf. Mix the almonds and sugar on the parchment. MICROWAVE ON HIGH FOR 11 TO 13 MINUTES until the sugar melts to form a dark brown syrup, frequently stirring and turning the mixture with a wooden spoon during cooking.

Leave to cool in the oven, then remove the praline from the oven and crush with a rolling pin or pulverize in an electric blender.

Use crushed praline in confectionery, and to decorate cakes and desserts.

MAKES 275 g/10 oz/1¾ Cups PRALINE

Note: Mixtures with a high sugar content reach very high temperatures during cooking. The praline will continue to cook rapidly after the oven is switched off. Take care not to overcook, as this will give the praline a bitter flavour.

COFFEE

Make the coffee in the usual way at a convenient time. To reheat, pour the quantity required for the first serving into a suitable jug and MICROWAVE ON HIGH for the time specified below. Set aside the remaining coffee for reheating later to give your guests a second cup.

Milk heats slightly quicker than black coffee and reheating time is, of course, dependent on the starting temperature. The coffee and milk may be reheated simultaneously, but to make certain neither boils, set the oven on the lower recommended time and continue cooking to the maximum time only if necessary.

HEATING TIMES FROM COLD:

Black Coffee:

600 ml/1 pint/2 ½ cups	MICROWAVE ON HIGH FOR 4¼ TO 4¾ MINUTES. Cover immediately.
1.2 litres/2 pints/5 cups	MICROWAVE ON HIGH FOR 7 TO 7½ MINUTES. Cover immediately.

Milk:

150 ml/¼ pint/⅔ cup	Whisk with a fork and MICROWAVE ON HIGH FOR 1 TO 1¼ MINUTES. Cover immediately.
300 ml/½ pint/1 ¼ cups	Whisk with a fork and MICROWAVE ON HIGH FOR 2 TO 2¼ MINUTES. Cover immediately.

Coffee and milk simultaneously:

600 ml/1 pint/2 ½ cups cold black coffee and 150 ml/¼ pint/1 ¼ cups cold milk	Place the jugs in the oven, whisk the milk and without covering, MICROWAVE ON HIGH FOR 5 TO 5½ MINUTES.

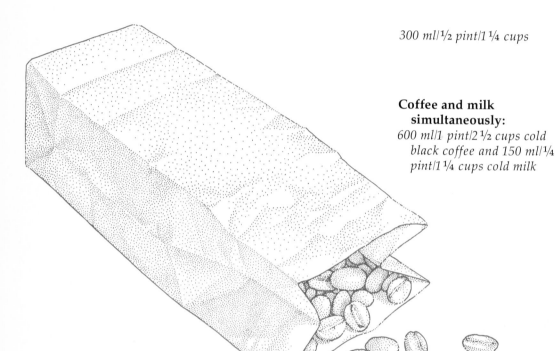

GAELIC COFFEE

METRIC/IMPERIAL	AMERICAN
750 ml/1 ¼ pints cold strong black coffee	3 cups cold strong black coffee
12 tablespoons Scotch whisky	12 tablespoons Scotch whisky
8 to 12 teaspoons sugar	8 to 12 teaspoons sugar
4 tablespoons double cream	4 tablespoons heavy cream

Put the coffee in a suitable jug, whisk with a fork and MICROWAVE ON HIGH FOR 4½ TO 5 MINUTES until steaming. Cover and set aside. Put 3 tablespoons whisky in each of 4 stemmed glasses and add sugar to taste.

Arrange the glasses in the oven and MICROWAVE ON HIGH FOR 1¼ TO 1½ MINUTES until the whisky is warm. Stir until the sugar is dissolved, then fill with coffee to within 1 cm/½ inch of the rim.

Carefully pour a tablespoon of cream over the back of a spoon onto the surface of each coffee so that it forms a separate layer. Serve immediately.

SERVES 4

ICELANDIC COFFEE

METRIC/IMPERIAL	AMERICAN
600 ml/1 pint strong coffee	2½ cups strong coffee
150 ml/¼ pint Grand Marnier	⅔ cup Grand Marnier
4 tablespoons demerara sugar	4 tablespoons light brown sugar
120 ml/4 fl oz double cream, whipped	½ cup heavy cream, whipped

Put the coffee in a suitable jug, whisk with a fork and MICROWAVE ON HIGH FOR 4½ TO 5 MINUTES until steaming. Cover and set aside. Divide the Grand Marnier between 4 drinking glasses, arrange on the oven shelf and MICROWAVE ON HIGH FOR 30 SECONDS. Remove from the oven, ignite and add the sugar and coffee while still flaming.

Top each glass with a generous spoonful of whipped cream and serve immediately.

SERVES 4

MULLED WINE

METRIC/IMPERIAL	AMERICAN
750 ml/1¼ pints red wine	3 cups red wine
12 cloves	12 cloves
2 small pieces of cinnamon stick	2 small pieces of cinnamon stick
grated rind and juice of 1 lemon	grated rind and juice of 1 lemon
grated rind and juice of 1 orange	grated rind and juice of 1 orange
2–3 tablespoons brown sugar	2–3 tablespoons brown sugar

Combine the wine, cloves, cinnamon, lemon and orange rinds and juice in a large bowl and MICROWAVE ON HIGH FOR 5 MINUTES until nearly boiling. Strain into a heated bowl, add sugar to taste and serve warm.

SERVES 6

Note: Take care not to sweeten too much. More sugar may be added to the wine when serving.

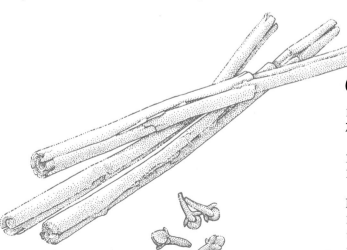

ORANGE AND LEMON TEA

METRIC/IMPERIAL	AMERICAN
750 ml/1¼ pints cold weak tea, strained	3 cups cold weak tea, strained
1 lemon, washed and sliced	1 lemon, washed and sliced
1 orange, washed and sliced	1 orange, washed and sliced

Pour the tea into a large serving jug and MICROWAVE ON HIGH FOR 4¾ TO 5¼ MINUTES until boiling. Add the fruit, then cover tightly. Leave to infuse for 5 minutes before pouring into heated glasses, adding a lemon and orange slice to each glass.

SERVES 4

DINNER PARTY MENUS

MENU 1

Corn and crab soup (*page 120*)

Escalopes de veau cordon bleu (*page 130*)
Potato and green pepper ratatouille (*page 138*)
Baked tomatoes
Green salad

Crème de chocolat praliné (*page 143*)

Coffee (*page 146*)
Glacé (candied) grapes (*page 144*)

Suggested wine: Beaujolais

ADVANCE PREPARATION

1 week before:	Cook and freeze soup. Make and freeze chocolate dessert.
Night before:	Transfer soup to refrigerator to thaw slowly. Cook ratatouille.
On the morning:	Cook escalopes; prepare garnish. Wash salad. Wash and dry grapes; stir sugar into water and leave to dissolve. Halve tomatoes, set in a circle on a plate.
2 hours before:	Remove dessert from freezer. Make coffee. Cool wine. Finish cooking syrup and dip grapes.
30 minutes before:	Heat conventional oven on low setting; set plates to warm. Reheat ratatouille (5 minutes on HIGH). Keep warm in conventional oven. Microwave tomatoes (3 to 4 minutes on HIGH). Keep warm in conventional oven.
Just before meal:	Reheat soup (5 to 7 minutes on HIGH).
During 1st course:	Reheat veal (10 to 12 minutes on LOW).

MENU 2

Soured cream and caviar tartlets (*page 113*)

Casserole de boeuf Santaubun (*page 132*)
Pommes de terre à la parisienne (*page 138*)
Mange-tout (*page 135*)
Glazed carrots (*page 97*)

Gâteau allemande (*page 141*)
or Apfelromtopf (*page 108*)

Cheeseboard

Coffee (*page 146*)

Suggested wine: St. Emilion

ADVANCE PREPARATION

1 week before:	Cook and freeze casserole. Make and freeze gâteau.
Day before:	Make caviar tartlet cases; store in airtight tin. Make apfelromtopf; leave in refrigerator.
On the morning:	Cook vegetables. Transfer casserole to refrigerator.
2 hours before:	Remove gâteau from the freezer. Make coffee. Uncork wine; leave at room temperature.
30 minutes before:	Heat conventional oven on low setting; set plates to warm. Reheat casserole (8 to 10 minutes on HIGH); keep warm in conventional oven. Heat tartlet cases (1 minute on HIGH). Warm cream, fill tartlets and keep warm in conventional oven. Reheat potatoes (2 minutes on HIGH); keep warm, uncovered.
During 1st course;	Reheat mange-tout and carrots together (5 minutes on HIGH).
After main course:	Reheat apfelromtopf (4 minutes on MEDIUM).

MENU 3

Vichysoisse (*page 118*)

Caneton lychée (*page 125*)
Broccoli spears (*page 92*)
Courgette (Zucchini) and tomato casserole (*page 95*)
Brown rice (*page 99*)

Bakewell tart
or Zabaglione (*page 143*)

Cheeseboard

Coffee (*page 146*)
Chocolate marzipan cherries

Suggested wine: Pouilly Fuissé

ADVANCE PREPARATION

1 week before:	Prepare chocolate marzipan cherries and refrigerate. Cook bakewell tart and freeze without icing. Cook and freeze rice.
Day before:	Make soup. Chill. Transfer tart to refrigerator; top with icing when thawed.
On the morning:	Cook vegetables. Cook duck but do not add lychees or garnish.
2 hours before:	Make coffee. Chill wine.
30 minutes before:	Heat conventional oven on low setting, set plates to warm. Reheat duck (4 to 6 minutes on MEDIUM); garnish and keep warm in conventional oven. Reheat courgette (zucchini) casserole (2 minutes on HIGH); keep warm in conventional oven. Prepare zabaglione; leave in bowl.
During 1st course:	Heat rice (4 to 6 minutes on MEDIUM).
After main course:	Warm zabaglione (1 minute on LOW); whisk, then pour into glasses.

MENU 4

Aspèrges au beurre maltaise (*page 114*)

Saumon meunière (*page 122*)
Juliennes de pommes nouvelles (*page 136*)
Jade spinach (*page 92*)

Jamaican Savarin (*page 139*)
or Strawberry shortcake (*page 142*)

Coffee (*page 146*)
or Orange and lemon tea (*page 147*)

Suggested wine: Gewüztraminer

ADVANCE PREPARATION

1 week before:	Make and freeze savarin. Make shortcake base, store in airtight tin.
On the morning:	Cook potatoes. Wash and prepare spinach; put in roaster bag. Unwrap savarin; thaw at room temperature.
2 hours before:	Cook asparagus; make beurre maltaise. Make coffee, or make and strain tea. Chill wine. Decorate shortcake.
30 minutes before:	Heat conventional oven on low setting; set plates to warm. Reheat potato dish (5 to 6 minutes on MEDIUM); keep warm in conventional oven. Cook salmon; keep warm in conventional oven.
Just before meal:	Reheat asparagus (3 to 5 minutes on MEDIUM). Warm sauce (2 minutes on LOW).
During 1st course:	Cook spinach (5 minutes on HIGH).
After main course:	Warm savarin (30 seconds on LOW). Fill with fruit and top with cream.
During dessert course:	Heat and infuse tea (4¾ to 5¼ minutes on HIGH).

MICROWAVE COOKING CHARTS

GUIDE TO ROASTING MEAT AND POULTRY

If you have a microwave oven with a choice of setting, use the optimum setting stated; otherwise cook on HIGH.

As far as possible, choose regular-shaped cuts of meat for microwave roasting to ensure even cooking.

Weigh the meat or poultry and calculate the approximate roasting time according to the oven setting to be used. Roasting time will also depend upon the shape of the meat or poultry and its temperature before cooking by microwave.

Season the meat and place on a trivet or an upturned plate in a large dish. Cover with greaseproof (waxed) paper to prevent splattering. Alternatively, place in a roaster bag.

After microwaving, wrap in foil, or leave in the roaster bag, if used, and allow to stand for 10 to 15 minutes before serving.

Type of Meat	Optimum Setting	Cooking Time on MEDIUM per 500 g/1 lb	Cooking Time on HIGH per 500 g/1 lb	Internal Temperature after Standing Time	Special Points
BEEF					
rare	MEDIUM	11–13 minutes	6–7 minutes	60°C/140°F	Choose top quality beef. Boned and rolled
medium	MEDIUM	13–15 minutes	7–8 minutes	70°C/160°F	rump and topside are ideal.
well-cooked	MEDIUM	15–17 minutes	8½–9 minutes	75°C/170°F	
CHICKEN,					
whole	MEDIUM	9–10 minutes	6–8 minutes	90°C/190°F	Cook whole chicken in a roaster bag, adding a
1 serving piece	HIGH	—	2½–3½ minutes	90°C/190°F	little stock. Cover tips of wings and legs with foil.
2 serving pieces	HIGH	—	3½–5½ minutes	90°C/190°F	
3 serving pieces	HIGH	—	4½–6½ minutes	90°C/190°F	
4 serving pieces	HIGH	—	6–9 minutes	90°C/190°F	
DUCKLING	MEDIUM	9–11 minutes	6–8 minutes	90°C/190°F	Cook in a roaster bag. Turn half-way through cooking.
LAMB	MEDIUM	11–13 minutes	8–10 minutes	80°C/180°F	When roasting leg of lamb, cover pointed end with a small piece of foil half-way through cooking.
PORK	MEDIUM	13–15 minutes	9–10 minutes	75°C/170°F	Score fat and sprinkle liberally with salt to obtain crisp crackling.
TURKEY	MEDIUM	11–13 minutes	9–11 minutes	90°C/190°F	Cook in a roaster bag. Turn at least once during cooking.
VEAL	MEDIUM	11–12 minutes	8½–9 minutes	75°C/170°F	

MEAT THERMOMETERS

A meat thermometer registers the internal temperature of meat and is useful for assessing whether a roast is cooked. Although ordinary meat thermometers must NOT be used in the microwave oven, they can be inserted into the centre of the meat when it is removed from the oven. Special microwave meat thermometers are obtainable; these may be left in large pieces of meat or poultry during roasting.

Note: If your microwave oven is fitted with a probe, set it at the temperature indicated above and allow standing time as stated.

GUIDE TO MICROWAVE OVEN SETTINGS

Different oven models use different symbols to denote settings. The following chart enables you to identify the settings used in this book (by arrows) with your own particular oven.

Note: There is no significant change in microwave cooking time unless the difference in setting is greater than 150 watts.

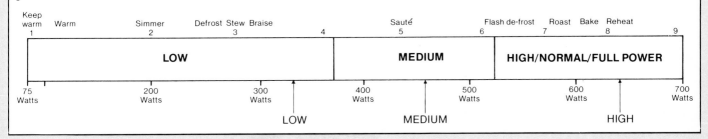

GUIDE TO COOKING FISH

Type of Fish	Quantity	Cooking Time on HIGH	Special Points
BASS (*whole*)	500 g/1 lb	5–7 minutes	Cover the head and tail with foil and make 2 or 3 slits in the skin to prevent bursting
COD STEAKS	500 g/1 lb	4–5 minutes	Cover with greaseproof (waxed) paper
HADDOCK FILLETS	500 g/1 lb	5–7 minutes	Cover the head and tail with foil and make 2 or 3 slits in the skin to prevent bursting
HADDOCK STEAKS	500 g/1 lb	4–5 minutes	Cover with greaseproof (waxed) paper
HALIBUT STEAKS	500 g/1 lb	4–5 minutes	Cover with greaseproof (waxed) paper
KIPPER (*whole*)	1 kipper	1–2 minutes	Cover with plastic cling film
LOBSTER (*whole*)	500 g/1 lb	6–8 minutes	Allow to stand for 5 minutes before serving
LOBSTER TAILS	500 g/1 lb	5–6 minutes	Turn over half-way through cooking
PRAWNS AND SHRIMPS (*peeled*)	500 g/1 lb	5–6 minutes	Arrange in a circle
RED SNAPPER (*whole*)	500 g/1 lb	5–7 minutes	Cover the head and tail with foil and make 2 or 3 slits in the skin to prevent bursting
SALMON STEAKS	500 g/1 lb	4–5 minutes	Cover with greaseproof (waxed) paper
SALMON TROUT (*whole*)	500 g/1 lb	7–8 minutes	Cover the head and tail with foil and make 2 or 3 slits in the skin to prevent bursting
SCALLOPS	500 g/1 lb	5–7 minutes	Cover with greaseproof (waxed) paper
SMOKED HADDOCK (*whole*)	500 g/1 lb	4–5 minutes	Cover with plastic cling film
TROUT (*whole*)	500 g/1 lb	8–9 minutes	Cover the head and tail with foil and make 2 or 3 slits in the skin to prevent bursting

Note: Allow slightly longer cooking times if the fish is to be cooked in a sauce.

DEFROSTING FISH

The most suitable setting for defrosting fish, particularly whole fish, is LOW.
To thaw whole fish, MICROWAVE ON LOW, allowing 8 to 12 minutes per 500 g/1 lb, giving the dish a half-turn after 4 minutes.

To thaw fish fillets, MICROWAVE ON LOW FOR 6 TO 8 MINUTES per 500 g/1 lb.

To thaw shellfish, MICROWAVE ON LOW FOR 7 TO 8 MINUTES per 500 g/1 lb.

To defrost fish using the HIGH setting, MICROWAVE ON HIGH FOR 15 SECONDS, then allow to stand for 2 minutes. Repeat until evenly thawed, turning the fish frequently.

GUIDE TO DEFROSTING MEAT AND POULTRY
ON DEFROST

Type of Meat	Defrosting Time per 500 g/1 lb	Special Points
BEEF,		
cuts for roasting	9 minutes	Turn once during defrosting
minced (ground)	10 minutes	Break up lumps with a fork occasionally during defrosting
steak, large	8 minutes	Turn once during defrosting
small	4 minutes	Turn once during defrosting
CHICKEN,		
whole	6 minutes	Turn every 1½ minutes during defrosting
pieces	5 minutes	Turn once during defrosting
DUCKLING	6 minutes	Turn every 1½ minutes during defrosting

Type of Meat	Defrosting Time per 500 g/1 lb	Special Points
KIDNEY	4 minutes	Turn once during defrosting
LAMB,		
cuts for roasting	10 minutes	Turn once during defrosting
chops	5 minutes	Turn once during defrosting
LIVER	4 minutes	Turn once during defrosting
PORK	8½ minutes	Turn once during defrosting
VEAL	9 minutes	Turn once during defrosting

Note: These are only approximate timings. Defrosting time is influenced by the size and shape of the meat or poultry, and by the starting temperature.

DEFROSTING ON HIGH

To defrost meat and poultry using the high setting, MICROWAVE ON HIGH allowing 1 minute for every 500 g/1 lb, then leave to stand for 10 minutes. Repeat until the meat is thawed.

GUIDE TO HEATING TIME FOR LIQUIDS

Liquid	Amount	Time on High
CHOCOLATE	1 cup	1 minute
COCOA	1 cup	1½ to 2 minutes
COFFEE	600 ml/1 pint (2½ cups)	5 minutes to boiling
black	1 cup	2½–2¾ minutes
	2 cups	3¼–3½ minutes
	3 cups	4¼–4½ minutes
	4 cups	5½–5¾ minutes
	5 cups	6¾–7 minutes
	6 cups	8¼–8½ minutes
TEA	1 cup	1¼–1½ minutes

Liquid	Amount	Time on High
MILK	1 litre/1¾ pints (3¾ cups)	7–8 minutes to steaming
	150 ml/¼ pint (⅔ cup)	1½ minutes to boiling
	300 ml/½ pint (1¼ cups)	2½ minutes to boiling
	600 ml/1 pint (2½ cups)	4 minutes to boiling
SOUP	600 ml/1 pint	5–7 minutes
	200 ml/⅓ pint (1 cup)	2½–3 minutes
WATER	150 ml/¼ pint (⅔ cup)	1¾ minutes to boiling
	200 ml/⅓ pint (1 cup)	1½–2 minutes to boiling
	300 ml/½ pint (1¼ cups)	3 minutes to boiling
	600 ml/1 pint (2½ cups)	5 minutes to boiling

Drinks should be heated to 60°–65°C (140°–150°F). A cup may be filled to the brim if it is to be heated to this temperature. If however, the liquid is to be boiled, leave at least 1 cm/½ inch at the top to avoid boiling over. Whisking liquids with a fork occasionally during heating also helps to prevent boiling over.

If several cups are being heated at one time, arrange them in a circle on the oven shelf.

Heat for the minimum time recommended above, then check the temperature of the liquid.

Do not heat liquids in tall narrow bottles, such as milk bottles. Small amounts of liquid are better not covered during reheating.

For ovens with a choice of setting, heat milk and milk-based drinks on MEDIUM rather than HIGH; increase the above timings by one-third.

GUIDE TO COOKING RICE

Because of the different manufacturing processes for treating rice, the cooking times and the amount of water required will vary considerably. As a general rule, when cooking rice by microwave, follow the packet instructions for conventional boiling, but allow a little extra water.

Make sure you use a large enough casserole. The rice will swell to about 3 times its dry volume during cooking.

MICROWAVE ON HIGH.

LONG-GRAIN RICE (*Traditional method*)

Quantity	Water (boiling)	Salt	Microwave Cooking Time	Special Points
50 g/2 oz (⅓ cup)	300 ml/½ pint (1¼ cups)	½ teaspoon	8–10 minutes	Rinse rice thoroughly. After cooking, rinse,
100 g/4 oz (⅔ cup)	450 ml/¾ pint (2 cups)	1 teaspoon	10–12 minutes	drain and reheat.
225 g/8 oz (1⅓ cups)	600 ml/1 pint (2½ cups)	1½ teaspoons	12–14 minutes	

LONG-GRAIN RICE (*All-in-one method*)

Quantity	Water (tap hot)	Salt	Microwave Cooking Time	Special Points
50 g/2 oz (⅓ cup)	150 ml/¼ pint (⅔ cup)	¼ teaspoon	6–8 minutes	Cook covered. Stir once during cooking.
100 g/4 oz (⅔ cup)	300 ml/½ pint (1¼ cups)	½ teaspoon	10–12 minutes	Leave to stand for 5 to 8 minutes before
225 g/8 oz (1⅓ cups)	600 ml/1 pint (2½ cups)	1 teaspoon	15–17 minutes	serving.

BROWN RICE

Quantity	Water (tap hot)	Salt	Microwave Cooking Time	Special Points
100 g/4 oz (⅔ cup)	450 ml/¾ pint (2 cups)	½ teaspoon	20 minutes	Cook covered. Stir once during cooking. Leave to stand for 5 minutes before serving.

ROUND-GRAIN PUDDING RICE

Cook as directed in the appropriate recipes.

GUIDE TO COOKING PASTA

Type of Pasta	Quantity	Container	Water	Oil	Salt	Cooking Time	Standing Time
SPAGHETTI	100 g/¼ lb	Small casserole	600 ml/1 pint (2½ cups)	1 teaspoon	½ teaspoon	6 minutes	10 minutes
CANNELLONI	175 g/6 oz (12 tubes)	Casserole to fit	1 litre/1¾ pints (4½ cups)	1 teaspoon	1 teaspoon	6 minutes	10 minutes
LASAGNE	175 g/6 oz (8 sheets)	Large deep dish	1 litre/1¾ pints (4½ cups)	1 teaspoon	1 teaspoon	6 minutes	10 minutes
MACARONI	225 g/½ lb	Large casserole	1 litre/1¾ pints (4½ cups)	1 teaspoon	1 teaspoon	6 minutes	10 minutes
NOODLES	225 g/½ lb	Large casserole	1 litre/1¾ pints (4½ cups)	1 teaspoon	1 teaspoon	6 minutes	8 minutes
RAVIOLI	225 g/½ lb	Large casserole	1½ litres/2½ pints (7 cups)	—	½ teaspoon	6 minutes	10 minutes

Note: Pasta must always be cooked in plenty of water to prevent sticking.

Avoid pieces protruding over the edge of the dish, as these will become brittle.
Stir once during cooking.

GUIDE TO COOKING VEGETABLES

FRESH VEGETABLES
Microwave on HIGH unless otherwise stated.
Choose whole even-sized vegetables.
Vegetables to be cooked in their skins should be pricked well.
Cover with plastic cling film unless otherwise stated.

Leave to stand for 3 minutes before draining.
Vegetables which have similar cooking times may be cooked in separate dishes in the microwave oven simultaneously; it is necessary to double the cooking time.

Type of Vegetable	Quantity	Water	Salt	Microwave Cooking Time	Special Points
ARTICHOKES, GLOBE	1	8 tablespoons (½ cup)	½ teaspoon	5–6 minutes	Turn upside down to drain before serving.
	2	8 tablespoons (½ cup)	½ teaspoon	7–8 minutes	
	4	8 fl oz (1 cup)	1 teaspoon	14–15 minutes	
ASPARAGUS	750 g/1½ lb	8 tablespoons (½ cup)	½ teaspoon	11–14 minutes	Arrange thicker stems towards the outside. Give the dish a half-turn after 6 minutes.
AUBERGINE (EGGPLANT)	2 medium, halved	2 tablespoons	—	7–9 minutes	Scoop out the cooked flesh and use as required.
BEANS, GREEN (*except thin French beans*)	500 g/1 lb	8 tablespoons (½ cup)	½ teaspoon	12–16 minutes	Stir twice. Do not overcook.
BEETROOT	2 medium	8 tablespoons (½ cup)	½ teaspoon	12–16 minutes	Leave to stand for 10 minutes before peeling. Do not overcook.
BROCCOLI	500 g/1 lb	8 tablespoons (½ cup)	½ teaspoon	10–12 minutes	Cut into even-sized pieces. Stir once.
BRUSSELS SPROUTS	500 g/1 lb	4 tablespoons (¼ cup)	½ teaspoon	7–8 minutes	Choose evenly-shaped sprouts. Stir once.
CABBAGE, *quartered*	500 g/1 lb	8 tablespoons (½ cup)	½ teaspoon	10–12 minutes	Rearrange once.
CABBAGE, *shredded*	500 g/1 lb	8 tablespoons (½ cup)	½ teaspoon	9–11 minutes	Stir once.
CARROTS, *whole*	6 medium	8 tablespoons (½ cup)	½ teaspoon	10–12 minutes	Thicker ends should be towards the outside. Rearrange once.
CARROTS, *sliced*	350 g/¾ lb	8 tablespoons (½ cup)	½ teaspoon	10–12 minutes	Slices must be no more than 1 cm/½ inch thick.
CAULIFLOWER, *whole*	750 g/1½ lb	8 tablespoons (½ cup)	½ teaspoon	12–16 minutes	Cook on MEDIUM; turning half-way through cooking.
CAULIFLOWER, *florets*	500 g/1 lb	8 tablespoons (½ cup)	½ teaspoon	10–12 minutes	Stir once.
CELERY, *whole or sliced*	500 g/1 lb	4 tablespoons (¼ cup)	¼ teaspoon	14–16 minutes	Stir once.
CHICORY (ENDIVE), *whole*	4 medium pieces	4 tablespoons (¼ cup)	—	5–8 minutes	Rearrange once. Add salt after cooking.
CORN-ON-THE-COB	1 cob	—	—	3–4 minutes	Cook in husk if preferred.
	2 cobs	4 tablespoons (¼ cup)	—	6–8 minutes	
COURGETTES (ZUCCHINI), *topped and tailed*	8 small	—	—	7 minutes	Sprinkle with nutmeg and dot with butter before cooking. Rearrange once.
LEEKS, *trimmed and sliced*	500 g/1 lb	4 tablespoons (¼ cup)	½ teaspoon	10–12 minutes	Stir once.
MARROW (SQUASH), *sliced*	500 g/1 lb	—	—	8–10 minutes	Use greaseproof (waxed) paper to cover. Add salt after cooking.
MUSHROOMS	225 g/½ lb	2 tablespoons	—	2–4 minutes	Do not overcook.

ONIONS	4 medium	4 tablespoons (¼ cup)	½ teaspoon	10–12 minutes	Stir once.
PARSNIPS, *cubed*	500 g/1 lb	8 tablespoons (½ cup)	¼ teaspoon	12–14 minutes	Add lemon juice before cooking. Stir once.
PEAS, *shelled*	500 g/1 lb	8 tablespoons (½ cup)	½ teaspoon	9–11 minutes	Stir once.
POTATOES, *peeled and quartered*	500 g/1 lb	8 tablespoons (½ cup)	½ teaspoon	10–14 minutes	Stir twice.
POTATOES, *baked in skins*	2 medium	—	—	7–8 minutes	Prick thoroughly. Cook on kitchen paper.
SPINACH	500 g/1 lb	—	—	6–8 minutes	Microwave in a cookbag. Add salt after cooking.
TOMATOES, *halved*	2	—	¼ teaspoon	1–1½ minutes	Add pepper and a knob of butter before cooking. No standing time required.
TURNIPS, *cubed*	2 medium	8 tablespoons (½ cup)	¼ teaspoon	14–16 minutes	Stir twice.

FROZEN VEGETABLES

Microwave on HIGH unless otherwise stated.
Cover except where stated.

Combine salt and water before adding vegetables.
Leave to stand for 3 minutes before draining.

Type of Vegetable	Quantity	Water	Salt	Microwave Cooking Time	Special Points
ARTICHOKE HEARTS	225 g/½ lb	2 tablespoons	½ teaspoon	4 minutes	Stir once.
ASPARAGUS TIPS	225 g/½ lb	4 tablespoons (¼ cup)	½ teaspoon	6–7 minutes	Rearrange after 4 minutes.
BEANS, GREEN (*except thin French ones*)	225 g/½ lb	8 tablespoons (½ cup)	½ teaspoon	7–9 minutes	Stir once.
BROCCOLI	225 g/½ lb	8 tablespoons (½ cup)	½ teaspoon	7–9 minutes	Rearrange after 4 minutes.
BRUSSELS SPROUTS	225 g/½ lb	8 tablespoons (½ cup)	½ teaspoon	6–7 minutes	Stir twice.
CABBAGE, *shredded*	225 g/½ lb	6 tablespoons	½ teaspoon	8–10 minutes	Stir once.
CARROTS, *whole or diced*	225 g/½ lb	4 tablespoons (¼ cup)	½ teaspoon	5–7 minutes	Stir twice.
CAULIFLOWER FLORETS	225 g/½ lb	—	—	5–7 minutes	Stir once. Add salt after cooking.
CORN-ON-THE-COB	2 cobs	—	—	8 minutes	Arrange in a single layer. Dot with butter. Turn once.
	4 cobs	—	—	10–12 minutes	
CORN KERNELS	225 g/½ lb	2 tablespoons	½ teaspoon	5–7 minutes	Stir once.
COURGETTES (ZUCCHINI), *sliced*	225 g/½ lb	—	—	5–6 minutes	Add salt after cooking.
MUSHROOMS	225 g/½ lb	—	—	5–7 minutes	Stir once. Add salt after cooking.
ONIONS, *small whole*	225 g/½ lb	—	—	4–6 minutes	Sprinkle salt over onions.
PEAS	225 g/½ lb	4 tablespoons (¼ cup)	½ teaspoon	5–6 minutes	
PEAS & CARROTS *mixed*	225 g/½ lb	2 tablespoons	½ teaspoon	6–7 minutes	
PEAS & ONIONS *mixed*	225 g/½ lb	2 tablespoons	½ teaspoon	6–7 minutes	
PEPPERS, *diced*	175 g/6 oz	4 tablespoons (¼ cup)	½ teaspoon	6–7 minutes	
POTATOES, NEW	225 g/½ lb	4 tablespoons (¼ cup)	½ teaspoon	7–8 minutes	Stir twice.
SPINACH, *leaf or chopped*	225 g/½ lb	—	—	6–7 minutes	Break up block 2 or 3 times. Add salt after cooking.

SUITABLE AND UNSUITABLE COOKWARE FOR USE IN THE MICROWAVE OVEN

Item	Uses	Reasons	Special Points
ABSORBENT KITCHEN PAPER	Cooking bacon	Absorbs fat	Remove as soon as bacon is cooked.
	Thawing bread rolls	Absorbs moisture	Remove as soon as bread is thawed.
	Cooking baked potatoes	Absorbs moisture	Remove immediately to prevent sticking.
ANCHOR HOCKING	Cooking most foods	Durable, easy to clean. Can be used from freezer to microwave. Can also be used in a conventional oven up to 200°C/400°F	Range includes items specially designed for roasting, cooking bacon, savarin and small cakes.
BAKEWELL PAPER	See *non-stick parchment*		
CARDBOARD, CHOCOLATE AND CANDY BOXES	Making cookies and cakes	Good shapes often un-obtainable in other materials	Do not use metal trimmed boxes. Line with plastic cling film.
CERAMIC PORCELAIN DISHES	Cakes, pies, tarts	Attractive to serve from	Avoid metal trimmed dishes.
CHINA CUPS, PLATES AND DISHES	Reheating	Attractive for serving. Saves washing up	Suitable for reheating only. Do not use metal trimmed china.
COFFEE POTS, HEATPROOF	Reheating beverages		Avoid jugs with metal trim and those with handles held by metal screws.
COOKING BAGS	Convenience foods	Saves washing up	Slit across the top to prevent bursting.
CORNING WARE	See *Glass ceramics*		
CUSTARD CUPS	Custards, small cakes		Avoid metal and paint trimmed cups.
FOAM DISHES	Warming food and drinks	Disposable and easy to hold	Will melt at high temperatures; do not use for foods with a high fat or sugar content.
GLASS CERAMICS	Casseroles, stews, cakes	Easy interchange between conventional and microwave ovens	Avoid metal trimmed dishes and plates.
GLASS JUGS, HEATPROOF	Heating liquids		Use a size larger than required.
GLASS, OVENPROOF BOWLS AND CASSEROLE DISHES	Bowls – sauces, custard, soups. Casserole dishes – casseroles, desserts	Easy to wash, practically unbreakable, transparent	Avoid metal trimmed glass. Use lids as required. If in doubt choose a larger size than you think you need.
GREASEPROOF PAPER	Covering moist foods	Keeps in some steam	Use a piece larger than the cooking dish.
IRVINWARE OVENMATES	Casseroles, individual pies, cakes	Can also be used in a conventional oven up to 200°C/400°F	The oven tray cannot be used on a turn-table. Some items are not suitable for use in a conventional oven.
KITCHEN PAPER TOWELS	See *Absorbent kitchen paper*		
MICROWAVE BROWNING SKILLET	Chops, steaks, doughnuts, browning onions	Suitable for foods where a heat-sealed surface is required	Do not overheat. Use the lid when directed. Clean with bicarbonate of soda (baking soda) on a damp soft cloth.
NATURAL SHELLS	Fish starters	Attractive for serving	Suitable for short-term cooking only.
NON-STICK PARCHMENT	Lining cake boxes and dishes	Non-stick and can be re-used	When lifting from oven hold parchment taut to prevent sliding.
	Baking cookies, melting chocolate, making praline	Ideal for lining oven shelf	

PAPER CUPS	Heating drinks	Easily disposable	Do not use for heating oil.
PAPER NAPKINS	Heating burgers and doughnuts	Absorbs hot fat. Does not stick as much as kitchen paper	Avoid the soft and coloured types.
PAPER PLATES	Reheating dry foods	Easily disposable	Not suitable for large quantities. Plates tend to lose rigidity on heating.
PLASTIC BOXES	Defrosting blocks of food		Freeze with the lid on but remove before microwaving. Most types will not withstand temperatures above 80°C/180°F, so avoid foods with a high sugar content.
PLASTIC CLING FILM	Covering vegetables, fish and meat dishes Lining cake dishes	Forms an excellent seal and is disposable Saves washing up	Do not overstretch. Remove carefully, slitting first to avoid steam burns. Fit loosely into the dish.
PLASTIC CUPS	Drinks	Disposable	Do not boil liquid or plastic will melt.
POLYPROPYLENE BOWLS	Puddings, sauces and soups	Reusable many times	Avoid pouring hot syrup or fat into the base. Do not use supplied lids in the oven – they may be forced off by steam.
POLYTHENE (PLASTIC) BAGS	Brief thawing small quantities of food from the freezer Rising yeast doughs	Convenient for freezer to microwave	Remove metal tags. Will not withstand high temperatures – use for thawing only. Bag should be lightly greased.
POTTERY CUPS, PLATES AND DISHES	Cooking and reheating	Cover with lid or plastic cling film	Test before using for the first time. Avoid metal trimmed and metallic glazed pottery. Unglazed pottery may absorb moisture and become hot.
PYREX	See *Glass, ovenproof/Glass jugs, heatproof*		
ROASTER BAGS	Softening potatoes Roasting	Hastens cooking Aids browning	Do not use metal tags. Remove from oven carefully as bags are liable to burst.
SOUFFLÉ DISHES, GLASS AND CHINA	Round cakes Soufflés	Excellent for straight sided cakes	Avoid metal trimmed dishes. Painted decorations will slow down the cooking.
STRAW BASKETS	Warming rolls	Attractive for serving	May become brittle if heated too long.
TOUGHENED GLASS	Reheating beverages, dissolving gelatine	Transparent, easy to wash	Use oven gloves to remove from the oven.
TUPPERWARE	See *Plastic boxes*		
WAXED PAPER	Covering	Prevents splattering	
WAXED PAPER CARTONS	Reheating drinks	Suitable for freezer to microwave	Open carton before heating. Do not heat too long or carton may burst.
WAXED PAPER PLATES	Reheating most foods	Does not absorb moisture	Do not reheat for long or wax may melt.
WINE GLASSES	Desserts, drinks	Attractive for serving	Use for warming only; delicate glasses may crack.
WOODEN BOARDS, BASKETS ETC.	Warming rolls	Attractive for serving	Wood absorbs moisture and may warp if heated for too long.

THE FOLLOWING ITEMS ARE NOT SUITABLE FOR USE IN THE MICROWAVE OVEN:–

Corning Centura	Melamine	Metallic trimmed containers or
Dessert pots	Metal containers	those with metal screws or handles
Foil-lined cartons	Metal tie tags	Yogurt pots

INDEX

ACKNOWLEDGMENTS

The publishers wish to acknowledge the following:

Special photography by Melvin Grey
Illustrations by Elsa Willson
Food prepared by Heather Lambert
Photographic stylist: Carolyn Russell

The publishers would also like to thank the
following companies for sponsoring photographs:
Amana Inc: 6–7, 22; Anchor Hocking Ltd, 50 Pall
Mall, London SW1: 14–15; Microwave Throwaways,
245 Church Road, Mitcham, Surrey: 10–11; Pyrex
Ltd: 62–3; Thermidor: Cover photograph, 18, 39.

Accessories for photography kindly supplied by: The
Craftsmen Potters Shop; Liberty & Co. Ltd.